Extramural

To
Philip Healy,
with thanks for making me re-read Newman

To open the mind, to correct it, to refine it, to enable it to know, and to digest, master, rule, and use its knowledge, to give it power over its own faculties, application, flexibility, method, critical exactness, sagacity, resource, address, eloquent expression, is an object as intelligible ... as the cultivation of virtue.

Thoughts and speech are inseparable from each other. Matter and expression are part of one: style is a thinking out into language. This is what I have been laying down, and this is literature; not *things*, not the verbal symbols of things; not on the other hand mere *words*; but thoughts expressed in language.

J.H. Newman, *The Idea of a University* (1852).

Extramural

Literature and Lifelong Learning

Adrian Barlow

The Lutterworth Press

The Lutterworth Press
P.O. Box 60
Cambridge
CB1 2NT
United Kingdom

www.lutterworth.com
publishing@lutterworth.com

ISBN: 978 0 7188 9279 1

British Library Cataloguing in Publication Data
A record is available from the British Library

First Published by The Lutterworth Press, 2012

Contents

Acknowledgements

This book was born out of my affection for Madingley Hall, home of the University of Cambridge Institute of Continuing Education, and I owe a debt of friendship to my colleagues there and to the students with whom I worked so closely until my retirement in 2011. All of them have contributed to my conviction that the work of lifelong learning in Higher Education is important, but too often undervalued.

I am grateful to all at Lutterworth Press for their enthusiasm for this book, with particular thanks to Oliver, my patient and perceptive editor.

Some of the chapters in Part 2 of this book have previously appeared in the following journals: *The Use of English*, *The Journal of the Friends of the Dymock Poets*, *The Rupert Brooke Society Newsletter* and the *Edmund Blunden Society website*. Permission to reprint them is acknowledged with thanks. Other chapters began life as lectures, in Cambridge, at Madingley Hall or elsewhere, including the University of Oxford Department for Continuing Education at Rewley House, and I am grateful for all the invitations to deliver these. A shortened version of the lecture 'Tom Paine's Plain Words' has previously appeared in *Tom Paine Bicentenary Papers* (2010) edited by John Weeks.

Permission to reproduce quotations from the following works in copyright is acknowledged with thanks: *The Habit of Art*, *The History Boys*, *Untold Stories* and *Writing Home* © Alan Bennett and reprinted by permission of Faber and Faber Ltd; *The Great Lover* © Jill Dawson, reproduced by permission of Hodder and Stoughton Limited; *Four Quartets* © the Estate of T.S. Eliot and reprinted by permission of Faber and Faber Ltd; *Howards End*, *The Longest Journey*, and *Two Cheers for Democracy* by E.M. Forster, reprinted by permission of the Provost and Scholars of King's College, Cambridge and The Society of Authors as the Literary Representative of the Estate of EM Forster; *The Memory of Love*, © Aminatta Forna 2010, courtesy of Bloomsbury Publishing Plc; 'Personal Helicon' from *Death of a Naturalist*, 'Chanson d'Aventure' and 'A Herbal' from *Human Chain* © Seamus Heaney and reprinted by permission of Faber and Faber Ltd; *Required Writing* and 'Aubade' from *Collected Poems* © the Estate of Philip Larkin and reprinted by permission of Faber and Faber Ltd.

Introduction

At Madingley Hall, home of the University of Cambridge Institute of Continuing Education, there is an unfinished portrait of the founding father of university extramural studies, James Stuart. It shows him as still a young man, serious and thoughtful: his brow is somewhat furrowed. That the portrait, by Hubert von Herkomer, is unfinished seems appropriate, for the work that Stuart began one hundred and forty years ago is not yet complete. Today, indeed, the principle that universities should see access to lifelong learning by part-time adult students as an obligation or, at least, as more than just an opportunity for public engagement is one few vice-chancellors would fight for. Changing priorities in higher education and in government policy have seen to that.

In Part 1 of *Extramural* I offer a personal and polemical view of the evolution of extramural studies from the missionary enthusiasm of James Stuart to the present time, when departments of continuing education are closing at an unprecedented rate. Stuart was a remarkable man — not least because he was able, when still only thirty years old, to persuade Cambridge University to embark on a programme of social and educational intervention which had national and international consequences. In 'By extension: a Cambridge perspective' I trace Stuart's influence in the work of later educationalists and cultural commentators such as Raymond Williams and Richard Hoggart. In doing so, I explore the whole idea of liberal education as applied to lifelong learning.

Nearly a quarter of a century ago, Richard Hoggart lamented the way extramural departments were giving in to 'the overweening demands for proved cost-effectiveness and for a vocational slant at the expense of those kinds of study which were undertaken for the love of God and the development of the personality'. He followed this lament with a challenge to universities:

> Vice-Chancellors should take time off from the endless struggle with resources and with the undeniable need to protect their best internal departments as well as they can, so as to renew their sense of a need

outside the walls which has never gone away and which has in some sense represented the best in university ideals.[1]

This leads me to ask what sort of idealism is needed by those who teach in adult higher education. Is this idealism different from that of mainstream academics teaching standard-entry undergraduate and graduate classes, whose priority may more often be to publish than to teach, and for whom imperatives such as the Research Excellence Framework and the Impact Agenda loom all too large?

Nothing convinces me more strongly of the value of continuing education than the commitment and enthusiasm of the students themselves. At different points in *Extramural* I include comments from my own students, who speak eloquently of what lifelong learning means to them:

> Lifelong learning is, I believe, a founding principle in any society that wishes to invest in its population, especially as maturing citizens exert greater influence over the shape of that society. Odd, it seems, that at the very age of maturity — with all the responsibilities that entails — the entitlement to learning appears to fall away.

The speaker here is Anil, a student who has attended my courses in Literature over several years. It has been a feature of most of the classes with whom I have worked in the past dozen years that they rapidly develop a cohesion that makes them very effective learning groups, supporting each other and creating an atmosphere of shared commitment. Sometimes I have launched a discussion and then stood back, watching and listening as a class teaches itself. No matter how disparate the educational background or experience of the students, no one is made to feel inadequate: the students encourage and challenge each other. It is also fascinating to watch how groups that have studied together, sometimes for a number of years, welcome and involve newcomers: I have never seen a student feel unwelcome or excluded.

Every academic subject has its particular virtue; but it is rare, I find, for a student not to pick up quite quickly the defining contribution of English as a discipline of thought. Anil again:

> The particular importance of literature must not be understated. What is it? I believe literature reflects a uniquely human obsession with enquiring about and understanding the world around us, and specifically our instinctive urge to peer into the minds of others. Literature expresses like nothing else the incalculable complexity of our experience, and the reading of literature is enriched by the widening of

---

1   Richard Hoggart, 'Foreword' to McIlroy, J and Spence, B *University Education in Crisis* (University of Leeds: Leeds Studies in Adult and Continuing Education 1988) pp.v–vii.

these individual experiences. The study of literature, then, enables us to construct and test theories about the lives of others in parallel with the daily analysis of our particular, individual situations.

I discuss and illustrate this in the second section of Part 1, 'On course: teaching literature in lifelong learning'. The teaching on which I focus here is all to do with working with groups of students and getting, over time, to know them well. By contrast the lectures, essays and reviews in Part 2 were all originally prepared for general audiences — that is, audiences that would certainly include those with specialist or expert knowledge, alongside others having little or no prior acquaintance with the subject at all. Such a description, of course, nearly always fits an open-access class or group of continuing education students. The difference is that these audiences are not my students: they do not know me, nor I them. The lectures cover a wide range, historically and in terms of subject — from Tom Paine in the eighteenth century to Alan Bennett in the twenty first. The contexts in which the lectures were delivered were different each time, and I preface each one with a brief account of where, why and when.

One thing they all have in common, though, is that I use quotation a lot in my lectures, unashamedly. I do this partly because students find it reassuring: they do not have to worry I'll assume they know the texts so well that quotation is superfluous. Partly it's because I always engage in close reading in my lectures: I don't want students to deal in vague generalities, so their arguments, like mine, must be rooted in the texts we are discussing. I want them to see that it is by close reading that texts force us to ask the questions that provoke further questions that lead to deeper understanding. Close reading, as Stefan Collini has argued,[2] is inseparable from hard thinking, and literature deserves our full attention.

The lectures in Part 2 are followed by a small selection of essays and reviews. Much of my own teaching and research has focused, throughout my career, on the literature of the Great War, and in particular on some of the lesser known contributors to that war. My postgraduate research was on the poet and novelist Richard Aldington, and I believe strongly in supporting the small societies and fellowships that have sprung up to promote or sustain the reputations of the writers of the Great War. 'Poets need friends' is a mantra I often repeat, and groups such as the Friends of the Dymock Poets, the Edward Thomas Fellowship, the Siegfried Sassoon Fellowship, the Wilfred Owen Association and the Ivor Gurney Society offer practical friendship on a number of levels. The essay on Edmund Blunden was commissioned by the Edmund Blunden Website, the first instance (to my knowledge) of a virtual community of Friends of a particular poet. The review of a book about the Marlowe Dramatic Society in Cambridge was written for the Newsletter of the Rupert Brooke Society.

2   See Part 3 below, p. 162.

It is a point literary historians will need to ponder that several of these societies have been founded in the past twenty years or less: further evidence of the undiminished afterlife of the Great War. The people who join such societies are very often the same people who participate in continuing education programmes. It is interesting, too, that these societies and fellowships are nearly always run from outside, not within, universities — though they may have strong support from individual academics. They represent a striking new dimension in the evolution of extramural literary study.

Much of my teaching in continuing education has centred on new (often very new) works of fiction, and the last piece to appear in Part 2 is a previously unpublished review of a controversial 2009 novel by Jill Dawson, *The Great Lover*, about an imagined relationship between a Fenland servant girl and Rupert Brooke. This is a book by a writer who herself lives in the Fens and has written previous novels with a Fenland setting. I grew up in the Fens myself, and one of the attractions of Cambridge for me has always been that it is a fen-edge city. From the window of my attic study in Madingley Hall, I look north and east to the straight-edge skyline which includes (on a clear day) Ely Cathedral. Some of the most rewarding courses I have taught have been about the Fens, their literature and their architecture. I like standing in flat landscapes — whether here, in Holland and Germany, on the Veneto or even in Cambodia — and once wrote thus about them:

In Praise of Flat Landscapes

Nothing so flat will move the man who loves mountains alone,
But even he, if he lie on his back on the bank of the dyke
And look up for the larks or watch the willow wands
Dipped and silvered by a moment of wind,

Even he with his head for heights might concede
Flat landscapes do not threaten and glower as mountains may;
No, they command a stillness, they are the earth at rest,
Set free at last from the weight of the sea.

Flat landscapes are generous: their arms stretch out,
Their soil gives richly, their skies are measureless.
They enrage the world in a rush with its ceaseless chatter,

But those who will walk all day on the line of the land,
Defining their place in a flat landscape,
Will never say twice flat landscapes are dull.

Part 3 of *Extramural* is a selection of postings from my blog, *World and time*. I began to write this blog in August 2009. From the start it was designed to promote the courses and programmes being offered by the Institute of Continuing

Education, but this was only part of its purpose. I wanted to make a record of the things that interest me in the context of my work and my teaching; at the same time I was keen to explore new ways of presenting my thoughts on books and writers, on poetry, on architecture, on Cambridge and Madingley, on the university and lifelong learning — on all of these things. My readership was to be open access, just like the classes I teach. I have tried over the past two years to make no assumptions about what would or would not interest them; it would be my job to make what is of interest to me of interest to anyone who found themselves — by accident or design — reading *World and time.*

More personal and less formal than lecturing, closer in fact to an essay or a monologue with the potential to turn into a conversation, the blog works best when it is prompted by some event that has just happened, some book I've been reading, some lecture I've just delivered or class I have taught. I once heard U.A. Fanthorpe introduce herself to a student audience as 'a practising poet — that is, I'm still trying to do the job better.' Though I never knew any poet with less cause to be modest than Ursula Fanthorpe, in the same spirit I consider myself to be a practising blogger.

The selection from *World and time* which makes up Part 3 of *Extramural* is divided into sections as follows:

3.1   About Madingley

3.2   On lit. crit. and teaching literature

3.3   Concerning E.M. Forster

3.4   On writers, mostly novelists

The pieces are not necessarily presented in chronological order, but I give the date of posting for each one.

A key idea informing the teaching of literature and running through *Extramural* is the idea of a community of literature to which readers and writers can equally belong. All literature involves a dialogue with the past — the writers of the present always consciously or unconsciously talking to those who have gone before — and it is part of the job of teaching literature to help students tune in to this dialogue. To illustrate this idea of a community to which readers are invited to belong the image of a hand being held out from writer to reader is sometimes used, as for example by Alan Bennett in his play *The History Boys* (2004) where Hector, the eccentric English teacher, explains to one of his pupils:

> The best moments in reading are when you come across something — a thought, a feeling, a way of looking at things — which you had thought special and particular to you. Now here it is, set down by someone else, a person you have never met, someone even who is long dead. And it is as if a hand has come out and taken yours.[3]

3   Alan Bennett, *The History Boys* (London: Faber and Faber 2004) p.56.

I refer to this passage twice during *Extramural*, once in the lecture 'Literature Now!' and again in 'Alan Bennett and *The Habit of Art*'. On both occasions I also refer to a commentary on the passage by the writer Blake Morrison. Indeed the hand reaching out to clasp another is a powerful image both about literature and in literature, and I discuss it again, in a different context, in Part 1 when exploring its use by Seamus Heaney in a poem of his which discreetly echoes a poem by John Keats. Making these connections is one of the purposes, as well as one of the pleasures, of literary study.

It will be obvious, I hope, both from what I have already written and from what follows, that I have found working and teaching in continuing education intensely rewarding. I have great admiration for many of my colleagues and for my students; all of them, directly or indirectly, have contributed to this book, and I am grateful.   *Madingley Hall, 17 August 2011*

Part 1

1.1 By extension: a Cambridge perspective

Extension lectures, extramural studies, lifelong learning, continuing education: the labels change over time. Partly, this is because the very concept of extramural studies keeps evolving; partly it is because each earlier label carries connotations later to be thought unfortunate. In some corners of every university, the very idea of extramural studies is treated with condescension: how do part-time adult learners, studying for personal fulfilment or for professional development, really fit into the modern world of the research-intensive university? The condescension can be heard trickling down the walls of Whitehall too: the last Labour Government dismissed university continuing education as 'recreational' or 'lifestyle' learning — implying that a weekend spent by mainly well-heeled, mainly white middle-class, often retired, students studying Latin, say, or Forensic Archaeology, was a lifestyle choice no different from spending a weekend improving your golf or enjoying 'treatments' at an expensive health farm.

The term 'extramural', though now out of favour, is still apt and reasonably accurate. I shall stick with it. Universities — especially old ones — do often resemble medieval walled towns with their gatehouses, towers and halls. University College Durham, where I spent five years as a student, is housed in a castle dating back to the earliest years of the Norman Conquest. Trinity College, Cambridge, boasts an intimidating turreted and crenellated gatehouse. Even the twentieth century Wills Tower of Bristol University echoes the great cathedral towers of the fifteenth century. The cliché 'ivory tower' is itself redolent of an exotic, exclusive world, one that is out of date and out of touch. So, the idea of scholars leaving their research to go and take their scholarship to those outside the academic community is well summed up in 'extramural'. Indeed, the University of Cambridge defines the function of its Institute of Continuing Education as 'a conduit for the transmission of the University's research and scholarship'. However, this 'top-down' definition of extramural study is inadequate, both as a description of what actually happens in extramural studies within Higher Education (HE) and as a manifesto for what ought to happen. The work of continuing education departments involves both less and more than this.

Such a form of educational outreach is not simply a kind of Victorian paternalism, though the genesis of extramural studies in the modern sense certainly stems from the 1870s and had its origins in Cambridge. As early as 1112, the Lincolnshire Abbey of Croyland, in those days one of the great European centres of Benedictine learning, sent monks out across the Fens to give lectures in local barns — anywhere in fact that could conveniently house a group of eager listeners. Where did the Croyland monks come first to deliver courses on Philosophy to the benighted locals? To Cambridge. According to this tradition, then, Cambridge begins its university life as a Local Centre, an extramural outpost of Croyland, which already had more than two centuries of academic study behind it.

Is an extramural department, is extramural study itself, compatible with the ideals of a university? There are those in Cambridge (and probably in other places too) who doubt it. 'Open-access Cambridge qualifications' sounds a contradiction in terms. Again, Cambridge is one of the few universities to insist upon the uniqueness of what it offers as having something to do with its location, with Cambridge itself. There is no Cambridge campus in Kuala Lumpur or Calcutta or Qatar: why, then, should there be extramural outposts of Cambridge in Clacton, King's Lynn or Colchester?

This sounds amazingly parochial in an age when the concept of an 'Open University' has won almost universal acknowledgement, and when 'online learning' is taken absolutely for granted. Today Cambridge itself acknowledges 'blended learning', the combination of online tuition and support with face-to-face teaching. Part-time qualifications — at least at postgraduate level — are becoming a fact of life here: students jet in from all over the world for regular teaching sessions (perhaps for a week or for a summer school) during, say, a two-year Masters' programme. At other times they keep in touch with their course director, their supervisor and their fellow students through a VLE, an online 'virtual learning environment'. Nevertheless, the University takes the view that all courses and qualifications offered in its name should have some element of 'Cambridgeness' about them. No doubt, those other universities still offering formal extramural teaching and learning opportunities feel the same.

Faced, then, with these tensions and changes in the way part-time adult higher education is perceived and provided, especially when seen from a Cambridge perspective, the following questions need to be asked: *What is continuing education (in the sense of extramural study)? Where did the idea come from? What is it for? Who is it for? How does it relate to the central functions and values of a university at any time but particularly today?*

'Today' is an important context: since 2007[1] fundamental changes to the way in which part-time adult students in higher education are funded in England have drastically reduced the opportunities for such education. The roll call of universities that have closed their departments of continuing education since that date is a melancholy one. Even those to have survived struggle to support the traditional liberal arts and humanities curriculum: funding in an age of austerity focuses on SIVS (Strategically Important or Vulnerable Subjects) and STEM subjects: Science, Technology, Engineering and Mathematics. Providing continuing professional development (CPD) at one end of the Higher Education spectrum, and up-skilling or re-skilling the workforce at the other, is the priority now. The old tensions between 'education' and 'training'; between 'professional' and 'academic'; between 'inutility' and 'utility' — to borrow terms used by Newman in his classic work, *The Idea of a University*, 1852 — are as strong and perhaps as corrosive today as they have ever been.

****

In 1995, not long after the re-unification of Germany, I was invited to give a lecture in Magdeburg (formerly in East Germany) on British education. The Otto-von-Guericke University had only been founded in 1993, and its Education Faculty was largely concerned with retraining teachers of Russian to become teachers of English. So rapidly indeed had the Faculty grown that it had had to find new accommodation and the only available building in Magdeburg of sufficient size was the former headquarters of the Stasi, the State Secret Police. My audience was a rather sullen cohort of former card-carrying Communists. When my lecture was over, however, the first question came quickly. A middle-aged woman said, 'Professor Barlow,' (flattering but inaccurate) 'you have said some startling things. If you had said in this room five years ago that the object of education is to make people think for themselves, you would probably have been arrested. Did you really mean that?' Sensing an opportunity for an expression of *perestroika*, I replied that I had certainly meant it. It seemed — and seems — self-evidently true. 'How many of you in this room believe that the job of education is to teach young people to ask questions and to challenge received wisdom?' I expected a forest of hands, but not one went up. 'Professor Barlow,' said my questioner with mordant satisfaction, 'if you had asked that question five years ago in this room you would probably have been shot.'

---

1   In 2007 the introduction of the ELQ [Equivalent or Lower Qualifications] policy removed funding from almost all part-time adult students studying any course accredited at a level equivalent to, or lower than, a qualification they already possessed. This drastically affected many university departments of lifelong learning with their traditional focus on liberal arts programmes.

There was nothing remotely original about what I was saying. In 1871, James Stuart, then a very young Fellow of Trinity College, Cambridge, had given a lecture to the Leeds Ladies' Educational Association. This lecture, entitled *University Extension*, is usually taken to be the starting point for extramural studies in any modern sense. Stuart began with the following definition and description:

> The object of all education is to teach people to think for themselves, that is the direct or specified object of what is called Higher Education. Reading and writing are one of the many means of acquiring education, they constitute what is called primary education, and supply men with better tools, so to speak, to work with. But reading and writing are not education any more than a fork and knife constitute a good dinner, and a man who is educated in the truest sense may even be unable to read or write, for an educated man is a man who is capable of thinking about what he sees.[2]

Stuart's argument was radical for its day: the idea that an illiterate person might yet be truly educated would have amused or irritated his colleagues back at Trinity. But Stuart went further:

> The object of true higher education is to lead out the faculties of the mind, a process which may be done by means of any subject, and is frequently better performed when the subject by means of which the education is imparted is not of a nature which can be immediately utilized; in fact, the subject by means of which higher education may be best given depends rather on the teacher than on the taught, and a man leads out the faculties of the human mind best by means of that subject which he is best able to teach.[3]

Here Stuart is following directly in the footsteps of Newman who had argued twenty years earlier that 'Liberal education, viewed in itself, is simply the cultivation of the intellect, as such, and its object is nothing more or less than intellectual excellence.'[4] For Newman, the word 'liberal' (in the sense of 'free') was an important qualification. He contrasted it with work he defined as 'servile': 'bodily labour, mechanical employment and the like, in which the mind has little or no part'. He argued:

> As far as this contrast may be considered as a guide into the meaning of the word, liberal education and liberal pursuits are exercises of the mind, of reason, of reflection.[5]

---

2   James Stuart, *University Extension* (Cambridge: Cambridge University Press 1871) p.3.
3   *ibid.*
4   J.H. Newman, *The Idea of a University* (London: Longmans, Green and Co.1852) p.121.
5   *ibid.*, pp.106–7.

Newman's definition of education is, however refreshing, an exacting one. He distinguishes fiercely between education as a systematic process and study as recreation. 'I consider', he says, 'such innocent recreations as science and literature are able to furnish will be a very fit occupation of the thoughts and the leisure of young persons, and may be made the means of keeping them from bad employments and bad companions'; but he continues:

> Recreations are not education; accomplishments are not education. Do not say, the people must be educated, when, after all, you only mean, amused, refreshed, soothed, put into good spirits and good humour, or kept from vicious excesses.... . Education is a high word; it is the preparation for knowledge, and it is the imparting of knowledge in proportion to that preparation.[6]

How does Newman's view of education, as expressed here, help us to understand the purpose and value of lifelong learning? There is an echo perhaps of the lisping circus owner, Mr Sleary, in Dickens's *Hard Times*, who reminds Mr Gradgrind that 'People mutht be amuthed, thquire, thomehow ... they can't be alwayth a-working, nor yet they can't be alwayth a-learning'.[7] But, more ominously, it is as if Newman sees the provision of quasi-intellectual entertainment as a strategy designed to keep the lower classes from revolting. He would, on this reading, see the idea of 'recreational learning' as having little to do with real education, and he certainly appears to see the whole process as one that requires the learner to be entirely passive — like, in fact, Gradgrind's 'little vessels' having facts poured into them. We can, however, better see the value Newman places on education by noting that he is an advocate of self-education. Self-education, he asserts, is a better form of education than one which has the absorbing of information or the passing of exams as its primary aim. People who are self-educated, he argues, are likely

> to have more thought, more mind, more philosophy, more true enlargement, than those earnest but ill-used persons, who are forced to load their minds with a score of subjects against an examination.[8]

Liberal education is, for Newman, ultimately a form of self-education, for he actually suggests that a university which had no teachers and no curriculum might be preferable to one dominated by instruction, rote learning and exam cramming. In such a place, he argues, men (it is, again, only men who feature in Newman's idea of a university) are more likely to learn 'principles of thought and action'.

---

6   *ibid.*, pp.143–4.
7   Charles Dickens, *Hard Times* (1854) Bk. III Ch.viii.
8   Newman, *The Idea of a University*, p.149.

It is clear Newman sees examinations as belonging to schemes of training, not of education — certainly not of liberal education. My own teacher of English started my A level course by announcing to us: 'Gentlemen,' (my schooling was men only, so Newman would have approved of that) 'for five terms I shall teach you, and together we will explore English Literature and why it is worth studying. In the sixth term, I shall not teach you, but I will train you to pass the examination.' And he did.

****

The value that Newman attached to liberal education for *young* undergraduates has applied equally to education for adult learners *of any age* in Higher Education. But whereas Newman envisaged university experience as only possible in a place like Oxford, where students would live an enclosed collegiate life, James Stuart envisaged from the start 'a sort of peripatetic university the professors of which would circulate among the big towns, and thus give a wider opportunity for receiving such teaching.'[9] Stuart's approach was more practical but no less idealistic than Newman's. In 1867 he accepted an invitation from the newly-formed North of England Council for Promoting the Higher Education of Women to give a series of eight weekly lectures on Astronomy in each of the cities — Manchester, Liverpool, Sheffield and Leeds — that made up the Council.

Anxious to make these lectures as educational as possible, Stuart invented the lecture hand-out (though he called it a syllabus). As originally conceived, this was a very brief summary of the lecture, simply a series of headings or single sentences. It was designed to help the students both follow the lecture as it unfolded and also to write up fuller notes of their own afterwards. Later Stuart added a series of questions to each syllabus, inviting students, if they wished but without obligation, to produce written answers to be marked by the tutor before the next lecture. From this simple beginning the syllabus developed to become a prime feature first of University Extension Lectures, then of extramural, and now of continuing education courses. To satisfy the demand for discussion with the tutor and for opportunities when the tutor could respond to questions afterwards, or before the next week's lecture, Stuart instituted the principle that tutors should be available to talk to students before the start of an evening, and that the evening itself should then be divided into two sessions: an hour-long lecture, followed by an optional class which would take the form of a discussion — firmly directed by the tutor — of the subject introduced in the lecture. This format is still recognisable in many of the remaining continuing education courses today.

By 1871 Stuart thought he had generated sufficient enthusiasm for his peripatetic university to justify asking Cambridge to support the scheme. He sensed that the University would soon need to demonstrate its commitment

9   James Stuart, *Reminiscences* (London: Chiswick Press 1911) p.155.

to the world outside its walls, public engagement being as much an issue then as today. He was right about the timing, and the University eventually adopted his proposal for a trial period of three years, placing the Extension Lectures programme under the aegis of the Local Examinations Syndicate, later re-named the University of Cambridge Local Examinations and Lectures Syndicate. Three lecturers were appointed to give lectures on behalf of the University in Nottingham, Derby and Leicester, travelling between the three cities each week. This idea of lecturers being appointed specifically to lecture outside Cambridge on behalf of Cambridge thus enshrined, from the start, the idea of 'Cambridgeness': the work of these teachers both emanated from Cambridge and was supervised by Cambridge. The Syndicate was responsible for assuring the quality of what was what being taught and examined, and was responsible too for guiding the programme as it grew in size and scope.

The same principles apply today. The work of the Institute of Continuing Education is controlled by the General Board of the University, which appoints a 'Strategic Committee' to manage the affairs of the Institute on its behalf. The permanent academic staff (the lecturers) of the Institute are all university appointments, and it is these lecturers who are responsible for the academic quality of all the Institute's teaching — their own, of course, and that of the tutors who are teaching on their behalf, whether in Cambridge or outside.

Stuart persuaded the University that 'one of the advantages of the system about to be inaugurated would be that it would offer a more liberal education to those about to become teachers in elementary schools.'[10] In this he was not promoting the idea of teacher training, but of teacher education. He had seen at first hand how the mechanics' institutes and the elementary schools he visited were struggling to provide good teaching to students and pupils of all ages because the teachers themselves were not adequately educated:

> The more ignorant our pupils, and the more they are necessarily engaged in the task of earning their daily bread, the more necessary it is that the one who attempts to teach them should be well versed in his subject far beyond the limits up to which he teaches it. It is only then that the process becomes truly educational, and ceases to be a simple imparting of unsuggestive and undigested facts.[11]

From the start, therefore, Stuart's extension lectures were designed to combine the 'inutility' (Newman's word) of the liberal arts with the utility of improving the education of those who were themselves to become educators. The majority of these would be women, and it is not the least important part of Stuart's legacy that the Extension Lectures responded from the start to

---

10 Stuart, *Reminiscences* p.172.

11 James Stuart, *A Letter on University Extension*, 23 November 1871, Cambridge University Library [UL] mss. BEMS 1/1.

the demand for higher education for women: Stuart himself was one of the earliest lecturers to travel to Hitchin to lecture to women at Emily Davies's nascent Girton College, and he was instrumental in encouraging Jemima Clough (who had been Hon. Secretary of the North of England Council for Promoting the Higher Education of Women) to establish what would become Newnham College, in Cambridge itself.

There was nothing élitist about Stuart's view of extramural studies: he wished to raise the level of education available from working men's and mechanics' institutes, and he was fully prepared to meet, mix with, and learn from, the people he wished to teach. This has always been an essential aspect of extramural teaching. He went, for example, to Northumberland and stayed with miners in their own homes:

> I spent a very interesting week in the pit villages. I stayed with some pit men; and we all slept in an upstairs room, and washed ourselves at a tap in the back garden. There were many of the pitmen whose houses I visited who had very remarkably good though small libraries, with such books as Mill's *Logic*, Carlyle's *Hero-Worship*, Fawcett's *Political Economy*, and others of that kind.[12]

Stuart did not make the mistake of patronising his students. Through his work he quickly discovered there was often far more appetite for learning, and sometimes far more genuine erudition, among his adult students than among the young undergraduates back in Cambridge. He helped to establish the principle that adult students could work — if they wished to — for credit by submitting written assignments, and that this credit could be accumulated. He also introduced end-of-course examinations, so that students who had both performed well during the course and reached an acceptable standard in the examination should be awarded a Certificate, signed by the Vice-Chancellor of the University. He went even further (though not successfully), proposing that such a qualification could lead to admission to a full-time degree programme at Cambridge with exemption from the first year of the programme.

Stuart's concept — of extension lectures providing continuing education for previously disenfranchised adult learners in the form of recognised Higher Education level Certificates which could become a passport to part-time or full-time university study leading to a degree — was visionary. His vision has today been largely realised, with many universities now accepting and indeed welcoming such students onto first degree programmes, often with exemption from part of the course; but, ironically, not at Cambridge.

Stuart worked tirelessly for extramural education, while still holding a professorship at Trinity. His work with educationally disadvantaged communities and sections of society led eventually to his becoming an MP, first in Hackney

---

12 Stuart, *Reminiscences*, pp.176–7.

(1884–1900) and, later, for a North-East constituency, Sunderland (1910–1914). As early as 1882 he had stood as a Liberal candidate for the University of Cambridge where, exceptionally, the system of election was by open voting, and he records in his *Reminiscences* that 'The largest number of clergymen voted against me, I suppose, than has ever voted against any individual person.'[13] When to his Parliamentary work he successfully added membership of London County Council, it was time to sever his formal academic links and he resigned his professorship in 1890. As a gift of thanks from the University, he received a silver salver and an Address signed by most members of the Senate (but not all; there were still some who disapproved of the very idea of extramural studies):

> We, the undersigned Resident Members of the Senate, having learned from your letter to the Vice-Chancellor your intention of resigning your Professorship in the University, desire to express our sense of the great public service which you have rendered in connexion with the University Extension movement.
>
> By yourself first delivering specimen courses of lectures, and afterwards strenuously advocating and ably organising their wide-spread establishment, you did for the country at large, and for our own and other Universities, work which we regard with sincere respect and admiration.
>
> The degree in which Cambridge has, during the last twenty years, come into useful relations with sections of the community which were previously regarded as beyond the sphere of its influence is, we hold, largely attributable to your inspiring initiative and to the wise principles of administration which, mainly under your guidance, the University laid down.[14]

It was right that this Address should have recognised the importance of Stuart's work, both nationally and in other universities, for the influence of his project spread far beyond Cambridge. It is appropriate to note that as long ago as 1890, Cambridge acknowledged its responsibility to those who had previously been 'beyond the sphere of its influence'. Extension lectures, extramural studies, lifelong or leisure learning, continuing or even post-professional education — all of these have owed a debt to James Stuart and all of them, by whatever current label they are known, contribute a great deal more to the University's commitment to widening participation, than simply accepting more 18-year old students from state schools and colleges.

Not, it must be acknowledged, that everything Stuart did succeeded at first attempt. He himself admitted, in the Inaugural Address he delivered to the Second Summer Meeting of University Extension Students in Oxford,

---

13 Stuart, *Reminiscences* p.235.
14 Stuart, *Reminiscences* p.176.

1889, 'we started on too ambitious a scale and we had to suffer for it.' As early as 1891, one of the first histories of the movement, *University Extension Past, Present, Future*, an Oxford perspective written by H.J. Mackinder, Staff Lecturer to the Oxford University Extension, and M.E. Sadler, Secretary to the Oxford Delegates for University Extension, had concluded:

> The promoters had in their mind three different classes of person: women, young men in the position of clerks or shop-assistants, and working people. The first idea was to have in each town a course specially adapted for each of these classes, and delivered on different days. But this proved, in almost every case, too costly. The larger towns were naturally the first to avail themselves of the new proposals. They contained a greater number of leisured or educationally-minded people; they furnished a larger area from which to draw subscriptions.... [But] the fact was that in most places no really general demand for higher education existed. It had to be created almost everywhere, and in many towns the work has still to be done. In every place a few of the leading inhabitants, the majority, perhaps, of the professional classes, a fair number of tradesman, and not a few working-men, were keenly alive to the value of the lectures which the University of Cambridge had decided to offer. There was abundant reason that their desire for higher education should be met; but the difficulty was that there were so few people who really felt the desire.[15]

There is plenty in this analysis of the situation in the nineteenth century which one can recognise from other sources. As early as the 1840s, novelists such as Elizabeth Gaskell had noted the appetite of working men to extend their education:

> In the neighbourhood of Oldham there are weavers, common hand-loom weavers, who throw the shuttle with unceasing sound, though Newton's "Principia" lies open on the loom, to be snatched at in work hours, but revelled over in meal times, or at night.[16]

And twenty years after Mackinder and Sadler were writing, E.M. Forster's Leonard Bast, in *Howards End*, is a classic instance of an insurance clerk anxious to improve himself by reading Ruskin and going to concerts in the Queen's Hall. Forster had met and knew people such as Leonard Bast: he himself taught for Working Men's Colleges and for the University of Cambridge Local Examinations and Lectures Syndicate. Much, indeed, that *University Extension* describes still obtains: Willy Russell's *Educating Rita*,

---

15 H.J. Mackinder and M.E. Sadler, *University Extension Past, Present, Future* (Oxford: Oxford University Press 1891) pp.26–7.

16 Elizabeth Gaskell, *Mary Barton* (1848) Ch. 5.

after all, only updates both Bernard Shaw's *Pygmalion* and the archetype of a working-class woman who aspires to better herself through education — with the Open University replacing the Workers' Educational Association (WEA). But the rigid social hierarchy implied by the original scheme to segregate women, clerks and working-men has largely vanished, along with Working Men's Institutes and single-sex universities; though of course Jemima Clough's Newnham College remains resolutely women-only.

It is, incidentally, ironic that Newnham should have been the setting for Virginia Woolf's celebrated polemical lectures, later transposed into *A Room of One's Own*. Not only did she complain that her father Leslie Stephen had deemed higher education inappropriate for women — or at least for his own daughter — but Stephen himself had contributed to the latest Macmillan 'English Men of Letters' series, advertised explicitly as being 'for university extension students'.

That the concept of extramural studies should have been, in spite of setbacks, so successfully developed in the twenty years since Stuart launched his first series of Lectures is a tribute to his vision and energy: it was an idea whose time had come. By the end of the First World War this momentum, accelerated as it had been by the founding of a number of university colleges, by the influence of the WEA and by organisations such as the YMCA providing lectures and classes for soldiers during the war itself, meant that the adult education movement had come of age. Cambridge recognised this fact in 1924 by approving the splitting of the combined Local Examinations and Lectures Syndicate and setting up an autonomous Board of Extramural Studies.

The headquarters of the old Syndicate were in a building at the entrance to Mill Lane in Cambridge; when the University opened the offices of the newly-established Board next door to the Syndicate, they called the building Stuart House. It was (and is) one of the most impressive buildings of the inter-war period in the city; and Cambridge's pride in it can be judged from the elaborate achievement of the University's arms dominating the pediment of its Queen Anne-style façade. Stuart House, then, at the time of its opening in 1926, was a powerful statement of the University's debt to James Stuart and an equally powerful statement of its commitment to lifelong learning.

****

From this date to the start of the Second World War, the fully evolved pattern of local centres, semi-independent of the parent university though sometimes managed by resident tutors who spent six months of each year 'up-country', organising, teaching and supporting students, had been established. Book boxes, supplying books for each course from a special university-based extramural library, were transported to local centres. Of particular importance was the creation of university tutorial classes, usually of twenty-four weekly meetings running for three years and provided jointly by universities and the WEA. These classes offered a challenging level of student democracy which many universities would still find alarming today. As a post-war WEA leaflet, *The University Tutorial Class: Questions answered for Students*, explained:

> A university tutorial class is much more than a group of students listening to a lecture. It is an exercise in self-government, a joint enterprise which depends for its success upon co-operation between all concerned: WEA branch, students and tutor. The WEA branch recruits students for the class and undertakes all the necessary local organisation. The students choose their own subject of study. They express preference for the tutor under whom they wish to work. They co-operate with him in the preparation of the syllabus, or master plan, of the three-year course. They appoint their own class secretary and librarian. The tutor teaches.[17]

The idea of a three-year programme was to allow time for students to reach a sufficient standard of proficiency in study skills for their work to be marked at university standard in the third year. What is important here is that nothing is imposed: everything is negotiated, and the teaching — as this same leaflet explains — is 'approached through the experience and interests of the students themselves, moving at a pace set by their needs'. In many ways, this remains today the fundamental skill of tutoring a continuing education class. A WEA leaflet of the same period, *A Statement for Tutors*, spells out the crucial difference (now, as then) between lecturing to 18-year-old students who have all got three A grades (and, now, at least one A* into the bargain) and teaching adult students on an open-access course:

> Although he will be expected to give much the tutor will have much to gain from the university tutorial class. He will have to reconsider the subject matter of his specialist knowledge and re-examine its assumptions constantly under the weekly scrutiny which they receive from men and women with a much wider range of experience and specialist knowledge than he is likely to meet anywhere else... . The exchange of speculation with men and women who, by virtue of their character and human experience assimilated during a long life, may in some respects be his superior gives him a standard against which to measure his own conception of life and the place of his specialist knowledge in it.... If he is honest he will recognize the influence of his students upon his own formation and count this as a rich reward.[18]

---

17 Workers' Educational Association (WEA), *The University Tutorial Class: Questions answered for Students*, (nd.) p.1.

18 Workers' Educational Association (WEA), *A Statement for Teachers* (nd.) p.3.

Speaking personally, I certainly recognise this description; so, I am sure, will most teachers who have worked in adult education. Throughout the twentieth century, writers and cultural commentators from E.M. Forster and T.S. Eliot to Raymond Williams and Richard Hoggart all developed their philosophy of education and of literature through such teaching, often in the first half of their careers. For me, it has been the other way around. The most significant decision of my career was taken before my career even began: in the week before my A levels, prompted by my English teacher (the same one who told us he would teach us for five terms and only train us to pass the exams in the sixth), I abandoned my initial idea of reading Law at university and determined to become a teacher myself. It was absolutely the right decision, and one I have never for a moment regretted. At different times and in different places I have taught pupils and students and teachers from the ages of 8 to 88 (and occasionally older still) but no teaching has been as challenging nor — certainly — as rewarding as the classes I have taught which are still most accurately described by the single term, extramural.

At the heart of such teaching, it seems to me, lie three principles. First, there is the awareness that you are likely to learn as much from your students as they will learn from you. Second, your own knowledge, scholarship and research must underpin every class you take: you cannot busk your way through two hours of lecture and discussion with extramural students. However, thirdly you are not there to dispense wisdom, nor necessarily the latest knowledge from the ivory tower, to grateful students who will lap up every word you utter: you are there to teach people to think in new ways through sharing your own subject with them, and giving them an insight into why that subject matters.

For me, that subject has been English Literature.

1.2 On course: teaching literature in lifelong learning

The following statements argue that English Literature is an important and rewarding subject. The first is by Rachel Falconer, Professor of Modern and Contemporary Literature at Lausanne University. The second is by C.K. Stead, the New Zealand academic, critic, novelist and poet. The third is by Raymond Williams, a leading figure in adult lifelong learning in the mid twentieth century, and author of *Culture and Society* (1958).

> Literature and literary criticism are about life – ordinary and extraordinary. When they cease to be lively, provocative and life-enhancing, they cease to have any defensible function at all.[1]

> Language — spoken and written — is power. If as a society we want to be effective in the world we need large numbers of people who are both articulate and literate; and the best promoter of those talents is literature itself. Literature is also a source of comfort and learning. In reading we learn from virtual rather than actual experience — in imagination, experiences we haven't had to live through in fact … . Sometimes our literary experiences can be more real to us than our own. We forget most of the detail of our own lives but remember a story. Narratives give shape to a shapeless world.[2]

> Literature was welcomed in adult education, it seems to me, because of the fact that many of the greatest nineteenth-century writers were active critics of society; their writings had an obvious interest for those who demanded change. The only question was the level of seriousness; were not fiction and poetry self-defined as frivolity and escape? The

---

1   Rachel Falconer, quoted by Matthew Reisz, in 'Style Points', *Times Higher Education*, 15 July 2010.
2   C.K. Stead, *Book Self* (Auckland, NZ: Auckland University Press 2008) pp. 96-97.

question has continued to be put, for the Gradgrinds have accumulated ... . But still, with the fierceness of Ruskin and of Morris against them, with Matthew Arnold quietly negotiating education in the name of culture, and with the strong tradition of self-educated working men still reading Bunyan and Shelley and Dickens, the accumulators were never sure of their ground. Literature stayed, and the best teaching of Ruskin and of Arnold developed into the practical criticism of our own generation.[3]

Of these writers only the last, Raymond Williams, was talking specifically about continuing education, but their statements add up to a manifesto for literature as a subject that is life-enhancing, liberal in Newman's sense, valuable for the training it offers as a 'discipline of thought' – a phrase always to be associated with F.R. Leavis – and at the heart of what lifelong learning should be about.

The first weekly continuing education class I ever taught was in Bedford. The group had been in existence for over twenty years, meeting in a church hall. It was a university tutorial class in the traditional sense, run jointly by Cambridge and the WEA, and I had negotiated a course with the students who had previously interviewed me to see whether they wanted to be taught by me or not. The course we had agreed was on ideas of Englishness in Literature from 1900 to the end of the Second World War. At first, the students had been nervous about my proposed subject, thinking there was something uncomfortably jingoistic about the theme, but I reassured them that my aim was to get them thinking about different ways in which writers from before the First World War onwards had represented nationality, national identity and a sense of 'Englishness', as distinct from Britishness, through their writing. It proved a lively topic, not least because there were Welsh, Scots, Irish and German students among the twenty four there.

The group was mostly of retired people, and included teachers, librarians and journalists. Nearly all of them knew each other well, and nearly everyone had plenty to say – except one, the only new student among them. Hilary was the wife of a farmer who had just retired and had told her to go out and find something to do now she was no longer needed to help on the farm. She had been encouraged to join by one of the others, but was nervous that she would not cope. At the start of the first class, she had passed me a note which read 'PLEASE DON'T ASK ME TO SAY ANYTHING'. At the end, she told me she would not come again because, as she explained, she had left school at twelve during the war and, though she liked reading, had never heard of any

---

3   Raymond Williams, in John McIlroy (ed.) *Border Country*, (Leicester: NIACE 1993) p.186.

of the books on my reading list and felt completely ignorant alongside all the
others. In addition to which, she said, she was deaf and could not hear what
most of the students were saying.

The class sat around a large table which all but filled a rather snug parish
meeting room. I told Hilary she could sit near to me the next week so that at
least she should hear everything I said, and she promised to give the class one
more go. The book we were studying was *Howards End* and Hilary said she
was quite enjoying it, though she felt the Schlegel sisters were less interesting
than Mrs Wilcox – and her favourite character was Miss Avery, because she
was the only character who had lived on a farm all her life. Well, it was a start;
and before she left, I made her agree that if I didn't expect her to speak during
the class she would at least talk to me about the book for five minutes at the
end of the morning.

That next class was full of surprises. I began by passing round a copy
of the once-popular Edwardian anthology, *The Open Road*, edited by E.V.
Lucas. This is the book that inspires Leonard Bast to go walking through the
Surrey woods one night when the stars fail to shine. None of the students had
actually seen a copy of the book before; few had heard of it. This led to an
animated debate about anthologies generally: about how many of them had a
copy of the *Oxford Book of English Verse*, edited by Q, as opposed to Palgrave's
Golden Treasury; about how far anthologies helped to shape taste or how far
they reflected it.

I asked what sort of picture of England and Englishness a foreigner might
get from reading *The Open Road*, with its bucolic descriptions of friendly
inns, thatched cottages and ploughmen homeward plodding. Erika from
Munich said it was exactly how she had imagined England to be from the
books she had read growing up in Germany before the war. Someone said it
was all very well for Forster to patronise Leonard for liking E.V. Lucas when
he himself had written some pretty purple passages. Such as, I asked?

> If one wanted to show a foreigner England, perhaps the wisest course
> would be to take him to the final section of the Purbeck Hills, and
> stand him on their summit, a few miles to the east of Corfe. Then
> system after system of our island would roll together under his feet.
> Beneath him is the valley of the Frome, and all the wild lands that
> come tossing down from Dorchester, black and gold, to mirror their
> gorse in the expanses of Poole. The valley of the Stour is beyond,
> unaccountable stream, dirty at Blandford, pure at Wimborne, sliding
> out of fat fields, to marry the Avon beneath the tower of Christchurch.
> The valley of the Avon – invisible, but far to the north the trained
> eye may see Clearbury Ring that guards it, and the imagination
> may leap beyond that on to Salisbury Plain itself, and beyond the

Plain to all the glorious downs of central England. Nor is suburbia
absent. Bournemouth's ignoble coast cowers to the right, heralding
the pine-trees that mean, for all their beauty, red houses, and the Stock
Exchange, and extend to the gates of London itself. So tremendous is
the City's trail! But the cliffs of Freshwater it shall never touch, and
the island will guard the Island's purity till the end of time. Seen from
the west, the Wight is beautiful beyond all laws of beauty. It is as if a
fragment of England floated forward to greet the foreigner – chalk of
our chalk, turf of our turf, epitome of what will follow.[4]

What did it mean to call a passage 'purple'? And if this was indeed
purple, did Forster intend his narrator to be taken seriously? Could the
tone of a passage such as this be both serious and comic at the same time?
And if it was comic who was being mocked, the sentimental Englishman
or the gullible foreigner, or even Forster himself? The discussion filled at
least half an hour. Forster's geography – or at least his sense of perspective
– was called into question: where were his 'glorious downs of central
England'? Berkshire, for goodness sake!

One of the students, who knew Forster's novels well, suggested that what
he was doing here was to poke fun at precisely the kind of writing which found
its way into anthlogies like *The Open Road*; she reminded us of the scathing
way he deals with tourists in Italy who go around with their noses so deep in
Baedeker's Guide that they pay scant attention to the treasures they are reading
about. Then someone pointed out that the landscape Forster was describing
was exactly the landscape of Hardy's Egdon Heath, and I made a mental
note to photocopy passages from *The Return of the Native* and from *Tess of the
d'Urbervilles* for the next class. Better still, one of the students said the passage
reminded her of Auden's poem 'Look Stranger!' and for a while I sat back and
listened to the students educate each other. The confidence with which they
had started to speak and the way they were embracing the search for ways to
define and describe England and Englishness was impressive.

Equally impressive was the turn the conversation took when one
student, who had up to now said little, asked wasn't it surprising that
Forster was so concerned about suburbia and the changing face of the
English countryside as early as 1910? Others quickly picked up this
theme, pointing out how the encroachment of suburbia was a recurring
motif in *Howards End* with the motor car as the demonic instrument
responsible for this pollution of the countryside. No one actually used
the word 'ecocriticism' at this point but when I discussed that term later
in the course, they all remembered the conversation in the car between
Charles and Margaret on the way to Hilton:

---

4   E.M. Forster, *Howards End* (London: Penguin English Library, 1983), p.170.

'The motor's come to stay... . One must get about. There's a pretty church – oh, you aren't sharp enough. Well, look out, if the road worries you – right outward at the scenery.'

She looked out at the scenery. It heaved and merged like porridge. Presently it congealed. They had arrived.[5]

There were those in the group who spoke up for Bournemouth, declaiming against Forster for calling its coasts 'ignoble', but most of them admired the novelist's prescience in imagining the commuter belt stretching all the way from the Stock Exchange to Sandbanks. I could see Hilary puzzling over this, and for a moment I was afraid she was going, in spite of herself, to speak up and ask if Forster really thought there were pine trees all the way from Hampshire to the gates of London. But I had underestimated her. At the end of the class, she asked me what was the word to describe something not meant to be taken literally. The friend who had brought her said at once, metaphorical, and I said yes, but … . (Forster himself, I recalled, had once declared, 'I am a Cambridge man, and my favourite word is 'but'.) The following week I came back to this image of the pine trees, and was able to introduce the difference between metaphor and metonymy.

What I have described here, my memory of the discussion in a university tutorial class long ago, exemplifies my technique of teaching literature to a goup of adult readers who between them had a formidable range of life and literary experiences. You have to build on what the students bring to the discussion; you never patronise them, and you never underestimate them. All the time the students learn from each other, and they end up teaching you as much as you teach them.

****

Just as a teacher of English in a school will teach different aspects of the subject to different classes at different levels so, too, in continuing education one teaches the subject in different ways to different sets of students, under different circumstances and with different objectives. Yet the subject is always English, whether being taught to primary or PhD students; and in this context it is only now, at the end of my career, that I have come to realise the importance of a teacher of whom I have been aware since the age of ten, when I was first introduced to his work by the Headmaster of my prep school. On a winter's evening, while we sat at our desks in the School Room (it was a very small school: we could all fit into a single large room) he read to us the chapter 'On Jargon' from *On the Art of Writing* (1916), by Sir Arthur Quiller-Couch.

I want to say more about Quiller-Couch, who is today too often overlooked as an important figure in the history of the teaching of English,

---

5   E.M. Forster, *Howards End*, pp.198-199.

but I must introduce him by returning briefly to James Stuart, the father of extramural studies. Stuart was asked in 1878 to give the inaugural address to the Nottingham University Students' Association - that is, an association of those students who were enrolled on the courses of Extension Lectures run by Cambridge and delivered in Nottingham. Stuart, by now Professor of Engineering and a pragmatist as much as an idealist, spoke on 'The Educational Value of Some of the Principal Branches of Study'. He had this to say about the study of what he called 'mere' or pure literature – poetry, drama and fiction:

> The danger of such study is that it becomes vague, that it becomes discursive, that in fact it ceases to become of the nature of a study and degenerates into a mere intellectual luxury. On the other hand, when we read with method and with attention, critically and reverentially approaching the works of genius, the faculties of imagination and of sympathy are kindled to a brighter glow, new and wider ideas arise in our minds, and our souls become smitten with that greater magnanimity which has belonged to those great souls with whom we endeavour thus to associate. These may be esteemed, perhaps, rather as moral than as intellectual qualities; yet the separation is not wholly possible, and most certainly a mind too deficient in the faculty of ready sympathy cannot be at its fullest development where the moral force is defective.
>
> Certainly at the present time of the world, we are somewhat in danger of neglecting too much merely literary study.... Yet we must beware of a danger arising from a devotion to mere literature; namely, that it becomes a mere mental luxury. I am convinced that there is nothing more enervating to the mind and body than luxury: it is the curse of our age and country.[6]

Stuart's idea of the study of literature as a way of opening minds and expanding horizons is one to which almost all teachers of English as a liberal art would assent. The terms he uses here – imagination, the faculty of ready sympathy, moral force – anticipate the rhetoric and arguments of later, mid-twentieth century, Cambridge teachers from F.R. Leavis to Raymond Williams and David Holbrook. Stuart's own tastes in literature were very much of his time. In the same lecture he lamented that 'There is no one just now, for example, who writes with the excellent elegance of Charles Lamb.' And his anxiety about the study of 'mere literature' becoming 'mere mental luxury' articulated a widespread fear in Cambridge circles that led to the idea of a School of English in the University being strongly opposed. Such indeed was this opposition that it was not possible for a student to take a degree in

6   James Stuart, *Nottingham University Students' Association Inaugural Address*, April 10 1878 (Cambridge UL mss. BEMS/1/40), pp.12-13.

English until 1917, when the syllabus for Section A, 'English Literature: Modern and Medieval', as proposed in the *Cambridge University Reporter* (8 May, 1917) included the following papers:

i   Questions and essays on the general history of English Literature since 1603.

ii Passages from specified and unspecified works of Shakespeare for explanation and discussion; with questions on language, metre, literary history, and literary criticism.

iii Questions on a prescribed period of English Literature.

iv Questions on English literature, life, and thought from 1350 to 1603.

v   Questions on a special subject in the general history of literature, ancient and modern, in connexion and comparison with English Literature.

vi Questions on the life, literature, and thought of England from 1066 to 1350; with passages from specified English and French works for translation and explanation.

This all looks traditional enough, and it is ironic that the Edward VII Professor of English at Cambridge who saw through this proposal was Sir Arthur Quiller-Couch, for Q (as he was always known) had a strong belief in the importance of teaching modern literature. Lecturing during the First World War on the poetry of George Meredith, he admitted:

> I have possibly as much reason as anyone in this room to know how faulty one's judgment may be about modern work, and specially about modern poetry. Still the task of appraising it has to be done, for the books of our time *are* the books of our time. They tell us in their various ways 'How it strikes a Contemporary': and we shall not intelligently prepare ourselves, here at Cambridge, by drawing an imaginary line somewhere between the past and the present and announcing, 'On this side are the certified dead, who are alive; on that, the living, who are non-existent.'[7]

Presumably, then, Q would have approved of the programme in literature for the University of Cambridge Local Lectures Summer Meeting of 1914, which ran uninterrupted by the outbreak of war:

- The Work and Ideas of William Morris
- The Modernisation of the Study of Literature
- Walt Whitman
- Some Tendencies in Poetry at the Present Day

---

7   Sir A. Quiller-Couch, *Studies in Literature*, Cambridge: Cambridge University Press 1924, p.59.

- Realism and Mysticism
- Samuel Butler
- Thomas Hardy
- Henry James, *Psychological Analyst*
- Pity and Terror in the Works of Rudyard Kipling
- The Modern Drama.[8]

High profile lecturers on this course included A.C. Benson, the essayist and Master of Magdalene, on William Morris, and E.M. Forster - by this date one of the best-known novelists in Britain - on Samuel Butler. It is interesting that the emphasis here was so firmly on the modern: only the course on Realism and Modernism went back as far as the 17th century metaphysical poets. To this day, you may more easily find contemporary literature forming the basis of undergraduate level courses taught in continuing education than in the English Tripos. This emphasis, incidentally, extended to other courses that summer: Roger Fry on Modern Art, for instance, and lectures on rising philosophers such as G.E. Moore and Bertrand Russell.

In many respects Quiller-Couch echoed James Stuart's own, earlier, ideas and literary enthusiasms (he shared Stuart's admiration for Charles Lamb, for instance) but he fundamentally rejected the concept of 'mere literature':

> There is in fact, Gentlemen, no such thing as 'mere literature'. Pedants have coined that contemptuous term to express a figmentary concept of their own imagination … . The thoughts, actions and passions of men become literature by the simple but difficult process of being recorded in memorable speech.[9]

****

I have just finished running a day school at Madingley Hall. It is part of a 10 week course on Modern English Literature, taught at Diploma level, equivalent to second year undergraduate study. There are eighteen students in the group, some of whom have been studying with me, on and off, for several years; others have joined this term. The youngest is in her early twenties, the eldest is several decades older.

They are a mixed group in every respect, except for their tremendous commitment to the course. I have practising and retired teachers; university officers, a writer, two students who are currently unemployed; an IT

---

8   University of Cambridge Local Lectures Summer Meeting 1914 Syllabus of Lectures (Cambridge: Cambridge University Press 1914) pp.29-46.

9   A. Quiller-Couch, *On the Art of Reading* (Cambridge: Cambridge University Press 1924) p.128.

specialist, a retired Arts administrator, a retired bookseller, an editor, a mother with two small children; some students I know little of, others over time I have come to know a good deal about.

Some of the students (the majority) are actively working for credit; that is, they are submitting work term by term and accumulating credit so that, when they have completed the required amount, they can qualify for a Diploma of Higher Education in Modern English Literature. After that, some hope to move on to take an Advanced Diploma in English Literature, a research-based course leading to submission of a 10-12000 word dissertation. Others have no need, or no intention, of collecting credit or indeed of submitting written work. They have come for various reasons, but writing essays is not one of them.

Do I mind that not everyone wants to pursue the programme to its conclusion, successfully completing six modules and gaining their Diploma? Not in the least; though, like Desdemona, 'I do perceive here a divided duty'. These Certificate and Diploma programmes (the higher-level Diplomas especially) are primarily intended to be taken by students who are serious about wanting to study for a qualification. Indeed there was a time when it was necessary to insist that students submitted written work as evidence of 'completion', without which the Institute of Continuing Education was not entitled to draw down the funding which underpinned the financial viability of the whole enterprise. Now, however, owing to the loss of funding for liberal arts and humanities part-time adult education announced by the Government in 2007, such arguments no longer hold. I welcome students who want to study English at the Institute, whatever their motives, credit-seeking or otherwise. The only criteria for admission are commitment to studying English Literature, plus willingness to read the texts and to participate fully in each session.

Does it matter, actually, whether every student actively contributes to discussion? I certainly want every student to feel able to speak up, and - if they feel they urge - to speak out. Some students can always be relied upon to answer a question, to get a discussion going; others may have to be reined in occasionally to give others the chance to speak. One quite quickly gets to know which students would like to speak but feel wary of committing themselves. A tutor's job with such a mixed group of students must always include checking that students are engaged, are following what is being said and are learning from one another as well as from the tutor.

The course I have been teaching is entitled 'Cambridge Critics and Cambridge Criticism'. It is the last of six 'core' modules taught over the past three years, one each Michaelmas and Lent Term. In the Easter Terms I have offered the students a project module. The course started with Sir Arthur Quiller-Couch, who established the first School of English at Cambridge, and has moved forward from I.A. Richards and William Empson to F.R. Leavis and *Scrutiny*. It will finish with Frank Kermode and Tony Tanner. I have devised the course in such a way that, rather than simply reading *The Great Tradition* or *Seven Types of Ambiguity*, we have been studying texts and authors. We have looked in detail for example at the poetry of George Herbert and the arguments Cambridge critics deployed to champion metaphysical poetry. We spent much of one two-hour evening class studying Herbert's sonnet 'Prayer' ('Prayer the churches banquet, angells age'), exploring in particular the line 'Heaven in ordinarie, man well dress'd'. With the aid of the Oxford Dictionary, we weighed the merits of eight different meanings of the word 'ordinarie' available to Herbert in the early 17th century; and for each possible meaning or pair of meanings, we used Empson's seven types of ambiguity to evaluate the effect Herbert's use of the word – indeed of the whole phrase 'Heaven in ordinarie' - might have on the way we read the poem. It was a fascinating experiment, and one I had not tried before. At the end of the class, a student told me he'd never before seen so clearly how learning a critical method could enhance one's way of reading closely and deeply.

****

Being able to devise one's own syllabus, to suit the programme both to the needs and experience of one's students and to one's own interests and research, is not least among the rewards of teaching literature to adult continuing education classes of this kind. The teacher of GCSE or A level English Literature is rigidly constrained by the demands of the 'specifications' which not only dictate to a large extent what texts he must teach but also how they must be taught – what assessment objectives will be targeted, and how much weighting they will carry; what strategies must be adopted for covering the syllabus – this military language suggesting all too accurately the siege of English. Lecturers, tutors or supervisors teaching undergraduates have more freedom than this, but still have to prepare their students at some speed for the exams on which too much these days depends. The time available to study individual texts or authors in depth is all too restricted.

The literature tutor working in continuing education is unbelievably lucky by comparison. John McIlroy, writing in *Border Country* (NIACE, 1993) about the early career of Raymond Williams, makes this point:

> Had Richard Hoggart and Raymond Williams been working in most English departments they may well have been simply literary critics. They would as junior lecturers have been teaching subjects designated by others. Even later their curriculum would have been subject to the policy of departments in which theirs would probably have been minority voices. They would, as many contemporaries with experience

of adult education and internal teaching attest, have lacked a great deal of autonomy and freedom to range widely across disciplines, benefiting from the impetus to innovative thinking such travel can stimulate.[10]

McIlroy sums this up by listing three advantages of teaching literature in adult education:

1 The freedom to choose one's own syllabus and gear this to whatever one happens to be researching or writing on.

2 The opportunity to study literary texts and topics at much greater depth than the pressures of time and crowded survey syllabuses in English departments allowed for.

3 The opportunity to teach beyond the usual frontiers of English.[11]

I agree with all these points, though I would qualify the first by saying that a continuing education teacher of literature (or of any subject) must be a generalist: it's no good squeezing the content of your course into the wrong-shaped mould, just because your own research interests are so all-absorbing to you that you assume they must be of interest and value to everyone else. They may be, but it doesn't necessarily follow.

The second point is critically important: you have to give the students time to reach the level of confidence needed to travel with you in each class. New skills are being learnt, new ways of thinking being discovered. One of my students, Sarah, has put this into her own words:

> Studying literature with close reading has enabled me to get more out of works that have long been favourites as well as stretching my appreciation by exposing me to writers new to me. Literature offers insights into social history, human behaviour and the values of other cultures, which, as a social scientist, I still find fascinating.
>
> As I have always known that I should have read English at university, to be able to study literature now and gain the skills of close reading has enriched my life, not least in the field of poetry.

The third point, teaching beyond the usual frontiers of English, is the one that most excites me. The usual frontiers are defined both by custom and practice: *what* has traditionally been taught, and *how much* can be taught in the time available. In continuing higher education, one has much greater freedom to challenge both custom and practice.

One of my first tasks, when I became a Staff Tutor, was to devise and teach a new Certificate of Higher Education in English Literature, which could be taught over two years and would appeal both to students with no

---

10 John McIlroy (ed.), *Border Country* (Leicester: NIACE 1993) p.4.
11 *ibid.*

previous experience whatever of studying English and to those who might have considerable knowledge of the subject already. Indeed, the first group of students to enrol included students who had left school with no formal qualifications, overseas students for whom English was certainly not even their second language, a retired teacher of A level English and someone completing a PhD in French art of the nineteenth century.

I developed a course consisting of four core modules (which all students aiming to achieve the Certificate must take) and two optional modules. It was to be a modular syllabus, so the modules could be taken in any order, though the first module was introductory.

Module 1   Writers, texts and readers

Module 2   Shakespeare

Module 3   Making the modern world: literature in the 17th century

Module 4   London in literature

Option 1   Close Reading and Context

Option 2   Project essay.

The first module introduced the study of literature texts from the perspectives equally of the writer and of the reader. I wanted to insist that writers and readers are both critics of the same text; that the act of writing is simultaneously an act of criticism, with the writer constantly discriminating between different options, spending more time (perhaps much more time) on the process of revision than on the initial act of writing. I focused therefore first on texts by writers who also wrote about writing – the act of writing their own novels, poetry or drama and the act of reading other people's. I began with David Lodge, whose novels are themselves self-reflexively about the business of writing and teaching literature and whose collection of brief critical essays, *The Art of Fiction*, offers a non-threatening, but still challenging, introduction to critical terms and critical thinking.

Next we turned to Trollope, and to *Barchester Towers*. There were three reasons for this choice. First, I wanted a writer whom the students were unlikely to have encountered before. Second, I wanted a novel dealing with an area of life that would have been unfamiliar (to say the least) to these students as readers. Victorian provincial society in a cathedral city is one thing; nineteenth century debates about theology and churchmanship are another. How important was it, I wanted the students to ask themselves once they started to question themselves and each other about how they read this novel, to be aware of the historical context in which Trollope located Barchester: that of the ongoing struggle between the different factions within the Church of England?[12] The novel pits different strands of churchmanship

---

12 See below, Part 2, 'Trollope and Religious Controversy', pp.64–80.

against each other: the old Anglican piety represented by Mr Harding, the Warden ('Heaven in ordinarie, man well dress'd'); the new influence of the Tractarian movement embodied by Mr Arabin; the aggressive traditionalism of Archdeacon Grantly; and, equal but opposite, the aggressive evangelicalism of Mrs Proudie and Mr Slope. Third, I wanted to make the students read Trollope in the light of the author's own *Autobiography*. How would we judge *Barchester Towers* by Trollope's own standards?

> A novel should give a picture of common life enlivened by humour and sweetened by pathos. To make that picture worthy of attention, the canvas should be crowded with real portraits, not of individuals known to the author, but of created personages impregnated with traits of character which are known. To my thinking the plot is but the vehicle for all this: and when you have the vehicle without the passengers, a story of mystery in which the agents never spring to life, you have but a wooden show.[13]

It is important to work outwards from the text itself; only then does it really make sense to start asking how we can understand and apply terms such as 'a picture of common life', 'real portraits' 'created personages' to a work of fiction. Is the reader only a passive spectator or is the act of reading as much a creative and creating act as the act of writing? It was the asking of questions such as these, based on the experience of reading significant but unfamiliar texts, which underpinned this introductory course.

Alongside the study of the main texts for this module, we spent a portion of every session, exploring a single poem, step by step, throughout the term. Sometimes we did this at the start of an evening, as a kind of limbering-up exercise; at other times we finished with the poem; but we never missed a week. The poem I had chosen was Wordsworth's sonnet 'Composed upon Westminster Bridge, September 3rd. 1802'. Following, at first, the strict principles of Practical Criticism, we began with just the fourteen lines of the poem itself: no title, no author, no date. What was the poem about? What if anything could we infer about the speaker? We didn't consider the form at all to begin with: that came in the second week. Gradually, as the term went on, we added more information, each time asking, whether (or how far) the new information – the title, the author, the date of composition, what the significance of that date might be in political terms, in biographical terms – altered or affected the way each member of the group responded to the poem. Having established that the poem was by Wordsworth, and why he was crossing Westminster Bridge with his sister early on a summer's day in 1802, we started to compare the poem with others he was writing

---

13 Anthony Trollope, *Autobiography*, (Oxford: Oxford University Press World's Classics 1923) Ch. VII, p.116.

about London and about his personal circumstances at this time. Each week I invited the students to write up a brief log of our discussion so that they kept a running record of our work on the poem. We always began by reading the whole poem aloud, and I encouraged them to learn it by heart; several of them did. We ended by looking at a range of contrasting critical approaches to this sonnet, both those which read the poem as an organic unity and those which deconstructed it to identify its *aporia*, the tensions, gaps and fissures which lay beneath its apparently unified, organic surface.

There were three reasons for making this an integral part of each week's work. I aimed, first, to demonstrate how different ways of reading a poem, using different contexts, deepened and adjusted one's initial response to the work. Next, I hoped by this approach to get students to decide for themselves which contexts and which approaches they found most helpful. At the same time, however, and as a result of this, I wanted thirdly to show that first impressions should never be last impressions: understanding how the poem was organised and structured (its internal architecture) and how the circumstances that influenced its production (its external relationship with the world) always existed in a dynamic relationship with each other.

Some of the students found the architectural analogy helpful: one can first study and appreciate the form, function and impact of a building in isolation; then one can examine the building in relation to those around it, and to those of a similar kind – both its contemporaries and its predecessors. Alternatively, one can reverse this order, taking in (as it were) the impact of King's Parade in Cambridge as a whole, before turning to focus on individual elements of the streetscape: the overwhelming dominance of King's College Chapel, for instance, or the modest provincial row of shops that faces it. So, some of the students were surprised to discover that the sonnet form had been largely unregarded during most of the 18th century, and that Wordsworth had found the impetus to start writing sonnets after reading some of Milton's, whose form he chose at first to follow. Others (those in particular who had some knowledge and experience of literary history) saw Wordsworth's poem as existing in a continuum that stretched both before and after, indeed up to the present day.[14]

There was a further reason for spending part of each session in this first term on this single poem: Wordsworth's celebrated sonnet — and, yes, we did also discuss how and why it might have become so celebrated and whether it deserved its fame at the expense of most of the other 100 plus sonnets Wordsworth wrote — provided a link to all the other taught modules in the programme. It provided a point of comparison and contrast when we

---

14 For a full discussion of Wordsworth's sonnet and its contextual history, developed from my teaching of this course, see Adrian Barlow, *World and Time: Teaching Literature in Context* (Cambridge: Cambridge University Press 2009).

started to read Shakespeare's sonnets and, later, when we read Milton's. By the time we came to explore representations of London both as a theme in literature, as a centre for the production of literature (both its writing and its publishing) and as a metropolitan hub of literary life, Wordsworth's poem had already got us thinking about all these things.

****

Working in this way with a group for a full term — and possibly over two or more years — you come to know your students very well. By contrast, on a weekend course (Friday evening to Sunday midday) the students may well be unfamiliar to you and to each other; however, because of the intensive teaching involved, tutor and class have to learn quickly to work together and the tutor must ensure that all who wish to contribute are encouraged to do so, though neither at the expense nor to the irritation of the rest of the group. As tutor, too, you must make no prior assumptions about who your students are and how much they will know about you or your subject.

I once taught a weekend course on T.S. Eliot's *Four Quartets*. There were nearly twenty students in the group. After fifteen minutes of the first session, with introductions over, I had launched into my opening discussion of the poem and its genesis and was talking about Eliot in the 1930s, when a student asked me a question about the poet and anti-semitism. This was a not unexpected question and I had already thought about ways of answering it, openly but cautiously. There came a moment when I said, 'Eliot's position on the Jews in the 1930s was implied in his book *After Strange Gods* and was much more oblique than the comments that would later be made by Ezra Pound, both in his poetry and ....' I got no further. A man sitting inconspicuously in the corner of the room interrupted me: 'Before you go any further, Mr Barlow, I'd better warn you, I'm Pound's cousin.'

Of course, one can often use such students to advantage, and I remember this *Four Quartets* weekend fondly. My introductory session took as its starting point Helen Gardner's landmark book, *The Composition of Four Quartets* (1978) and discussed the way in which the poem had grown and altered profoundly between 1936, when *Burnt Norton* appeared as the final poem in Eliot's *Collected Poems 1909-1935*, and 1942 when — in very different circumstances — Eliot published *Little Gidding* and completed the cycle. At the time he wrote *Burnt Norton* Eliot had no plans to write a sequence of poems on the subject of time, memory, language and history: he did not even think of *Burnt Norton* as a quartet, though the five-part format echoed that of *The Waste Land*. We noted the final words of the *Burnt Norton*:

> Ridiculous the waste sad time
> Stretching before and after.[15]

---

15 T.S. Eliot, *Burnt Norton*, in Collected Poems 1909-1962 (London: Faber and Faber 1963) p.195.

These lines had appeared on the last page of the *Collected Poems*, published at a time when Eliot thought his career as a poet had come to an end and was hoping that playwriting, lecturing and editing would be the main elements of his career from then on. We discussed ways in which people signal the end of a career, as well as the way these lines appeared to have been Eliot's own last words on his career as a poet — at least as it had seemed to him in the middle of the 1930s. By contrast, the final lines of *Little Gidding* offer a completely different summing up:

> And all shall be well
> And all manner of thing shall be well
> When the tongues of flame are in-folded
> Into the crowned knot of fire
> And the fire and the rose are one.[16]

This led us on to a discussion about the evolution of poems: whether it is true, as Paul Valéry had claimed, that 'a poem is never finished, only abandoned' or whether we agreed with Robert Frost that writing was an act of discovery: 'I write,' Frost claimed, 'to find out what I didn't know I knew.'[17] Several members of the group were themselves writers as well as readers. One quoted a couple of lines from Seamus Heaney that she said chimed with her experience:

> I rhyme
> To see myself, to set the darkness echoing.[18]

This brought us back to *Burnt Norton*, which we discussed in detail the following morning. We considered the image of the drained pool in the rose garden and the images of the children glimpsed when suddenly 'the pool was filled with water out of sunlight'. Helen Gardner suggests that there were two direct sources of inspiration behind this passage in the poem: Rudyard Kipling's story 'They' and a poem by Elizabeth Barrett Browning, 'The Lost Bower' — described by Gardner as a 'lax effusion'.[19] I had two further suggested sources. One was D.H. Lawrence's short story *The Shadow in the Rose Garden*, about which Eliot had spoken in a lecture published in 1934, (*After Strange Gods*, p.35) the same year he had visited the garden of Burnt Norton in Gloucestershire. The other was an essay of Elia by Charles Lamb ('Dream Children, a Reverie') which I thought (and still think) particularly telling.

---

16 *ibid., Little Gidding*, p.223.
17 Robert Frost, 'The Figure a Poem Makes' in *Collected Prose of Robert Frost* ed. Mark Richardson (Cambridge, Mass.: Harvard University Press, 2007) p.132.
18 Seamus Heaney 'Personal Helicon', *Death of a Naturalist* (London: Faber and Faber,1966) p.41.
19 Helen Gardner, *The Composition of Four Quartets* (London: Faber and Faber 1978) pp.39-41.

Burnt Norton begins and ends as a meditation on time and what has or has not happened in the past (the 'waste sad time')

> What might have been is an abstraction
> Remaining a perpetual possibility
> Only in a world of speculation.[20]

It's particularly poignant because, as Helen Gardner discreetly hints in her book and Lyndall Gordon later makes explicit in hers,[21] Eliot visited Burnt Norton with an old American friend, Emily Hale, who might well have become his wife had he not impulsively married shortly after arriving in London and decided to stay in England. By the time of his visit to Burnt Norton, however, that marriage had ended childlessly and in separation (though Eliot had no intention of seeking a divorce) so his meeting with Emily must have been full of unspoken 'what ifs?' In this context, then, the Charles Lamb essay offers a striking parallel: Elia dreams of the wife and family he hoped for but never had and at the end it is the imagined children who break the 'reverie':

> We are nothing; less than nothing, and dreams. We are only what might have been, and must wait upon the tedious shores of Lethe millions of ages before we have existence, and a name.[22]

What is one to make of such a parallel? We argued about whether such a link is only coincidental (there is no evidence that Eliot had this essay of Lamb's in mind or, indeed, that he ever read Lamb's essays at all). If coincidental, did this make the link and its insistent echo ('…what might have been') irrelevant or did it have value in making us as readers of *Burnt Norton* more aware of the currents and undercurrents in Eliot's writing? The discussion raised indeed the whole question of context: did one need to know about Emily Hale to appreciate what Eliot was talking about in this poem? Eliot himself never mentioned her and those who read the poem when it first appeared had no knowledge of her.

Our discussion quickly became a discussion about the nature of poetry, about the process of composition and about creativity itself. To have students in the group who were themselves writers gave the discussion added depth: we agreed that all writers make constant use, consciously and unconsciously, of everything they have read. This led us to articulate some views and reservations about the idea of intertextuality and, of course, the discussion continued throughout the weekend, though it was put temporarily aside on the final morning, Sunday, when we drove to Little Gidding itself and read

---

20 T.S. Eliot, *Burnt Norton*, Collected Poems 1909-1962 p.189.
21 Lyndall Gordon, *T.S. Eliot, an Imperfect Life* (London: Vintage, 1998).
22 Charles Lamb, *The Essays of Elia*, (London: George Harrap and Co., 1909) p.185.

the entire sequence of *Four Quartets* aloud to each other in the chapel that Eliot had visited in 1935 on a visit from Cambridge (we saw his name in the Visitor's Book). It was an absolutely memorable experience, one of the most profound of my entire teaching career.

By the end of the course, however, it was clear there was a strong appetite for further study of the poem and discussion of the questions of context that had been raised. It's a good example of the way in which study and learning of this kind, with adult students who become deeply involved in the topic, can become open-ended in a way that is rarely if ever possible in school or undergraduate teaching. By the time the course was over, I had sketched out with the students a possible second course which, in the end, became a further two courses on '*Four Quartets* in Context'. In the first of these, we explored the poems in the context both of Eliot's own writing (especially of his plays, *Murder in the Cathedral* and *The Family Reunion*, which immediately preceded and followed *Burnt Norton*) and of other writing between 1936 and 1942. We studied Auden's 'Spain 1937', 'In Memory of W.B. Yeats' and 'September 3rd 1939'; Louis McNeice's 'The Sunlight on the Garden' and 'Autumn Journal', E.M. Forster's wartime broadcasts in *Two Cheers for Democracy* and Virginia Woolf's late essay, 'Thoughts on Peace in an Air Raid'. All of these informed our re-reading of *Four Quartets* and illustrated the value of literary context in arriving at a deeper response to any given work.

The final course I ran (with many of the original students, together with new members of the group who all made their own contribution to the discussions) looked at *Four Quartets* from three different perspectives: critical, biographical and fictional. I began with Helen Gardner's own evolving critical response to the poem over a period of thirty years from *The Art of T.S Eliot* to *The Composition of Four Quartets*. Then we revisited the poem in the light of the biographical interpretation developed in Lyndall Gordon's *T.S.Eliot, an Imperfect Life* (1998). Third, and unexpectedly, I had read a recently published novel by the American novelist Martha Cooley, *The Archivist* (1998) about a reclusive widower who is the archivist responsible for safeguarding a collection of Eliot's letters to Emily Hale.

Creating a course, or sequence of courses, of this kind is something that can perhaps only be done in the context of extramural study, and the breadth of commitment and experience, as well as of reading, brought by the students who attend such courses is unparalleled. What I have described here, from early in my career in continuing education, extended over a period of three years; often, however, one's preparation for teaching is much more compressed. At the other end of that career I had been teaching Seamus Heaney's recent poetry and was preparing to give a lecture to the University's International Summer School on Heaney's *Human Chain* (2010). Indeed, on the morning that I was due to give the lecture I was also supervising a Diploma student writing a project essay on the same book.

The student, Emily, and I had been working separately on the same poem, 'Chanson d'Aventure'.[23] It consists of three twelve-line sections (4 x three-line stanzas each) and has as its starting point the ambulance journey the poet endured when he suffered a stroke in 2006. However, it is also profoundly a love poem addressed to his wife who accompanies him in the ambulance to hospital. Though he has to be 'forklifted … bone-shaken, bumped at speed' while she sits 'ensconced' in the nurse's seat, the communication between them is intense:

> Everything and nothing spoken,
> Our eyebeams threaded laser-fast, no transport
> Ever like it until then … .

Heaney has already prefaced the poem with an epigraph from 'The Extasie', so the threading together of the two bodies by the eyebeams comes with the shock of recognition to those who know Donne's poem. ('The Extasie' is of course also the source of the 'unseen eyebeams' in *Burnt Norton*.) This first section of 'Chanson d'Aventure' ends with the poet, now recovered and looking back on the experience, recalling how

> we might, O my love, have quoted Donne
> On love on hold, body and soul apart.

Most of the students to whom I was to lecture would have been aware of Donne but might not have read 'The Extasie', so in introducing Heaney's poem I paused to read and discuss the Donne before coming back to the 'Chanson', looking now with extra attention at the phrases 'Our postures all the journey still the same' and 'everything and nothing spoken' (echoing Donne: 'All day, the same our postures were / And we said nothing all the day'). This is explicit enough. But the second section of the poem immediately takes the reader into different territory, where every echo is implicit, and the cumulative impact is intense. It opens by picking up the last word of the previous line:

> Apart: the very word is like a bell
> That the sexton Malachy Boyle outrolled
> *In illo tempore* in Bellaghy
>
> Or the one I tolled in Derry in my turn
> As college bellman …

It's easy enough to point to Keats's 'Ode to a Nightingale' ('Forlorn! The very word is like a bell …') for the source of that first line, but the work to be done lies in getting one's audience to see the underlying connections between Keats's poem and 'Chanson d'Aventure'. Indeed, Keats's meditation

23 Seamus Heaney, 'Chanson d'Aventure' in *Human Chain* (London: Faber and Faber, 2010) pp.14-16.

on death and on the no-man's-land between waking and dreaming offers a helpful commentary on Heaney's situation: the 'drowsy numbness' of Keats anticipates, for instance, the stroke-stricken hand Heaney can no longer feel and which lay 'flop-heavy as a bellpull', held tightly by his wife while the ambulance raced for the hospital.

Heaney's poetry always interfuses the personal and the political, and the references to Malachy Boyle, to Bellaghy and to Derry (tracked down easily enough via the internet) do just that. Bellaghy, a small Catholic village in Northern Ireland near Heaney's one-time home, contributed two 'martyrs' to the 1981 hunger strikes — and Heaney knew both men. Derry was where as a boy, Heaney had been sent to a Catholic boarding school, St. Columba's College: here, in due time, he became the college 'bellman', responsible for ringing the bell for daily chapel services. There is an important discussion to be had about Heaney's choice and placing of '*In illo tempore*', the phrase from the Latin mass: is he seeking somehow to give a benediction to the hunger strikers or simply to suggest that those darkest moments of the Northern Ireland 'Troubles' belong to an era now long past? In my lecture, I had time only to raise such questions, not to answer them.

I admit it took me a while to register the significant echo of 'outrolled', which chimes (almost literally) with the 'outrollings' of the 'bell of quittance' in Thomas Hardy's poem 'Afterwards':

> And will any say when my bell of quittance is heard in the gloom
> And a crossing breeze cuts a pause in its outrollings,
> Till they rise again, as they were a new bell's boom,
> 'He hears it not now, but used to notice such things'?[24]

In fact the whole of the second section of 'Chanson d'Aventure' works like a muffled peal of bells in change ringing: answering the three explicit references ('bell ... bellman ... bellpull') are three implicit references: the Hardy poem first; then, behind 'bellman' there is the *Macbeth* allusion to 'the owl that shriek'd, the fatal bellman' that foretold the death of Duncan. Behind each of these, and harking back to the first section, there is, thirdly, an implied echo from John Donne again: 'Never send to know for whom the bell tolls; it tolls for thee.'[25] The fact that it had been the young student Seamus Heaney himself who had 'tolled' the bell at his school, St. Columba's in Derry, only adds to the poignancy of this dense intertextualising.

I assumed, when I had got this far, that I had tracked down all the significant echoes in this section of the poem. Emily, however, thought she had come across the image of a 'capable warm hand' somewhere else in Keats.

---

24 Thomas Hardy, 'Afterwards'. *The Collected Poems of Thomas Hardy* Michael Irwin ed. (London: Wordsworth Poetry Library, 2006) p.511.

25 John Donne, *Devotions upon Emergent Occasions* (1624).

She was quite right:

> This living hand, now warm and capable
> Of earnest grasping, would, if it were cold
> And in the icy silence of the tomb,
> So haunt thy days and chill thy dreaming nights
> That thou wouldst wish thine own heart dry of blood
> So in my veins red life might stream again,
> And thou be conscience-calm'd — see here it is —
> I hold it towards you.[26]

This extraordinary Gothic piece, an uncollected poem of 1819, both complicates and clarifies aspects of Heaney's poem. Keats himself borrows here, echoing Faustus's final agonised soliloquy from Marlowe's play ("See, see where Christ's blood streams in the firmament!"). So, when Heaney speaks of his 'once capable / Warm hand', that wistful note of 'once' is undercut by the urgency he feels to retain connection with his wife at this critical moment when he may be (for all he knows) about to die. Faustus could not bear the thought that he had severed himself from the love of Christ; Keats cannot bear the prospect of his coming separation by death from Fanny. By the same token Heaney has to confront the possibility of his own imminent death and the severing of himself from his wife. The holding of hands here serves as a poignant symbolic 'handfasting' in a poem which asserts the necessity of communicating at a time when ordinary communication has become impossible. Hence the horror of the poet's reaction to the word 'Apart' which links the first two sections of the 'Chanson d'Aventure'. Hence, too, the brutal image of the section's last line where eventually the 'ecstatic' gaze that binds them together is 'bisected' by the medical impedimenta in the ambulance: 'the hooked-up drip-feed to the cannula'.

The Shakespeare scholar Jonathan Bate has pointed out that 'the creation of the literature of the future is dependent on a dialogue with the literature of the past',[27] and Heaney's poem illustrates this powerfully. I find that exploring such a dialogue appeals strongly to adult students, who are quick to grasp that 'Literary writing means the rewriting of existing literature' (Bate again).[28] For this reason contextual close reading is always a major element in my courses, as I have illustrated in the three courses and lectures discussed above.

Being able thus to construct one's own syllabus in the ways and for the reasons I have described is one of the great freedoms and responsibilities of teaching in continuing education. I believe firmly in the value of asking young undergraduate students to become familiar with the chronology and

---

26 John Keats, *Bright Star: the Complete Poems and Selected Letters of John Keats* (London: Vintage 2009) p.365.

27 Jonathan Bate, *English Literature: a very short introduction* (Oxford: Oxford University Press, 2010), p.26.

28 *ibid.*, p.22.

development of literature (as the Cambridge Tripos still does) but I know how easily a tightly-prescribed curriculum can become a straitjacket and I know, too, that adult students have different needs and study literature for different reasons. I prefaced this discussion of teaching extramural English with quotations from contemporary teachers, critics and scholars of English Literature. So, to end, here are three statements by students of mine – some of them graduates of the courses I have discussed above – putting into words what studying English at later periods of their lives has meant to them.

> I think that its appeal centres vitally on its ability to involve the reader's imaginative faculties with lives (and places) quite beyond those of their own limited experience. If we read with an open mind, we can gain invaluable insight into human behaviour and culture(s). We can take significant steps towards empathising with people(s) who have hitherto tended to be 'other' to us, and we can begin to shed some of the — often shameful — prejudices we have held. None of which is to disregard the sheer pleasure of seeing the world through the eyes of those who have greater imagination that we have: Conrad, Dickens, Wells, Lawrence, Ishiguro — the list is endless. (*Peter, Cambridge*)

> Poetry and good novels make demands of us both emotionally and intellectually: they expose our fears and weaknesses, and force us to face realities other than our own. The intimacy between reader and writer is an interesting relationship, and it makes us feel less alone. (*Betty, Bedford*)

> In the first place lifelong learning enlarges one's world. Whereas children automatically learn in school which subjects interest them as well as making friends and increasing their intelligence, such opportunities become much more limited in adult life. One's ideas also become more limited and therefore adult learning is very important in trying to enlarge one's way of thinking. Literature can teach new concepts, especially in the ways that other people, who are apparently totally different from me, can feel things. Literature can teach not only the factual aspects of such differences but also how the world works. It also enables me to empathise better with others. (*Miko, Japan*)

None of these three statements offers an academic answer to the question, 'Why study literature?', though each of the students proved through their contributions in class and through their written work more than able to meet the intellectual demands of a course taught at university level. What matters more is the sense that literature expands one's horizons in a unique way, forcing one to examine one's own consciousness of being conscious, and developing at the same time a deeper sense of the 'odd, indeterminate business of being human'.

This applies, I should add, as much to teachers as to students. That phrase just quoted comes from an essay by the Oxford academic and novelist, Peter Conrad. In this essay, 'The Garden of Academus', Conrad describes his teaching as 'an annual routine ... a seasonal journey through three centuries of literary history that started with Sidney and Spenser each October and reached the Romantic poets by June.'[29] I recognise this cyclical pattern to teaching. When I taught A level English Literature, it was not just three centuries I had to cover in a year's introduction to the whole field of Eng. Lit. I summed up this mad race in a sonnet written to encourage a class struggling to find sonnets of any interest at all:

> Sonnets again! Our annual advance
>   On English Lit: with Oedipus we start
> Then Shakespeare to Stoppard at a glance,
>   (I know it's irony, but is it art?)
> We twist the Miller's Tale for all it's worth,
>   Acknowledge the obscurities of Donne,
> We share Romantic Agony, the birth
>   Of modern verse, but Larkin, Hughes and Gunn
> Are scarcely touched on, for the novel waits
>   Bulky and sober: narrative technique,
> Jane Austen's irony, or Hardy and the Fates
>   (Each topic strictly rationed to a week).
> Put bluntly thus, how can we not suspect
>   Wordsworth was right, we murder to dissect?

It has been, for me, one of the rewards of teaching in continuing education that I could step off this particular whirligig of time. For Peter Conrad, though, the cyclical teaching year has meant a great deal. 'Travelling round in circles,' he admits:

> I managed to find out a good deal about the development of culture, and even more about the development of language – about the way it defines and controls the world, imposing a personal imprint on obdurate reality. Above all else, I learned most of what I know about the odd, indeterminate business of being human .... My concern was to pass on some of the enjoyment and enlightenment I derived from literature.[30]

He puts it better than I could.

---

29 Peter Conrad, 'The Garden of Academus', in *Areté* (No. 34, Spring/Summer 2011) p.119.
30 *ibid.*

Part 2

2.1 Tom Paine's Plain Words

This lecture was delivered on the first day of the Tom Paine 200 Celebrations in Thetford, Norfolk, on 6 June 2009, a large-scale festival designed to mark the 200ᵗʰ anniversary of Paine's death. I had been invited to give the opening lecture, on the literary rather than the political character of Paine's writing, to an audience of people who might know quite a lot about Paine's history and historical significance but who might not be very familiar with the actual texts of his two main political works, Common Sense *and* Rights of Man. *For this reason, my lecture contained a number of quotations, all of which I had printed onto hand-outs so that my discussion of particular passages could be followed more easily. The lecture was delivered in the side chapel of a redundant church to an audience too large for the available space. In consequence I was asked to repeat the lecture later in the afternoon — the only time I have ever delivered the same lecture twice on a single day. I had originally been commissioned to give this lecture a year beforehand, so it was my good fortune that President Obama chose to quote Paine in his Inauguration Speech on Capitol Hill. This gave me a good introduction to my subject.*

On 20 January this year, Inauguration Day in America, the temperature in Washington D.C. was only 28 degrees Fahrenheit, but the sun shone on an estimated crowd of 1.8 million people who had come to hear (even if they could not see) their newly elected President, Barack Obama. What they heard were statements like this:

> Our founding fathers, faced with perils we can scarcely imagine, drafted a charter to assure the rule of law and the rights of man.

Appeals to 'our founding fathers', linked to 'the rights of man', are appeals to something deep in collective American memory. In a speech in Philadelphia a few days before his Inauguration, Obama had defined the founding fathers thus:

that first band of patriots ... who somehow believed that they had the power to make the world anew.

I suppose it's impossible, here in Thetford this morning, to hear the words 'the rights of man' and not associate them at once with Tom Paine (though it was not he who coined the phrase). Obama's reference to making the world anew should also remind us at once of Paine, writing in support of American independence:

> We have it in our power to begin the world over again. A situation, similar to the present, hath not happened since the days of Noah until now. The birthday of a new world is at hand, and a race of men, perhaps as numerous as all Europe contains, are to receive their portion of freedom from the event of a few months.[1]

The new President, in his inaugural speech, never mentioned Paine by name; but in the final moments of his nineteen-and-a-half minute address, Obama quoted directly from him:

> In the year of America's birth, in the coldest of months, a small band of patriots huddled by dying campfires on the shores of an icy river.
>
> The capital was abandoned. The enemy was advancing. The snow was stained with blood.
>
> At a moment when the outcome of our revolution was most in doubt, the father of our nation ordered these words be read to the people:
>
> 'Let it be told to the future world that in the depth of winter, when nothing but hope and virtue could survive, that the city and the country, alarmed at one common danger, came forth to meet it.'

In the immediate aftermath of Obama's speech, most Americans assumed the President was quoting words that had come from the pen of the 'father of our nation', George Washington himself. Not so: Washington was ordering his men to listen, not to himself, but to Tom Paine. The significance of Obama's tribute to Paine was defined the next morning when an American commentator, John Nichols, writing in a leading political weekly, *The Nation*, described Paine in these terms:

> It was right that Obama turned to Paine. When the Pennsylvania Assembly considered the formal abolition of slavery in 1779, it was Paine who authored the preamble to the proposal... . Paine, to a greater extent than any of his peers, was the founder who imagined a truly United States that might offer a son of Africa and of America not merely citizenship but its presidency. It was Paine, the most

---

1   Thomas Paine, *Common Sense* (London: Penguin 2004) p.69.

revolutionary of their number, who proved to be the wisest, and the best, of that band of patriots — for his time, and for this time.... When our new president says that his election proves 'the dream of our founders is alive in our time,' it is Paine's dream of which he speaks.[2]

Nichols might have added that it was Paine who coined the name 'the United States of America'. All this is reason enough for Thetford to be celebrating Tom Paine today. My contribution is to talk about Paine as a communicator, famous for his plain speaking. But I want to start by referring you back to what Obama said in his speech; 'the Father of our nation ordered these words *to be read* [italics added]': it was Paine's writing, not his actual speaking, that made what he had to say so memorable. Obama is already praised as one of the finest presidential orators; but oratory was not Paine's skill: writing was. George Holyoake, one of Paine's earliest admirers, noted how 'among friends his conversation had every fascination that anecdote, novelty, and truth could give it,' but that 'In mixed company and among strangers he said little, and was no public speaker.'[3]

How did a Thetford stay-maker, whose early years at least were spent on the margins of poverty and sometimes on the margins of the law, come to be one of the great prose writers in the English language? Even today there is no agreement about Paine's style, just as there is no agreement about his political influence. Some editors of his work have described his writing as 'uncomplicated, unscholarly and unsophisticated rhetoric',[4] and even among his contemporaries there were those who expressed contempt for his writing: Governor Morris, one of his opponents in the early American Congress, went so far as to say Paine was 'ignorant even of grammar'[5]. Other contemporaries were more appreciative, George Washington being one of the first to praise the 'sound doctrine and unanswerable reasoning' of Paine's pamphlet *Common Sense*. Most critics today have acknowledged that he was 'a master of popular exposition'. Bruce Kuklick, for example, an American academic from the University of Pennsylvania, has said that Paine:

> had a power of expression that has exceeded that of almost any political thinker in the English language. He had the rare gift — always presumed to be the product of his poor artisanal experience — of being able to write for the populace. The success of the struggle for independence demanded the support of the masses, and among the Founding Fathers only Paine

2   John Nichols, 'Obama's Vindication of Thomas Paine', *The Nation*, 21 January 2009.

3   George Holyoake (ed.) *Rights of Man* (London: George Bell and Co. 1906) p.xiii.

4   M. Foot and I. Kramnick (eds.) *Thomas Paine Reader* (London: Penguin Classics 1987) p.41.

5   *ibid.*, p.12.

entirely understood what the people wanted or needed to hear.… Unlike most of his fellow revolutionaries, he eschewed contemporary stylish discourse and learned jargon. His writing was concrete, using pithy phrases designed to stick in the mind.… . His language, in one sense, was that of the common man. In another sense, he went far beyond what an ordinary person could say — he was able to speak to the deepest political concerns at the same time as he shaped them.[6]

I think Paine himself would have endorsed this assessment. Commenting on his aims as a writer he once wrote: 'As it is my design to make those that can scarcely read understand, I shall therefore avoid every literary ornament and put it in language as plain as the alphabet'.

There are a number of questions arising from these comments:

• Is Paine's rhetoric really 'unsophisticated'?

• Was his writing really so unlike that of his contemporaries?

• Did Paine really 'avoid every literary ornament' and only use 'language as plain as the alphabet'?

It is to questions like these that I hope to suggest some answers.

****

Paine's own account of his early schooling and subsequent career is a good starting point:

At an early period, little more than sixteen years of age, raw and adventurous, and heated with the false heroism of a master [Rev. William Knowles] who had served in a man of war, I began the carver of my own fortune, and entered on board the Terrible privateer, Capt. Death. From this adventure I was happily prevented by the affectionate and moral remonstrance of a good father, who, from his own habits of life, being of the Quaker profession, must begin to look upon me as lost. But the impression, much as it effected at the time, began to wear away, and I entered afterwards in the King of Prussia privateer, Capt. Mendez, and went with her to sea. Yet, from such a beginning, and with all the inconvenience of early life against me, I am proud to say, that with a perseverance undismayed by difficulties, a disinterestedness that compelled respect, I have not only contributed to raise a new empire in the world, founded on a new system of government, but I have arrived at an eminence in political literature, the most difficult of all lines to succeed and excel in, which aristocracy, with all its aids, has not been able to reach or to rival.[7]

---

6   Bruce Kuklick (ed.) *Paine: Political Writings* (Cambridge: Cambridge University Press 1989) pp. xi–xii.

7   Thomas Paine, *Rights of Man* (London: Penguin Classics 1985) p.219.

This is a revealing and important passage, appearing unexpectedly in the middle of *Rights of Man*. That note of self-congratulation with which the passage ends is a characteristic that in his later life caused Paine to be dismissed or disparaged by many who had earlier admired him. In this — as surprisingly often in his writing — he reminds me of Alexander Pope, who famously said

> Yes I am proud, I must be proud to see
> Men not afraid of God afraid of me.

But what particularly pleases Paine is that he has been able to reach 'an eminence in political literature ... which aristocracy, with all its aids, has not been able to rival'. Acutely class conscious, he can't resist pointing out that he has made a greater success of being an author than aristocrats who have had all the advantages of cultural capital and classical education. You'll notice that the one thing he records about his schooling is that his headmaster, William Knowles, had sown in his mind the idea of running away to sea. With hindsight, Paine admits that what had initially attracted him about Knowles turned out to be a sham: his 'false heroism'. Indeed, he is severe upon his younger self, admitting his lack of a sense of purpose or ambition. He sounds grateful to his father, who was 'of the Quaker profession' for having rescued him from his youthful folly, even if a few years later he abandoned his apprenticeship and ran away to sea for a second time. It's clear that Paine's father had some influence on his son, at least, and Paine's Quaker upbringing places him firmly in the English dissenting tradition, a tradition embracing not only contemporaries such as Coleridge and Hazlitt but stretching back to the celebrated pamphleteer Daniel Defoe. It's a curious fact, indeed, that Paine's early adventures at sea mirror rather closely those of Robinson Crusoe, and I think it is a fair bet that Defoe's novel was among Paine's earliest reading.

There is an assumption that, as Holyoake puts it, apart from 'a little grammar school ploughing, he was self-taught.' That misrepresents the truth of Paine's education. True, he left school at 13, but most grammar school boys of his background would have done the same: this was the age at which apprenticeships often began. True, too, he appears to have had no interest at all in any Latin authors he may have had beaten into him; there is hardly a Latin reference to be found anywhere in his writing, apart from a quotation from Shakespeare's *Julius Caesar*. Nevertheless, by the time he left school he would I think have been a fully proficient writer; he was evidently a keen reader of Shakespeare and of poetry (of which his father disapproved) and, importantly, he had a developing interest in Science. Certainly, he had already begun to acquire a prodigious knowledge of the Bible — so much so that in the early 1790s (forty years after leaving school) he was able to quote and analyse the Old Testament in depth and from memory. As a prisoner in Paris during the French Revolution he had no access to a Bible while writing *The Age of Reason*, his attack on bible-based religion.

Is it fair then to call Paine 'self-taught'? I don't think so. Perhaps like many late-starters, or those who have a second chance and come back to education, he knew he had much to catch up on; but an image of Paine sitting up late at nights to read great works by candle-light after a hard day's diligent work as an excise man or a stay-maker or a shop-keeper, is not entirely convincing. He certainly bought books and scientific equipment from what wages he could spare but he also attended lectures and joined social clubs where political controversy and debate were as much a part of an evening's activity as drinking. At Lewes in Sussex he became well known both for his animated debating — and for his love of beer. In Lewes, too, he began his writing career: in June 1772, writing under the pseudonym 'Humanus', Paine published a letter in the *Lewes Journal* discussing a design for a fire-escape made out of iron and leather. Other letters on current issues, mostly to do with social and political controversies, soon followed. Most importantly, and again in 1772, Paine wrote *The Case of the Officers of Excise*, a polemic in support of his fellow excise-men and their claim for higher wages. It's a remarkable work, remarkable both for the persuasiveness of its argument and for the clarity of its writing; straight away, we see some of the signs of Paine at his most characteristic:

> If the increase of money in the kingdom is one cause of the high price
> of provisions, the case of the excise officers is peculiarly pitiable. No
> increase comes to them — they are shut out from the general blessing
> — they behold it like a map of *Peru*. The answer of Abraham to Dives
> is somewhat applicable to them, 'There is a great gulf fixed.'[8]

Here we see Paine at once basing his argument on a plea for fairness, and he does it by pointing out the unfairness of the situation, the way in which the excise officers are excluded and can only look on like children who can see a treat that they are not allowed to have. The map of Peru signifies the wealth that is leading to the 'increase of money' and adding to the 'general blessing' — but it is only a map, a piece of paper: tantalising, but worthless. Paine only uses a telling simile like this to render something abstract in concrete terms. At the same time, he is alert to the sound of his sentences; it is no accident that his indignant theme of unfairness is emphasised by a succession of plosive phrases: 'prince of provisions' ... 'peculiarly pitiable' ... 'map of Peru'.

At this stage in the development of his writing, he cannot resist a biblical reference even when it isn't entirely appropriate. Quoting from the story of Dives and Lazarus in St Luke's Gospel (Luke 16, vv.19-31), Paine remarks that between the rich and the poor 'there is a great gulf fixed', which in

8   *Thomas Paine Reader*, p.41.

this context implies that the rich are able to keep the poor well away from them and their wealth. In the biblical story, however, it is Abraham who tells the rich man Dives, now dead and tormented in hell, that there is a great gulf fixed between him and Lazarus who is safe in Abraham's bosom, being comforted by the angels. In the Bible, therefore, it is the rich who are deprived, admittedly after death, of the blessings that are given to the poor — the exact opposite of the situation Paine describes. No wonder he says that the words 'a great gulf fixed' are only 'somewhat applicable' to the situation he describes.

Elsewhere in *The Case of the Officers of Excise* Paine uses the actual language of discourse as an image to illustrate his argument:

> There is a powerful rhetoric in necessity... . No argument can satisfy the feelings of hunger, or abate the edge of appetite. Nothing tends to greater corruption of manners and principles than a too great distress of circumstances... . *Agur*, without any alternative, has made dishonesty the immediate effect of involuntary poverty. 'Lest I be poor and steal'.[9]

Most of us, I suspect, would have to reach for a reference book or go into Google to identify Agur, but Paine assumes his readers will know that Agur was the prophet in the Old Testament Book of Proverbs who cried out, 'Remove far from me vanity and lies: Give me neither poverty nor riches; Feed me with food convenient for me: Lest I be full, and deny thee, and say, Who is the Lord? Or lest I be poor, and steal, And take the name of my God in vain.' (Proverbs 30, vv.8-9). Poverty, Agur says — and Paine agrees with him — forces a man to become dishonest simply to keep himself alive. This is the nub of Paine's case for giving the excise men more pay: they are so badly rewarded that they are bound to be dishonest, either accepting bribes to supplement their pay or simply doing their job badly because there is no incentive to do it well. Paine even goes on to suggest that there is a perverse logic in people's stealing under these circumstances: if they don't steal they will starve to death and to do that, when one had the means of feeding oneself by stealing one's food, would be suicide — a worse crime even than murder.

I think the moral ambiguity of this situation is neatly caught in the contrast Paine draws between *rhetoric* and *argument*: 'There is a powerful rhetoric in necessity.... No argument can satisfy the feelings of hunger, or abate the edge of appetite.' Rational discussion (argument) is unable to ease the pangs of hunger, and these pangs exercise a powerful appeal to the senses (rhetoric): they lead the individual to behave in ways a rational man would in normal circumstances eschew. Perhaps almost without realising it, Paine is suggesting that rhetoric is not to be trusted, that it can be used to make men act against their better judgement.

---

9   'The Case of the Officers of Excise', *Thomas Paine Reader*, p.40.

These references to rhetoric and argument show clearly, I think, that Paine was a very self-reflexive writer: in the act of writing, he borrows the terms of oratory as metaphors to illustrate his case. Later in *The Case of the Officers of Excise* he uses the same device, even more explicitly:

> He who never was an hungered may argue finely on the subjection of his appetite; and he who never was distressed may harangue as beautifully on the power of principle. But poverty, like grief, has an incurable deafness, which never hears; the oration loses all its edge; and 'To be, or not to be' becomes the only question.[10]

This, surely, is far from unsophisticated. The first sentence is formal and balanced, the subjection of appetite weighed against the power of principle. It is almost a perfect model of a classical period and certainly not 'the language of ordinary men'. By contrast, the next sentence — 'poverty, like grief, has an incurable deafness, which never hears' — has a directness which makes its meaning unambiguous. With a nice irony, it uses amplification to emphasise silence: 'deafness, which never hears' is tautological but rhetorically effective — at the very moment when rhetoric is shown to fail: 'The oration loses all its edge'. Even this is subject to a further, and very literary irony: Paine invokes Hamlet's most famous soliloquy to remind his reader that extreme poverty (the lot of the excise men) leads to 'the only question': should they steal food to keep themselves alive or should they simply give up and die?

These passages show Paine feeling his way towards a style which looks effortless but is actually very skilfully contrived. It is a style which is designed to appeal both to the groundlings and to those in the most expensive seats: both the uneducated and the sophisticated can respond to his writing without feeling either overwhelmed or patronised. Paine was an admirer of Oliver Goldsmith, and Goldsmith describes the balancing act that Paine brings off very well:

> Convincing eloquence is infinitely more serviceable to its possessor than the most florid harangue or the most pathetic tones that can be imagined; and the man who is the most thoroughly convinced himself, who understands his subject and the language he speaks in, will be more apt to silence opposition, than he who studies the force of his periods, and fills our ears with sounds, while our minds are destitute of conviction.[11]

****

No one reading Paine's work, from *The Case of the Officers of Excise* onwards, was left in any doubt that Paine understood both his subject and the language he spoke in. He also understood his audiences, both the sophisticated and the

---

10 *Thomas Paine Reader,* p.47.
11 Oliver Goldsmith, 'On Education', *The Bee,* No.6, Saturday 10 November 1769.

undereducated: the acclaim with which his pamphlet was greeted gave him a passport into a world he had not known before. Although by the time he left England to try his luck in America he remained on the one hand an artisan, a bankrupt shop keeper and an ex-tax collector; at the same time he had begun to meet and impress people with an intellectual energy and in a social position he had not encountered before: among these were people such as Benjamin Franklin who gave him a letter of introduction to take to Philadelphia. Franklin, whose own writing Paine greatly admired (he thought his proverbial sayings were better than anything in the Bible) was not quite sure how to place his young admirer, so he wrote to his brother-in-law in somewhat guarded terms:

> The bearer Mr Thomas Paine is very well recommended to me, as an ingenious, worthy young man. He goes to Pennsylvania with a view of settling there. I request you give to him your best advice and countenance, as he is quite a stranger there. If you can put him in a way of obtaining employment as a clerk, or assistant tutor in a school, or assistant surveyor (of all which I think him very capable) so that he may procure a subsistence at least, till he can make acquaintance and obtain a knowledge of the country, you will do well, and much oblige your affectionate father.[12]

At first, Paine got a job as a teacher but he soon showed a flair for journalism, writing articles for local Philadelphia papers. Like a typical eighteenth century essayist, he ranged widely across a variety of subjects: he published essays on science and on politics; significantly, he also wrote attacks on slavery. No one was in doubt that he spoke from a liberal, and increasingly radical, position; but when in 1776 he published his celebrated pamphlet, *Common Sense*, he took care not to be identified as the author and certainly not to represent any one political party or interest. He wrote in the Preface, 'Who the Author of this Production is, is wholly unnecessary to the Public, as the Object for Attention is the *Doctrine itself*, not the *Man*.' Paine added, 'Yet it may not be unnecessary to say, That he is unconnected with any Party, and under no sort of Influence public or private, but the influence of reason and principle.'[13]

In fact, Paine's identity as the author of *Common Sense* emerged almost at once, for the pamphlet was a phenomenal success. The historian G.M. Trevelyan summed up its impact like this:

> It would be difficult to name any human composition that has had an effect so instant, so extended and so lasting.... It was pirated, parodied and imitated, and translated into every language where the new republic had well-wishers. It worked nothing short of miracles.

---

12 David Freeman Hawke, *Paine* (New York: WW Norton and Co. 1974) p.30.
13 Thomas Paine, *Common Sense* (London: Penguin 2004) p.4.

This is an astonishing tribute to the writing of a man who had left England less than two years before, out of work, out of luck and with nothing much more than the luke-warm recommendation of Benjamin Franklin in his pocket. Yet the pamphlet sold nearly 100,000 copies in its first year, and nearly as many again in Europe. So much for its 'instant' impact; but Trevelyan was equally right to call the influence of *Common Sense* 'lasting': President Obama's inaugural speech this year has demonstrated as much.

In one important respect, *Common Sense* achieved such an instant impact in America because it made Americans feel good about themselves: to read Paine's words in the Preface — 'The cause of America is in a great measure the cause of all mankind' — was to see oneself in a new and brighter light. Here was someone prepared to take them seriously and not just to see them as a rabble of disaffected colonials who beefed about paying taxes to the mother country. Of course it helped that Paine identified himself from the start as an American too. One of his most famous statements, from the seventh issue of *The Crisis* (1776), makes this very clear:

> When my country, into which I had just set my foot, was set on fire about my ears, it was time to stir. It was time for every man to stir.

The other important factor that helped to ensure *Common Sense* made such an impact was of course the way it was written. 'In the following pages' Paine warned,

> I offer nothing more than simple facts, plain arguments, and common sense; and have no other preliminaries to settle with the reader, than that he will divest himself of prejudice and prepossession, and suffer his reason and his feelings to determine for themselves; that he will put *on*, or rather that he will not put *off*, the true character of a man, and generously enlarge his views beyond the present day.[14]

Enlarging their views beyond the present day meant taking the long view, seeing themselves caught up in an historical process and a moment when they had the opportunity to influence history. No one before had made Americans understand their situation so clearly, or illustrated the challenge so graphically. Telling them that now was the time to show resolution in the face of 'one common danger', Paine warned what would happen if they failed to stay united:

> The least fracture now will be like a name engraved with the point of a pin on the tender rind of a young oak; the wound will enlarge with the tree, and posterity read it in full grown characters.[15]

---

14 *Common Sense*, p.24.
15 *ibid.*, p.25.

The ability to crystallize a critical concept in an image at once domestic ('a name engraved with the point of a pin') and rural ('the tender rind of a young oak') yet at the same time civic and historic ('posterity will read it in full grown characters') is a sign of the sophistication of Paine's writing. So, too, is his continued preoccupation with the act of writing itself and his acute awareness of the danger of distorting his argument by too powerful a rhetoric. We have already seen him examine this tension in *The Case of the Officers of Excise*; he returns to the theme in *Common Sense* when launching a powerful critique of the constitutional principle of the separation of powers:

> Some writers have explained the English constitution thus; the king, say they, is one, the people another; the peers are an house in behalf of the king; the commons in behalf of the people; but this hath all the distinctions of an house divided against itself; and though the expressions be pleasantly arranged, yet when examined they appear idle and ambiguous; and it will always happen, that the nicest construction that words are capable of, when applied to the description of some thing which either cannot exist, or is too incomprehensible to be within the compass of description, will be words of sound only, and though they may amuse the ear, they cannot inform the mind.[16]

As you can see in this passage, Paine is well aware that rhetoric can be a snare, and that expressions 'pleasantly arranged' may turn out to be merely 'idle and ambiguous': 'the nicest construction that words are capable of' he knows may prove to be no more than 'words of sound only'.

Was Paine unique, or at least ahead of his time, in thinking and writing like this? I think not. It's a mistake to assume that all 'polite' writing in the eighteenth century was florid, Latinate and over-ornamented. The philosopher David Hume, who died in the year that *Common Sense* was published, 1776, wrote a valuable and witty essay, 'Of simplicity and refinement in writing', with which Paine would have agreed wholeheartedly, just as he certainly shared Hume's scepticism about religion:

> As the eye, in surveying a Gothic building, is distracted by the multiplicity of ornaments, and loses the whole by a minute attention to the parts; so the mind, in perusing a work overstocked with wit, is fatigued and disgusted with the constant endeavour to shine and surprise.... Besides, it is with books as with women, where a certain plainness of manner and of dress is more engaging than the glare of paint, and airs, and apparel, which may dazzle the eye, but reaches not the affections.[17]

---

16 *ibid.*, p.10.
17 David Hume, 'Of Simplicity and Refinement in Writing', *Essays Moral and Political* (1748).

This is not to say that Paine never could or never did go for the full effects of rhetoric and melodrama. He ends the first half of *Common Sense* with an extraordinary apostrophe:

> O ye that love mankind! Ye that dare oppose, not only the tyranny but the tyrant, stand forth! Every spot of the old world is over-run with oppression. Freedom hath been hunted round the globe. Asia, and Africa, have long expelled her. Europe regards her like a stranger, and England hath given her warning to depart. O! receive the fugitive, and prepare in time an asylum for mankind.[18]

Again one is struck by Paine's prescience: his plea to America to become a place of safety (an asylum) for those fleeing oppression (the fugitive) or those seeking a new life (mankind) precisely anticipates and in fact defines the way in which the United States has throughout its history presented itself to the world, from the Declaration of Independence onwards.

****

In the final section of this lecture, I'd like to consider some of the ways in which Paine's writing in *Rights of Man* differs significantly from the way he wrote *Common Sense*. In 1776 Paine had sedulously avoided mentioning anyone by name: 'Compliments,' he had said in the Introduction, 'as well as censure to individuals make no part thereof.' Even King George III, one of the very few individuals referred to in *Common Sense,* is always diminished to a mere cipher: 'k —'. The voice of the speaker, himself anonymous you'll remember, in theory at least gives no clue to the identity of the author. Most of the time, the tone is authoritative and didactic rather than passionate and personal.

With *Rights of Man* the case is altered. Now everything is personal. The book is a response to and an attack on Edmund Burke's *Reflections on the French Revolution*. It's a debate, in which Paine sets out to examine and refute all the arguments put forward by Burke; he employs all the devices of the seasoned debater: irony, satire, rhetorical effects; sometimes he speaks more in sorrow than in anger of his former friend; sometimes in downright denunciation. You won't find anywhere in *Common Sense* sentences like these:

- A greater absurdity cannot present itself to the understanding of man, than what Mr Burke offers to his readers.[19]

- I know a place in America called Point-to-Point; because as you proceed along the shore, gay and flowery as Mr Burke's language, it continually recedes and presents itself at a distance before you;

---

18 *Common Sense*, p.46.
19 *Rights of Man*, p.43.

but when you have got as far as you can go, there is no point at all. Just thus it is with Mr Burke's three hundred and fifty-six pages.[20]

- I have now to follow Mr Burke through a pathless wilderness of rhapsodies, and a sort of descant upon governments, in which he asserts whatever he pleases, on the presumption of its being believed, without offering either evidence or reasons for so doing.[21]

What is the effect of this kind of *ad hominem* confrontation? The most significant is to keep us as readers always aware that Paine is responding to someone else's ideas. In *Rights of Man* his own views emerge as a response to someone else's arguments, whereas in *Common Sense* (published fifteen years earlier) his views often had the appeal of novelty: he was saying something new, or at least saying something in a way that was new. What is striking about *Rights of Man*, however, is its astonishing topicality. Listen, for example, to his account of how Parliament conducts its financial affairs:

> Parliament, imperfectly and capriciously elected as it is, is nevertheless supposed to hold the national purse in trust for the nation: but in the manner in which an English parliament is constructed, it is like a man being both mortgager and mortgagee; and in the case of misapplication of trust, it is the criminal sitting in judgement upon himself. If those who vote the supplies are the same persons who receive the supplies when voted, and are to account for the expenditure of those supplies to those who voted them, it is *themselves accountable to themselves*, and the Comedy of Errors concludes with the Pantomime of HUSH[22] The national purse is the common hack which each mounts upon…. They order these things better in France.[23]

The note of rising incredulity which sounds throughout this passage achieves its climax with the phrase Paine puts in italics — '*themselves accountable to themselves*'— which is immediately turned into the anticlimax of Parliament likened to a Shakespearean farce and then reduced to a pantomime and a dumb show. The image of MPs all riding on the back of the national purse like a shared horse is too uncomfortably close to today to need further comment, except to say that it is easy to miss the ultimate point of the paragraph which resides in the final sentence, where Paine paraphrases the famous opening line of Laurence Sterne's best seller of a decade previously, *A Sentimental Journey*: 'They order, said I, this matter better in France'. What Paine does throughout *Rights of Man* is not only

---

20 *ibid.*, p.49.
21 *ibid.*, p.64.
22 i.e. a farcical performance in which no one will say or admit anything.
23 *ibid.*, p.76.

to attack what he sees as the absurdities of hereditary succession and the whole idea of monarchy; it is also to assure his readers that government in revolutionary France, as in post-Independence America, offers a better, fairer and less expensive model of government than the system in Britain: 'They order these things better in France'.

I hope you might agree with me that the construction and language of this paragraph are hardly written for the common man: the literary references aside, its argument is pitched at a readership who have already absorbed the 400-odd pages of Burke's pamphlet. His audience now is very different from the audience he aimed at with *Common Sense*. It's not, perhaps, a trivial point that Paine refers more than once to Burke's *Reflections* as a 'pamphlet' but to his own *Rights of Man* as a treatise and an essay. And yet, to my mind what animates Paine's most famous book is the spectacle, the theatricality, of his quarrel with Burke. Indeed, he himself frequently seems to be thinking in theatrical terms; apart from his repeated references to Shakespeare, he represents the monarchy and the British submission to the monarchy as a kind of absurd freak show. Talking for instance about the right to wage war, Paine says:

> In England, this right is said to reside in a metaphor, shown at the Tower for sixpence or a shilling apiece: So are the lions; and it would be a step nearer to reason to say it resided in them, for any inanimate metaphor is no more than a hat or a cap. We can all see the absurdity of worshipping Aaron's molten calf, or Nebuchadnezzar's golden image; but why do men continue to practice themselves the absurdities they despise in others?[24]

For Paine, gawping at the Crown Jewels is as absurd as worshipping a golden calf. In a sense, his attack on the English constitution is an appeal to Englishmen to grow up. And in the end it is the sheer absurdity of the whole idea of monarchy that leads him to write in a manner and with a tone of voice quite different from what we encountered in *Common Sense*:

> Whether I have too little sense to see, or too much to be impressed upon; whether I have to much or too little pride, or of anything else, I leave out of the question; but certain it is, that [which] is called monarchy, always appears to me a silly, contemptible thing. I compare it to something kept behind curtain, about which there is a great deal of bustle and fuss, and a wonderful air of seeming solemnity; but when, by any accident, the curtain happens to be open, and the company see what it is, they burst into laughter.[25]

24 *Rights of Man*, p.77.
25 *ibid.*, p.182.

I cannot help thinking that this hilarious send up of the whole edifice of monarchy anticipates the final scenes of *Alice in Wonderland* where the entire court of the Queen of Hearts collapses like a pack of cards. It's an unexpected conclusion to reach about *Rights of Man*, but at least it shows (I hope) that Paine's writing is a good deal more various, more subtle and even perhaps more sophisticated than many people — Paine not excluded — have suggested. I have tried to show that there are fundamental differences between *Common Sense* and *Rights of Man* but that in each book, and in all Paine's writing, there is a distinctive voice that wants to be heard by everyone who will listen. I agree with the critic who wrote that Paine 'helped to create the very language of politics, the vocabulary in which men and women expressed timeless discontents and voiced aspirations for a better world.' How, then, to define that language and its purpose? The best definition is Paine's own:

> I speak an open and disinterested language, dictated by no passion but that of humanity.... Independence is my happiness, and I view things as they are, without regard to place or person; my country is the world, and my religion is to do good.[26]

---

26 *ibid.*, p.228.

2.2 Trollope and Religious Controversy

This is an expanded version of a lecture given at Rewley House, Oxford (home of the University of Oxford Department for Continuing Education) on 30 April 2011 as part of a Study Day on Anthony and Frances Trollope. This was a very different audience from the audiences who had heard my Tom Paine lecture:[1] here the students were by and large specialists in — or at least serious enthusiasts for — Trollope's Barchester novels, most of whom could be assumed to have a good knowledge of the texts. Indeed, there were members of the Trollope Society in the audience and others who already had Trollope-related publications to their name. There were a few students whom I recognised from courses I had taught on Trollope at Cambridge, but on the whole I was lecturing to an audience of strangers. My lecture was the second session of the morning, and my brief was to speak for an hour and answer questions for up to twenty minutes afterwards. The lecture was accompanied by a PowerPoint presentation designed both to illustrate some of the key differences between Tractarian and Evangelical churchmanship and ecclesiology in the mid-nineteenth century and to project for the audience some of the key passages I would discuss during the lecture.

At the start of *Framley Parsonage*, Lady Lufton has just presented Mark Robarts — a 'gentlemanlike, young, High Church, conservative country parson'[2] — to the living of Framley, which is within her gift. Lady Lufton herself, the narrator tells us, 'liked cheerful, quiet, well-to-do people, who loved their Church, their country and their Queen, and who were not too anxious to make a noise in the world.' She also believed strongly in what she saw as the virtues of the country: she wanted the farmers to pay their rents, the elderly to be well looked after and to be 'obedient to their pastors and masters — temporal as well as spiritual.... That was her idea of loving her country'.[3]

---

1 See above, pp. 49–63.
2 Anthony Trollope, *Framley Parsonage* (Oxford: O.U.P. World's Classics 1980) Ch.II, p.17 [*Framley Parsonage* hereafter *FP*].
3 *FP*, Ch.II, p.16.

In her still almost feudal view of an ideal England she places the country far ahead of the city and would have agreed with William Cowper that 'God made the country and man made the town'.[4]

I want to argue in this lecture that although Trollope claimed to be more interested in the social than in the professional or spiritual lives of clergymen, he had a detailed understanding of the religious controversies of the mid-nineteenth century. I want further to suggest that his understanding of, and sympathy with, the pastoral and devotional side of Anglican ministry was something he as novelist explored with some sensitivity, even if his narrator pretended otherwise. I shall indeed argue that our understanding of Trollope's narrative strategy throughout the *Chronicles of Barset* depends on our recognising that the narrator is as much a created character as the Archdeacon or Mr Slope, and that the narrative voice which speaks to the reader so confidentially is capable of subtle modulations. He becomes the reader's confidential and modest companion who admits, 'I shall always be happy to sit, when allowed to do so, at the table of Archdeacon Grantly, [and] to walk through the High Street of Barchester arm in arm with Mr Robarts of Framley'. From his mother Fanny Trollope he may well have inherited his anti-evangelical sentiments, but from his father he also derived a powerful if eccentric sense of the fascination of matters ecclesiastical. The common view is that Trollope gained his strong work ethic from his mother, but actually his father could be similarly obsessive:

> He had at this time commenced a work — an *Encyclopaedia Ecclesiastica*, as he called it — on which he laboured until the moment of his death. It was his ambition to describe all ecclesiastical terms, including the denominations of every fraternity of monks and every convent of nuns, with all their orders and subdivisions. Under crushing disadvantages, with few or no books of reference, with immediate access to no library, he worked at his most ungrateful task with unflagging industry.[5]

I'm not suggesting that church history as such particularly interested Trollope, but church politics certainly did, and in the mid-nineteenth century church politics could not be detached from church doctrine. His evocations of Dr Grantly, Bishop and Mrs Proudie, Mr Slope and Mr Arabin, are all sharpened by his very precise definitions of their churchmanship. However, these controversies do not simply provide an historical context with which Trollope's original readers were very familiar, but which the modern reader may need to recover: they also animate the plots and indeed the narrative perspective of the Chronicles — in particular of *Barchester*

4   William Cowper, *The Sofa*, Bk.I.
5   Anthony Trollope, *Autobiography*, (Oxford: Oxford University Press World's Classics 1923, Ch. I, pp. 12–13.

Towers, *Framley Parsonage* and *The Last Chronicle of Barset*. They both complicate our understanding of the central characters in these novels and challenge our too-easy identification of Anthony Trollope himself with the genial chronicler of Barset.

First, some defining of terms is necessary. When Lady Lufton offers the living of Framley to a clergyman who is described as 'High Church', this does not mean that Mark Robarts had become a devoted follower of the Oxford Movement. True, he had been at Oxford in the period shortly after Newman had gone over to Rome, but he was not like the young Mr Arabin, who (as Trollope explains in *Barchester Towers*) had 'taken up cudgels on the side of the Tractarians at Oxford [where] he sat for a while at the feet of the great Newman',[6] very nearly following him to Rome. 'High Church' in the sense Lady Lufton approves, refers to the established Anglican forms of worship conducted by clergy who were content to follow custom and tradition:

> They all preached in their black gowns, as their fathers had done before them; they wore ordinary black cloth waistcoats; they had no candles upon their altars, either lighted or unlighted; they made no private genuflexions, and were contented to confine themselves to such ceremonial observances as had been in vogue for the last hundred years. The services were decently and demurely read in their parish churches, chanting was confined to the cathedral, and the science of intoning was unknown.[7]

This is an important passage. The black gowns were worn for preaching, and preaching was the dominant feature of services in Anglican churches, whether high or low — so much so that the three-decker pulpit rather than the altar was often the focal point of the church. 'Reading the service' was what was expected: parish churches on the whole did not have surpliced choirs in the chancel and certainly did not have weekly services of Communion. If there was music to accompany the service, it was more likely to be provided by the village band and choir — as for example described by Thomas Hardy in his account of the services in Mellstock church in *Under the Greenwood Tree*. When we read of Mr Arabin's first Sunday as a parish priest in the Barchester diocese, Chapter XXIII of *Barchester Towers* is headed 'Mr Arabin reads himself in at St. Ewold's'; when they arrive at the church, the archdeacon's servant is waiting for Dr Grantly and the new vicar 'with the vestments'[8] — that is, the gowns and preaching bands (worn in the collar), nothing as Roman as cope or chasuble, alb or dalmatic. Mr Arabin himself

---

6   Anthony Trollope, *Barchester Towers* (Oxford: Oxford University Press World's Classics series 1996) Ch. XX, p.188 [hereafter *BT*].

7   *BT*, Ch.VI, pp.45.

8   *BT*, Ch.XXIII, p.227.

is assailed by nerves before the service, and 'feared he should acquit himself badly in St. Ewold's reading desk'. In the event, all he had to do was read the lessons and preach a sermon; the Parish Clerk would have read the rest of the service and Dr Grantly would have delivered the Absolution.

Trollope describes the reading of the lessons as 'pulpit reading', where Mr Arabin 'did his work sufficiently well, in spite of the slightly nervous affliction which at first impeded him, and which nearly drove the archdeacon beside himself.'[9] Dr Grantly, we infer, had no such impediment, never having suffered from the 'annoying degree of bashfulness' which so surprisingly afflicted Mr Arabin.

'High Church' derived in fact from the idea of a traditional Anglicanism which placed a high value on certain key tenets: absolute acceptance of the Monarch, the Head of State, as Head of the Church of England, followed by equally absolute adherence to the Thirty Nine Articles (the Articles of Faith) and to the Prayer Book. 'High Church' had, as the passage above makes clear, nothing to do with candles on altars — lit or unlit — genuflexion or other rituals associated with what the narrator terms 'tendencies, which are somewhat too loosely called Puseyite practices'[10]

Edward Bouverie Pusey, the third member of the original Tractarian triumvirate — along with John Keble, who ignited the Oxford Movement with his Assize Sermon preached in St Mary's University Church in July 1833, and Newman — was the person accused of introducing dangerously Papistical practices into the Church of England. Unlike Newman, Pusey never went over to Rome, but whereas Newman (who came originally from an Evangelical background) always celebrated Communion by adopting the northward position at the altar, Pusey and his followers adopted the eastward position, controversially turning their backs on the congregation for the prayer of consecration. It is thus significant that Trollope is sufficiently aware of his facts and sufficiently scrupulous in his writing to preface his reference to Puseyite practices with the qualification 'somewhat too loosely called'. He is aware of the nuances of churchmanship in the Church of England and feels obliged to draw attention to the way people are too ready to apply the label 'Puseyite' to forms of religious observance which deviate from the Anglican norm and which — to some people at least — seem to smack of Rome.

By contrast, Trollope's narrator seems to me to be someone older (in temperament if not absolutely in years) than Trollope himself. It is this narrator who admitted, 'I never could endure to shake hands with Mr. Slope' adding that he has 'a pawing, greasy way with him'[11] It is this speaker,

---

9   *BT*, Ch.XXIII p.228.
10 *BT*, Ch.VI, p.45.
11 *BT,* Ch. IV, pp.29, 32.

in fact, who is as much a creation of the author as any of the characters in the novel; who presents himself as a thorough sympathiser with the views of Lady Lufton; who shares the indignation of Dr Grantly at the sermon preached in the cathedral by the bishop's chaplain; and who takes personal offence at the way 'all those peculiar habits and privileges which have always been dear to high-church priests, to that party which is now scandalously called the high-and-dry church, were ridiculed, abused, and anathematised.'[12] It was in fact the rapid advances made by the Evangelical wing of the Church of England on the one hand, and by the Tractarians on the other, which could be said to have left the old traditional rural and provincial Tory parish priests and their congregations 'high and dry'. In all his attitudes, as I hope to show, Trollope's narrator is actually more extreme than Trollope himself.

This polarisation between high and low is treated by Trollope in a number of ways. Sometimes it is plainly humorous and satirical, as when the Proudies introduced a new sofa, 'a horrid chintz affair, most unprelatical and almost irreligious; such a sofa as never yet stood in the study of any decent high church clergyman of the Church of England'.[13] This is of course the same sofa which will later be responsible for stripping the Bishop's wife of her dignity: at Mrs Proudie's Reception, Bertie Stanhope contrives to get her dress caught under the caster of the sofa, 'which carried away there is no saying how much of her garniture'.[14] This is the only occasion in the novel when Mrs Proudie is made an object of outright mockery. That it should be her own vulgar (scilicet 'low church') sofa which hoists her with her own petard is a neat comic achievement on Trollope's part — though one can detect almost too much relish in the way the narrator describes 'the wide ruins of her magnificence'.[15]

The sofa and Mrs Proudie are treated as broad farce. Elsewhere in the Barchester novels, however, Trollope can present the ideas of high and low church in subtler ways. When he introduces Framley Church he describes it and its former incumbent in these terms:

> It was but a mean, ugly building, having been erected about a hundred years since, when all churches then built were to be mean and ugly; nor was it large enough for the congregation, some of whom were thus driven to the dissenting chapels, the Sions and Ebenezers, which had got themselves established on each side of the parish, in putting down which Lady Lufton thought that her pet parson was hardly as energetic

12 *BT*, Ch.VI, p.50.
13 *BT*, Ch.V, p.34.
14 *BT*, Ch.XI, p.96.
15 *BT*, Ch.XI, p.97.

as he might be. It was, therefore, a matter near to Lady Lufton's heart to see a new church built, and she was urgent in her eloquence both with her son and with the vicar, to have the good work commenced.[16]

It sounds very unlikely that a village of Framley's size would have a potential congregation too large to fit inside the parish church, so that would-be worshippers were forced to go to the local Methodist or Baptist chapel; unlikelier still that it had not had a pre-Reformation village church of its own. Some possibilities can be inferred: the old parish church might have been allowed to become so neglected — particularly the all-but-redundant chancel, which would have been the responsibility of the patron to maintain — that it was found cheaper to pull it down and replace it. Eighteenth century churches were built without chancels, since there were no choirs, and the altar would have been a wooden communion table which hardly needed a sanctuary and which anyway, as already suggested, would have been overshadowed by the reading desk and pulpit.

The real reason the congregation would not fit into the church is that the upkeep of the building (and perhaps a portion of the vicar's stipend) would have come from pew rents. Trollope is careful to tell us in passing that the local grocer's wife is the pew-opener in the church. The title of pew-opener is a misnomer. In fact, the function of pew-opener was to ensure that nobody sat in a box pew — one with a door — which was not 'theirs' by right of having rented it for the year or in perpetuity. The farm labourers and servants who would have made up the bulk of the Framley population would not have afforded to pay pew rent from their wages; they would have be forced to sit either at the back, or side aisles or (more likely in an eighteenth century church) in a dark gallery, probably at the west end.

Three other facts are implied by this description of Framley Church which, incidentally, stands opposite the main entrance to Framley Court and therefore offends Lady Lufton's eye every time she leaves her estate. The fact that her 'pet parson', Mark Robarts, is hardly 'as energetic as he might be' in 'putting down' the local non-conformist chapels, as if they were a form of vermin, suggests that he has a greater level of tolerance of dissent than his patron would wish. The existence of the chapels is not a major concern of his: in such matters he is more of a latitudinarian, more liberal as a clergyman than his predecessor, the aptly named Dr Stopford, would have been.

The second fact, not to be noticed so early in the story, but significant nonetheless, is that Mark is here criticised for the first time — for lack of energy in pursuing what Lady Lufton conceives to be his duty. This, of course will soon emerge as a major theme of the novel. Mark's readiness to become a 'hunting parson', who is more likely to be spending time with the liberal

---

16 *FP*, Ch.II, pp.12–13.

Whig grandees associated with the Duke of Omnium than with his own flock in the staunchly Tory domain of Framley, is what will shortly lead Lady Lufton to call on Mr Crawley, the perpetual curate of Hogglestock, to admonish his fellow clergyman and bring him back to a proper sense of his pastoral duties and spiritual responsibilities.

It is interesting, thirdly, that Lady Lufton expects her son and Mark to take forward the fund-raising and building of a new church, 'this good work', rather than involving herself in the project. Church building was indeed seen as 'good work' in the mid-nineteenth century, and the leading local family would have been expected to contribute liberally towards the cost of the new church. The Cambridge Camden Society (later the Ecclesiological Society) began publishing tracts from the 1830s onwards aimed specifically at those with the responsibility (churchwardens) or with the money (patrons) to undertake church building work. Thus, for instance, Pugin himself quoted with approval from the tract *A Few Words to Church Builders* which claims in its introduction to be intended:

> for the use of those to whom God has given, not only the means, but the will, to undertake a work, *the noblest perhaps in which a man can engage*, the building of a house in some degree worthy of His majesty.[17]

Ludovic Lufton, Lady Lufton's son and Mark Robarts' old school friend, would have been just such a churchwarden as Pugin and the Ecclesiologists were hoping to reach. (Lady Lufton herself, as a woman, could not have been churchwarden — hence her expectation that her son would take forward her pet project of building a new church outside the family gates.) *Framley Parsonage* is set in the early 1860s, a key decade for church building. The new church would be built in accordance with the principles being set down by the Ecclesiological Society, the arbiter of taste or correctness (depending on your point of view) in all matters to do with the external design and internal ordering of churches. The approved style for a small village church was something near 'middle pointed', late Early English in style, with a chancel and an organ. If funds allowed, the church would have a spire and certainly a pitched roof. For the Ecclesiologists, following Pugin, Gothic was an architecture of aspiration: pointed arches, steeply pitched roofs, spires — all of these reinforcing the idea that the architecture of a church should raise the eyes and hearts of worshippers towards heaven. No clerestory, therefore, since these usually demanded a low-pitched roof, and that indicated 'debased' Gothic. The higher the churchmanship, therefore, in the Puseyite sense of seeking to revive the rituals and catholicity of the pre-Reformation Church, the higher the pitch of a new church roof.

---

17 'A Few Words to Church Builders', quoted in A. Welby Pugin, *The Present State of Ecclesiastical Architecture in England* (London: Charles Dolman 1843) p.56.

Were such things really taken seriously? Yes, indeed, and Trollope knew this very well. In *Barchester Towers*, Mr Slope's attitude to religious leanings other than his own is described in these terms:

> In doctrine he, like his patron [Mrs Proudie], is tolerant of dissent, if so strict a mind can be called tolerant of anything. With Wesleyan-Methodists he has something in common, but his soul trembles in agony at the iniquities of the Puseyites. His aversion is carried to things outward as well as inward. His gall rises at a new church with a high-pitched roof.[18]

To have something in common with the Wesleyan-Methodists meant not considering that the apostolic succession was sacrosanct, the laying on of hands by two or more bishops at a priest's ordination less important than the ordinand's fitness to preach. It meant that worship in chapels, based on hymn singing, extemporary prayer and preaching, was regarded as a surer way of reaching the hearts of the congregation than 'reading the service'. It indicated that you did not hold the Thirty Nine Articles or the Prayer Book in high esteem, and therefore that you did not accept the authority of the Head of State as the Head of the Church. If you were sympathetic to the non-conformists, you were technically siding with those who had refused to accept the Conformity Act (1662) and thereby excluded themselves from holding any office in the Church of England. You could not be high church in any sense if you felt an affinity with the Methodists. The churchmanship of the bishop's chaplain is defined as much by his architectural as by his non-conformist leanings.

The narrator is at pains to tell us that Mr Slope's strongest supporters are 'enthusiastically religious young ladies'[19] and he reminds us too that the Bishop's Chaplain, a 'priestly charmer', behaves like a religious and sexual predator: 'the female heart, if it glow with a spark of low church susceptibility, cannot withstand him.'[20] This prefaces one of the most important elements of the plot: Mr Slope's pursuit of the Widow Bold and, less predictably, Eleanor's defence of the bishop's chaplain.

On the surface, Eleanor's two suitors — Mr Arabin and Mr Slope — simply represent the Tweedledum and Tweedledee of high and low churchmanship, but this is unfair to both clerics and to Trollope's handling of the situation. Eleanor is not 'an enthusiastically religious young lady': she shares the unassuming pietism of her father, Mr Harding, and the strong sense of fair play that had actuated her late husband, John Bold, in *The Warden*. When aroused, she also has a powerful defensive instinct: over the affair of Hiram's Hospital, she was the only person able to persuade her fiancé

---

18 *BT*, Ch.IV, p.28.
19 *BT*, Ch.VII, p.60.
20 *BT*, Ch. IV, p.32.

to call off the *Jupiter's* campaign against her father. So too, in *Barchester Towers*, she initially defends Mr Slope against the Archdeacon and her sister, Mrs Grantly, not because she is love with him, or is attracted to him, still less because she approves of his sermons and his churchmanship; she simply believes that Mr Slope's intentions in offering to help Mr Harding regain the Wardenship of the Hospital are good, and does not understand why she should be 'charged with improper conduct'[21] by the Archdeacon. When she says to her brother-in-law, 'I wish you had seen Mr. Slope, Dr. Grantly, because I think perhaps it might have done good', the archdeacon demands to know:

> 'Why am I to be called on to lower myself in the world's esteem and my own by coming in contact with such a man as that? I have hitherto lived among gentlemen, and do not mean to be dragged into other company by anybody.'[22]

Eleanor, 'as innocent as her own baby', is nonplussed by this reply and can only say in her defence that she had spent an hour talking to Mr Slope the previous day, 'and I did not feel myself lowered by it.' When even her father, Mr Harding, begins to suspect that she is likely to become engaged to the bishop's chaplain, the narrator is forced to intervene — and does so rather surprisingly. First, he agrees that Mr Harding never should have suspected her, and then adds:

> But Mr Harding was by no means a perfect character. In his indecision, his weakness, his proneness to be led by others, his want of self-confidence, he was very far from being perfect. And then it must be remembered that such a marriage as that which the archdeacon contemplated with disgust, which we who know Mr. Slope so well would regard with equal disgust, did not appear so monstrous to Mr. Harding, because in his charity he did not hate the chaplain as much as the archdeacon did, and as we do.[23]

Mr Harding is a saintly character — perhaps the most saintly in the whole of the *Barset Chronicles* — as the account of his funeral at the end of the *Last Chronicle* makes clear. Yet here Trollope's narrator unexpectedly insists that Mr Harding is not a perfect man, and lists four reasons why not. But he instantly qualifies this criticism by admitting that Eleanor's father, in his wish to think well, not ill, of others, was a more charitable man than the archdeacon — and than us the readers, who are assumed to share the narrator's and the archdeacon's hatred of Mr Slope. It is, to say the least, a

21 *BT*, Ch.XVIII, p.169.
22 *BT*, Ch.XVIII, p.168.
23 *BT*, Ch.XVIII, pp.170-171.

risky strategy to allow the narrator of a novel to make such assumptions —
unless, of course, the author wants to alert his readers to the narrator's own
prejudices, and to enable them to draw back from these. As, indeed, they do.

What is particularly offensive to the Archdeacon is not simply that Mr Slope
is an evangelical churchman, but that he is self-evidently not a gentleman. At
Cambridge he had been a sizar — that is, being partly supported financially by
his college and partly by paying his way by working part-time as a college servant.
His egregious and ingratiating behaviour towards women — not only towards
Eleanor but also to the Signora Madeline Neroni — is intended to betray that he
is no gentleman. And there is an amusing but appropriate irony about the way his
relationship with Eleanor comes to an end. At the Ullathorne Sports Day, when
he goes too far and attempts to insinuate his arm around Eleanor's waist, Eleanor
turns and 'raised her little hand and dealt him a box on the ear with such right
good will, that it sounded among the trees like a miniature thunder-clap.'[24]

Now the narrator pretends to be dismayed at the way the heroine has
behaved. He admits that Eleanor's instinct had been correct: she had known
that men like Slope 'can endure no taint on their personal self-respect, even
from a woman' and that therefore 'the slap on the face that he got from
Eleanor was ... the fittest rebuke that could have been administered to him.'
Nevertheless,

> She should not have raised her hand against the man. Ladies' hands,
> so soft, so sweet, so delicious to the touch, so graceful to the eye, so
> gracious in their gentle doings, were not made to belabour men's faces.[25]

He protests, of course, too much. And he knows it. For in the next paragraph
he adopts the pose of a would-be epic poet unequal to the task before him:

> But how shall I sing the divine wrath of Mr Slope, or how invoke the
> tragic muse to describe the rage which swelled the celestial bosom of
> the bishop's chaplain? Such an undertaking by no means befits the
> low-heeled buskin of modern fiction.[26] (*ibid.*)

Such mock afflatus on the one hand and self-mocking deprecation on
the other (buskins being the open-toed, calf-length boots worn by Athenian
tragic actors) serve only to make it impossible to take Mr Slope seriously
ever again. It was with his sermon against Eleanor's father and the musical
tradition of Barchester Cathedral that he had first announced himself as a
serious enemy to the Archdeacon and the old high church party. Now, at the
moment of his greatest humiliation, he wants to avenge himself by preaching
a sermon against Eleanor herself:

---

24 *BT*, Vol.2, Ch.XL, p.144.
25 *BT*, Vol.2, Ch.XL, p.146.
26 *ibid.*

He felt debasement coming on him, and he longed to shake it off, to
rise up in his stirrup, to mount to high places and great power, that
he might get up into a mighty pulpit and preach to the world a loud
sermon against Mrs Bold.[27]

Trollope's own views on sermons are frequently expressed in *Barchester
Towers*. 'There is, perhaps, no greater hardship at present inflicted on mankind
in civilised and free countries, than the necessity of listening to sermons', he
says in Chapter VI; and in Chapter XXIII he suggests that priests should only
be allowed to preach if they have shown themselves capable of preaching
well. If so, then 'Clergyman who could not preach would be such blessings
that they would be bribed to adhere to their incompetence.'[28] It is one of
the most significant contrasts between Mr Slope and Mr Arabin that the
former is 'gifted with a certain kind of pulpit eloquence'[29] while the latter
is nervous about speaking in public. After preaching his first sermon at St
Ewold's, Arabin has to admit that he will no doubt make himself better heard
'as soon as he had learnt how to pitch his voice to the building'.[30] It is hard to
imagine Mr Slope's ever having had such a problem.

Trollope is as capable of mocking Mr Arabin as he is Mr Slope. At the end
of the scene at Plumstead when Arabin has been unable to defend himself
against Eleanor's accusations that he has spread false rumours about her
relationship with Slope, the narrator closes the chapter (entitled 'Another
Love Scene') with the exclamation:

Poor Mr Arabin — untaught, illiterate, boorish ignorant man! That
at forty years of age you should know so little of the workings of a
woman's heart![31]

On the other hand, it is through his defence of the church and even of
the need for different parties in the church to fight one another, that Arabin
both attracts Eleanor for the first time and demonstrates that Trollope is too
hard on himself (I do not think he is being disingenuous) when he says,
both in *Framley Parsonage* and in *The Last Chronicle* that 'my object has been
to paint the social and not the professional lives of clergymen.' Trollope, *in
propria persona*, says this in defence against the accusation that he has spoken
of the clergy 'as though their professional duties, their high calling, their daily
workings for the good of those around them were matters of no moment'.[32]

---

27 *BT*, Vol.2, Ch.XL, p.147.
28 *BT*, Ch.XXIII, p.229.
29 *BT*, Ch.IV, p.28.
30 *BT*, Ch.XXIII, p.230.
31 *BT*, Vol.2, Ch.XXIX, p.39.
32 Anthony Trollope, *The Last Chronicle of Barset* (Oxford: Oxford University Press,
    World's Classics 2001) Ch. LXXXIV, pp.889–90 [Hereafter LC].

When Eleanor, dining with her brother-in-law and Mr Arabin, says, 'I never saw anything like you clergymen, you are always thinking of fighting each other,' she does not expect the serious vein in which Mr Arabin replies:

> What you say is partly true; our contentions do bring on us some scandal. The outer world, though it constantly reviles us for our human frailties, and throws in our teeth the fact that being clergymen we are still no more than men, demands of us that we should do our work with godlike perfection. There is nothing godlike about us: we differ from each other with the acerbity common to man — we triumph over each other with human frailty — we allow differences on subjects of divine origin to produce among us antipathies and enmities that are anything but divine. This is all true. But what would you have in place of it? There is no infallible head for a church on earth.[33]

The earnestness of Arabin's argument here, culminating in his rejection of papal infallibility and showing — by his final refusal to follow Newman to Rome — his commitment to the Church of England, takes Eleanor by surprise. In a remarkably critical passage, Trollope interprets her reactions thus:

> She had been used all her life to listen to clerical discussion; but the points at issue between the disputants had so seldom been of more than temporal significance as to have left on her mind no feeling of reverence for such subjects. There had always been a hard worldly leaven of the love either of income or of power in the strains she had heard; there had been no panting for the truth; no aspirations after religious purity.[34]

It is of course precisely the kind of religion and religious discussion that goes on around the Archdeacon's table which Trollope is condemning. This cannot be the same narrator who has so firmly aligned himself with the old high-and-dry church and who automatically takes the Archdeacon's side against Mr Slope. What is more, Trollope adds that 'she was sick of it without knowing that it was so.' It is in fact the theological seriousness of Arabin's response to her attack that provokes in Eleanor 'a certain pleasurable excitement' — she has never heard anything like it before.

All of this demonstrates not that Mr Arabin's Anglican religion is unworldly, but that he can recognise its worldliness as a sign not of strength but of human fallibility. In the end, Arabin's apparent weaknesses — his shyness, his nervousness in the pulpit and his lack of confidence in relating to women, for example — are actually manifestations of his honesty and human goodness. And in this respect Trollope places him, of course, at the

---

33 *BT*, Ch.XXI, pp.204-205.
34 *BT*, Ch.XXI, pp.205.

opposite extreme from Mr Slope, who would never admit to any fallibility at all. Arabin has a hard time wooing Eleanor, but it is clear that she is the woman he should marry, though it needs the much-too-worldly and disenchanted Signora Madeline Neroni to point out to him that he and Eleanor are simply waiting for each other.

I hope I have indicated sufficiently how the religious controversies that provide the context for the *Barset Chronicles* also animate the plots and deepen the characterisation of novels such as *Barchester Towers*. I want to end by showing how two characters in these novels, Mr Harding and Mr Crawley, do more than Grantly and Arabin, Slope or Mrs Proudie, to show the real depth of Trollope's understanding of the spiritual and pastoral life of a priest.

In many respects these two, Mr Harding and Mr Crawley, are exact opposites of each other. Mr Harding is universally respected and loved: when he dies, all Barchester attends his funeral in the cathedral. As warden of Hiram's Hospital, he looks after the bedesman very well. When he resigns from the Hospital because he doubts whether indeed he is entitled to the income he derives from Hiram's will, the hospital gardens and buildings soon go into decline — the life goes out of the place. He divides his ministry between his work as warden and his position as precentor at the cathedral. His legacy to the Church of England is his research into early post-Reformation English sacred music, preserved in the book which he had published at his own expense and which in effect affirms the historic continuity between the Anglican past and its present. He embodies all the virtues of the old High Church, and none of its vices. He is the absolute antithesis of his son-in-law, Dr Grantly, whose father (the former bishop of Barchester) had been his closest friend. The same phrase, 'meek authority', used by Trollope to describe old Bishop Grantly, could be precisely applied to Mr Harding. He becomes, too, a touchstone by which others measure their own spiritual lives. Talking to the Dean (the position now filled by Mr. Arabin) just before Mr Harding's death, the Archdeacon admits:

> 'The fact is, he was never wrong. He couldn't go wrong. He lacked guile, and he feared God, — and a man who does both will never go far astray. I don't think he ever coveted aught in his life, except a new case for his violon-cello and somebody to listen to him when he played it.'[35]

Having said this, Dr Grantly has a rare moment of self-doubt. He starts to review 'the sterner ambition of his own life…. What things had he coveted? Had he lacked guile? He told himself that he had feared God, but he was not sure that he was telling himself true even in that.'[36]

---

35 *LC*, Ch.LXXXI, p.860.
36 *ibid.*

By contrast Mr Crawley is described as 'a strict man, — a strict, stern, unpleasant man, and one who feared God and his own conscience.'[37] His moral certainty in all matters seems at first sight the opposite of Mr Harding's gentle diffidence. However, in one respect at least they are not so dissimilar: when Mr Harding discovers that he cannot be morally certain he is entitled to the rewards and comforts of the wardenship, he resigns and places himself in a position of relative poverty. Nobody can persuade him to do otherwise. Mr Crawley's poverty, however, stems (as Trollope is at pains to point out) both from his having married too young and having fathered too many children. It is, Trollope implies, almost as a result of this youthful impatience that Crawley has never been offered a living with a stipend sufficient for his family. Whereas Mr Harding has spent his whole life working in or near the cathedral, Mr Crawley has been in the wilderness. When first introduced in *Barchester Towers*, though never named in that book, he is described as 'the small curate of a small Cornish parish';[38] by the time he reappears in *Framley Parsonage*, the portrait painted of him is chilling:

> The first ten years of his life as a clergyman had been passed in performing the duties and struggling through the life of a curate in a bleak, ugly, cold parish on the northern coast of Cornwall. It had been a weary life and a fearful struggle, made up of duties ill requited and not always satisfactorily performed, of love and poverty, of increasing cares, of sickness, debt and death.[39]

It is while in this Cornish parish, however, that he rescues his old Oxford friend, the then young Mr Arabin, from the danger of following Newman and converting to Roman Catholicism. A decade and more later, Mr Arabin — having by now become Dean of Barchester — is able to repay this debt by offering Crawley promotion of a kind: the perpetual curacy of Hogglestock. Hogglestock, though, is still in the wilderness for it is a large ugly village on the furthest edge of the county of Barset and the diocese of Barchester. Mr Crawley's parishioners are the brickmakers, 'a race of men very troublesome to a zealous parson who won't let men go rollicking to the devil without interference'.[40] Yet, in *The Last Chronicle of Barset*, it is these same brickmakers who provide him with his own spiritual counsel when he most needs it: the motto 'It's dogged as does it', comes from them and sustains him as he approaches his trial for theft on suspicion of stealing the cheque for twenty pounds.

---

37 *FP*, Ch.XIV, p.171.
38 *BT*, Ch.XX, p.190.
39 *FP*, Ch.XIV, p.171.
40 *FP*, Ch.XIV, p.171.

The fullest estimate of Mr Crawley comes from his wife, who in *Framley Parsonage* almost dies of malnutrition and exhaustion, but who in *The Last Chronicle* supports him without hesitation and without regard for her own future:

> She knew he was good and yet weak, that he was afflicted by false pride, that his intellect was still very bright, yet so dismally obscured on many sides as almost to justify people in saying that he was mad. She knew that he was almost a saint, and yet almost a castaway through vanity and hatred of those above him.[41]

No one else in all the *Chronicles* (not even Mr Harding) is described as 'almost a saint'. Yet he proves to be not only an effective and beloved pastor to men such as the brickmakers, (they club together to give him a substantial gift when he resigns from Hogglestock) but also to his fellow clergy. He 'saves' Arabin from Rome, just as he later saves Mark Robarts, the vicar of Framley, from spiritual if not financial ruin. Acting as Lady Lufton's ambassador, he has got to know Mark well, so that 'Robarts would submit to his opinion on matters of ecclesiastical and even theological law'.[42] Again, no one else in all the *Chronicles* (not even Mr Arabin) exercises such a ministry among his fellow clergy. Now he warns Mark:

> I make bold to ask you, Mr. Robarts, whether you are doing your best to lead such a life as may become a parish clergyman among his parishioners?… But it cannot be that it should content you to place yourself as one among those thoughtless sinners, for the crushing of whose sin you have been placed here among them. You become a hunting parson, and ride with a happy mind among blasphemers and mocking devils — you, whose aspirations were so high, who have spoken so often and so well of the duties of a minister of Christ.[43]

It is a sermon that Crawley preaches to Robarts, and its effects are far reaching. It saves Robarts and enables him to endure the disgrace of financial ruin and the presence of the bailiffs in the Parsonage. It ensures that in *The Last Chronicle*, Crawley has a friend in Mark who is ready throughout to defend Crawley when all the other clergy (including Mr Harding) have begun to doubt him.

There is indeed one further important comparison to be made between Harding and Crawley: just as in *Barchester Towers*, Mr Harding's daughter Eleanor terrifies and outrages the Archdeacon who thinks that his sister-in-law is likely to marry Mr Slope, so in *The Last Chronicle* the Archdeacon has to cope with the prospect that his son Henry may marry Grace Crawley. The idea of

---

41 *LC*, Ch.XLI, p.412.
42 *FP*, Ch.XV, p.177.
43 *FP*, Ch.XV, pp.183–4.

having Mr Crawley as a member of his family circle is almost too much for Dr Grantly, who threatens to disinherit his son if he marries Grace — no matter that she is in herself a very well educated and sensible woman whose father is at least a gentleman, even if in self-imposed exile from the society of gentlemen.

Ultimately, Dr Grantly is reconciled to both daughters and to their fathers, and there is a sense in which the Archdeacon's blessing is always required in Barchester. More significantly still, it is Dr Grantly who is finally able to release Mr Crawley from poverty by presenting him with the living of St Ewold's. St Ewold's, of course had originally been presented in *Barchester Towers* to Mr Arabin, and afterwards — when Mr Arabin succeeded to the Deanery — to Mr Harding. Indeed, it was (according to the Archdeacon) Mr Harding's dying wish that Mr Crawley should succeed him. So it is important to see Mr Crawley as standing in this line of succession, a line finally confirmed when the Archdeacon, having finally met and entertained Mr Crawley at Plumstead as the father of his future daughter-in-law, gives him a very special gift. It is a volume of sermons published by the late Bishop Grantly, and containing the Bishop's own manuscript notes. Mr Crawley treasures the gift and promises to study the sermons and the notes carefully. Thus, symbolically and actually, Mr Crawley is brought in out of the wilderness.

Sermons, as I have suggested, play a particularly important role in Trollope's own conflicted thinking about the nature of Anglicanism. By accepting these sermons from the past, and promising to study them, Mr Crawley aligns himself to the traditional teaching of the Church of England. But of all the clergy to whom Trollope introduces us, Crawley alone defies categorisation: he cannot be described as High; or High and Dry; Low or Evangelical. Strict, yes; but strict in the way he submits himself to the teachings of the Church and in the way he applies them to himself and to Mark Robarts when such teachings are needed. He and Mr Harding, so unalike in most respects, are the two clergy on whom, in the end, Trollope as novelist confers the greatest praise. Mr Harding is described by the Archdeacon as providing the perfect example of a Christian life. Mr Crawley is described by his wife as 'almost a saint.' Finally, though, if it is Mr Harding who commands our affection, it is Mr. Crawley (with all his faults and all his sufferings) who demands, according to Trollope, our admiration. Dr Grantly tells him that Mr Harding had been moved to name him as his successor both 'by what he had heard of the cruel and undeserved persecution' Mr Crawley had suffered and also because of the character he bore 'in the diocese for zeal and piety'. His qualities as a pastor and as a priest are finally recognised and rewarded.

There is, however, one final indication of how Trollope views the priest who, above all others in the *Chronicles of Barset*, is a man of sorrows. By the end of the novel, he has learned humility and gratitude and come to recognise the seriousness of the faults that have damaged him and his family so badly. When the Dean returns at the end of *The Last Chronicle* from his extended tour of the Holy Land, he tells his old friend that the Holy Land has more than fulfilled his expectations. To this Crawley replies:

> 'For myself, it is, of course impossible that I should ever visit any scenes except those to which my immediate work may call me, — never in this world. The new Jerusalem is still within my reach, — if it be not forfeited by pride and obstinacy; but the old Jerusalem I can never behold. Methinks, because it is so, I would sooner stand with my foot on Mount Olivet, or drink a cup of water in the village of Bethany, than visit any other spot within the traveller's compass.... Rome makes my mouth water but little, nor even Athens much. I can realize without seeing all that Athens could show me, and can fancy that the existing truth would destroy more, than it would build up. But to have stood on Calvary!'[44]

When Arabin points out, 'We don't know where Calvary was,' Josiah Crawley replies simply, 'I fancy that I should know, should know enough.'

Is it not wholly characteristic of Trollope that he should choose as the most Christ-like of all the clergy who populate the Barchester novels the man who almost uniquely belongs to no ecclesiastical party; whose sermons genuinely save men's souls as they saved Mark Robarts; who alone reduced Mrs Proudie to silence with the simple command, 'Peace, woman!'; who is most emphatically both saint and sinner, and who finally can be identified with his Saviour — by his very initials?

---

44 *LC*, Ch.LXXVIII, p.840.

2.3 The Word is Said: Re-reading the poetry of John Drinkwater

This lecture is based on a talk given to the Friends of the Dymock Poets, 5 April 2008. The Friends are a literary society devoted to the enjoyment and study of the group of poets associated with the parish of Dymock on the Herefordshire-Gloucestershire border. In the months leading up to the outbreak of the First World War in 1914 Lascelles Abercrombie, Wilfred Gibson, Robert Frost, Edward Thomas, John Drinkwater and Rupert Brooke, plus their families and friends, all lived or came to stay in the hamlets surrounding Dymock. Most but not all of them were already published Georgian poets, but at the heart of the community lay the production of their own poetry magazine, New Numbers, *edited by Abercrombie and Gibson.*

This was the third occasion on which I had spoken to the Friends of the Dymock Poets. Previously I had lectured on my experience of editing the poetry of Robert Frost[1] and on Rupert Brooke's Letters from America. *On this occasion, I had been invited to speak on John Drinkwater, in whom I had had a long-standing personal interest — as the talk I gave reveals. I had been warned in advance that my lecture would be recorded and transcribed for later publication in the journal* The Dymock Poets and Friends. *What follows is therefore an edited version of my lecture since, when speaking at an event such as this, I always speak informally, without a script. I did, however, provide a hand-out containing all the poems discussed during my talk. I should add that the audience was on the whole very knowledgeable about the Dymock Poets though few of them were familiar with Drinkwater's work or about the period of his career that my talk focused on, the years immediately before and during the First World War.*

Poets need friends. I think this is particularly true of John Drinkwater, because over the past 60 years, of all the Dymock Poets, Drinkwater is possibly the one who has faded most rapidly from the scene. He now seems to be perhaps the least known of the group; in his time, however, he was probably better known than any of them. During the period from 1918

---

1   Adrian Barlow (ed.) *Robert Frost: Selected Poems* (Oxford: Oxford University Press 1998).

onwards he became one of the leading literary figures of his generation: when Robert Bridges died in 1930, Drinkwater was rumoured to be on the shortlist to succeed him as Poet Laureate. (The job went to John Masefield.) Clearly, he was a man of some considerable stature in terms of his poetic reputation, and that reputation had been greatly enhanced by his sudden achieving of real fame with the success of his first major play, *Abraham Lincoln*, which opened in 1918.

It's actually in 1918 that I want to start; not, however, at the theatre, not with *Abraham Lincoln*, but rather less probably in a hut in a large army encampment in a place called Buchy, not far from Rouen in northern France, on 18 January. What was Drinkwater doing there? He was giving a reading of his poems to an audience of British soldiers who had been allowed a few days' rest and relaxation from the Front, and were spending it at this camp at Buchy. During the First World War, Buchy was one of the major convalescent, rest and recreation centres for the British army. It was safely behind the lines but close enough to the Front for soldiers to be brought to and from there even if just for a short break.

John Drinkwater had left England on 23 December, 1917. He spent Christmas in Rouen. It was perishingly cold, possibly the coldest winter of the war. His job, for a month, was to go out and entertain the troops. He went as part of an entertainment unit, accompanying the Lena Ashwell Concert Party, one of the leading entertainment groups during the First World War. He travelled around the different camps, particularly the ones run by the YMCA. The YMCA played a very important part in maintaining troop morale: the 'huts' run by the YMCA were major centres in all such camps, and indeed right up to the Front Line itself.

Drinkwater arrived at Buchy on 17 January. He was greeted there by the YMCA padre, who had never met a poet before, and was rather overwhelmed to encounter somebody as well known as Drinkwater. He took him around and looked after him, and acted as master of ceremonies at his reading on 18 January. The day afterwards, the Lena Ashwell Concert Party had an audience of over 2,000 men. 'Hut' is a bit of a misnomer, for this YMCA hut was a substantial building in a very large camp, where at some events 2,600 soldiers turned up. Drinkwater read his own poems, and among them two made a particular impact on the YMCA padre at the time. One was called 'A Prayer', and the padre wrote it out afterwards in his notebook; the other, his much anthologised poem 'A Town Window', John Drinkwater wrote out in his own hand as a 'thank you' to the man who had looked after him at Buchy.

When he got back to England Drinkwater sent the padre a cutting of a newspaper article he had written about the life in these YMCA huts. He summarised his experience thus:

The scene inside one of these huts at night is of a truly heroic poignancy. Certain hours are set apart for the sale of hot drinks and cigarettes and such, and then from every hut comes out from YMCA headquarters each night, someone or other to do what he may towards cheering the evening. Here I have seen a repertory company, led by one of our most distinguished tragic actresses; concert parties, including elegant lights of the music hall stage; a Scotch theologian of European reputation, and with uncommonly pretty wit; the keeper of a great English gallery, showing slides of famous pictures, a professor talking of Whitman and Browning and Dickens; a man just reading the best English poetry, another man with his kinematograph machine. And all this variety, most eagerly received, is not haphazard makeshift under the assumption that the best for a difficult job need not be very good, since allowances will readily be made; it is in each case the best of its kind that can be secured, supplied by wholly admirable organisation.... The fruits of their work, the glowing activity of the huts in those stark and sullen camps, is one of the most excellent decencies of the war. For a man to nourish it in any way, by service or by gift, is to enrich his own stores.[2]

'A man just reading the best English poetry'. We don't know all the poems Drinkwater read, but we know he was a fine performer, as a poet and as a reader of poetry. By the 1930s he had an international reputation and was giving readings and lectures across the United States. An enthusiastic reviewer wrote:

His poetry sells in bulk among the middle classes (the big market for poetry), but it loses something in the printed page. For its full savour you should hear the poet recite the poems himself.... His personal presence and voice adds to his poetry what staging adds to a play. As a lecturer he's always a big draw. Bill him to appear and the "poetry public" turns out from their houses for miles around. He has a superb manner on the platform, a handsome countenance, eloquent eyes, a fine voice, and the training of an actor to see him through. He never sings above the heads of the bourgeoisie. He always is grave and measured, voicing a fine idealism and an unswerving moral sincerity, and he believes in the grandeur of the simple human heart.[3]

This description reminds us that Drinkwater was not only poet and playwright: he was also actor, stage manager, and theatre manager. He was absolutely a man of the theatre, so it's not surprising that Drinkwater the actor, the performer and the poet are one and the same.

---

2 The newspaper cutting from which I quote here is in an album of private papers. The identity of the newspaper has not been established: it may be the *News Chronicle*.
3 *New York Herald Tribune* (6 February 1932).

Drinkwater began life as an insurance clerk. Although born in Leytonstone, north London, he spent most of his early childhood in the Oxford area, and it's the Oxfordshire countryside and Cotswolds with which he is most closely associated. He also had a great deal of affection for the Warwickshire countryside, and over and over again his points of reference were Warwick and Warwickshire. That poem 'A Town Window' looks out beyond the Birmingham street where he was lodging:

Beyond my window in the night
    Is but a drab inglorious street,
Yet there the frost and clean starlight
    As over Warwick woods are sweet.

Under the grey drift of the town
    The crocus works among the mould
As eagerly as those that crown
    The Warwick spring in flame and gold.

And when the tramway down the hill
    Across the cobbles moans and rings,
There is about my window-sill
    The tumult of a thousand wings.

Drinkwater had published his first collection of poems privately in 1903, but his first serious attempt at publication for the wider public belongs to 1908. His reputation grew rapidly: by Christmas 1913, the *Birmingham Mail* was describing him as 'the only noteworthy poet Birmingham can cherish'. One of his first Dymock poems is 'Blackbird':

He comes on chosen evenings,
My blackbird bountiful, and sings
Over the gardens of the town
Just at the hour the sun goes down.
His flight across the chimneys thick,
By some divine arithmetic,
Comes to his customary stack,
And couches there his plumage black,
And there he lifts his yellow bill,
Kindled against the sunset, till
These suburbs are like Dymock woods
Where music has her solitudes,
And while he mocks the winter's wrong

> Rapt on his pinnacle of song,
> Figured above our garden plots
> Those are celestial chimney-pots.[4]

It's Drinkwater's ability to see heaven in the mundane — 'celestial chimney-pots' — to make a joke and a serious point at the same time. This is very much a characteristic of his work; it is part of the charm of his writing. I use the word 'charm' deliberately, because charm works both for and against him. I think it's a quality which people both admire and enjoy in his poetry, but which makes it all too easy to disparage, implying there is something superficial about the writing.

At the same time that his career as a poet began to take off, (while he was still working as an insurance agent in Birmingham) he became very much involved with a group of actors, the Pilgrim Players, whose genesis led ultimately to the creation of the first Birmingham Repertory Theatre. This led also to his friendship with Barry Jackson, and ultimately to his being appointed first manager of the theatre.

At that point he gave up his career in insurance and devoted himself to a life in the theatre. Not that it was an easy life. Setting up a new venture like a repertory theatre and being responsible for managing it, particularly once the war began, was for him a very demanding and precarious job.

Drinkwater, as war broke out, was both a poet and man of the theatre. But how did his reputation stand, as a Georgian and as a member of Dymock poets? Edward Thomas, reviewing the early *Georgian Poetry* anthologies, does not mention Drinkwater. Although he is in all the Georgian anthologies and in all issues of *New Numbers*, he is somehow on the edge. When *New Numbers* was still being discussed it was felt by Lascelles Abercrombie and W.W. Gibson that Drinkwater should be excluded: they feared he would only publish the poems that he couldn't get money for elsewhere. So there is a certain sense in which Drinkwater is *in* the group, but not quite *of* the group. After the War, he was notably not in the Golden Room:[5] at that key point in the history of the Dymock poets, Drinkwater is absent.

During the First World War, he became slightly detached from Edward Marsh and the other central figures in the Georgian poetry movement, not least because he didn't enlist and because his life was increasingly taken up with running the Birmingham theatre. So I see Drinkwater as being near the centre but also slightly on the periphery of the poetry scene. Yet his pre-war and war-time poetry deserves more attention than it has received. 'Dominion' is one of his pre-war poems that I would like to examine.

---

4   All poems by John Drinkwater reproduced in this lecture are taken from *Collected Poems*, 2 vols. (London: Sidgwick and Jackson, 1923).

5   'The Golden Room', a 1927 poem by W.W. Gibson, celebrates the only occasion when five of the six poets now collectively known as the Dymock Poets were together in Gibson's home, The Old Nailshop. The five were Abercrombie, Gibson, Rupert Brooke, Robert Frost and Edward Thomas, together with their families.

I went beneath the sunny sky
    When all things bowed to June's desire,
The pansy with its steadfast eye,
    The blue shells on the lupin spire,

The swelling fruit along the boughs,
    The grass, grown heady in the rain,
Dark roses fitted for the brows
    Of queens great kings have sung in vain;

My little cat with tiger bars,
    Bright claws all hidden in content;
Swift birds that flashed like darkling stars
    Across the cloudy continent;

The wiry-coated fellow curled
    Stump-tailed upon the sunny flags;
The bees that sacked a coloured world
    Of treasure for their honey-bags.

And all these things seemed very glad,
    The sun, the flowers, the birds on wing,
The jolly beasts, the furry-clad
    Fat bees, the fruit, and everything.

But gladder than them all was I,
    Who, being man, might gather up
The joy of all beneath the sky,
    And add their treasure to my cup,

And travel every shining way,
    And laugh with God in God's delight,
Create a world for every day,
    And store a dream for every night.

One of the criticisms of Drinkwater's poetry, and this applies to the Georgian poets in general, was of the overuse of the word 'little'. It is used here as an affectionate diminutive, 'my little cat'. He also uses that peculiarly poetic word 'darkling' to mean 'surrounded by darkness'. Mathew Arnold used it in 'Dover Beach', and it goes back via Keats to Milton, who used it in *Paradise Lost*, and even before then to Shakespeare. It's one of those words that almost immediately proclaims itself a word with poetic lineage.

Like his poem 'Blackbird', where in 'celestial chimney-pots' there is a linking with everyday life, the inner life seems to be at the heart of what

Drinkwater is trying to say here. Notice the title, 'Dominion', an echo straight from Genesis and the idea that God gave man dominion over all the animals that walked on dry land. Indeed there is a strong suggestion, in his early poetry particularly, of a Biblical basis for his quasi-theological view of life. That's not to say that Drinkwater would ever have wanted to be thought a specifically Christian poet. I think his own position was broader than that, and anyway his views evolved during his life time. More helpfully, poems like 'Dominion', 'Blackbird', and even 'Cotswold Love' associate him very clearly with a kind of pre-war ruralist aesthetic — one which fits very well with *New Numbers* and indeed the whole Dymock poetry project.

It's interesting, for instance, to notice how often in his early poetry he refers to the plough and the ploughman. These references suggest a clear connection to be made between Drinkwater and Thomas Hardy. I'm thinking particularly of that famous Hardy wartime poem 'In the Time of the Breaking of Nations' ('Only a man harrowing clods / In a slow silent plod'). Here is Drinkwater's poem, 'Plough':

> The snows are come in early state,
> And love shall now go desolate
> If we should keep too close a gate.
>
> Over the woods a splendour falls
> Of death, and grey are the Gloucester walls,
> And grey the skies for burials.
>
> But secret in the falling snow
> I see the patient ploughman go,
> And watch the quiet furrows grow.

This poem was written just as the First World War got under way, and the presence of the war is clear, although there is no explicit reference to it. The idea of burials and the gradual accumulation of death becomes a central idea of this very short poem. Notice that, just as with Hardy, the ploughman becomes a symbol of continuity, of survival, of the fact that although there may be a great trauma about to be unleashed, nevertheless the natural cycle of life is the natural cycle of ploughing, harvesting, reaping, and all of that suggests the hope for the future.

I would be wrong to imply, however, that his perception of the First World War was simply one of Hardy-esque detachment; far from it. Drinkwater's poem 'Nineteen-Fifteen' is one of the most interesting and under-read poems of this early phase of the First World War, and again it starts with ploughing:

On a ploughland hill against the sky,
    Over the barley, over the rye,
Time, which is now a black pine tree,
    Holds out his arms and mocks at me —

In the year of your Lord Nineteen-fifteen
    The acres are ploughed and the acres are green,
And the calves and the lambs and the foals are born,
    But man the angel is all forlorn.

The cropping cattle, the swallow's wing,
    The wagon team and the pasture spring,
Move in their seasons and are most wise,
    But man, whose image is in the skies,

Who is master of all, whose hand achieves
    The church and the barn and the homestead eaves —
How are the works of his wisdom seen
    In the year of your Lord Nineteen-fifteen?

The tone of serious irony makes this a remarkable poem, written so early in the cycle of the war. It contributes importantly to the evolution of war poetry, but, as I have said, Drinkwater did not enlist, neither was he conscripted. We do not know exactly why not: he was born in 1882, and by the end of 1915 the regulations for conscription required any unmarried or widowed man between the ages of 19 and 41 to enlist. According to the Conscription Act in January 1916 anyone in this category was 'deemed to have enlisted'; in other words you were *de facto* a soldier, and if you did not enlist you were technically deemed to be a deserter. However, by this stage Drinkwater was married and had a job that he must have regarded as a significant contribution to the war effort at home.[6] What we do know is that, right at the start of the war, in fact three days after the war began, he and Lascelles Abercrombie were speaking to a conference of teachers in Stratford-on-Avon Grammar School. Drinkwater was lecturing on 'The value of poetry in education' and specifically on the importance of Shakespeare now war was beginning. This is what Drinkwater said:

> When you have first taught the child that [he had just recited 'Fear no more the heat of the sun' from *Cymbeline*], you have done more for his moral sense than will ever be done by the whole maze of text-book information and precept... . We tell people that they must seek beauty, but we take no steps to enable them to recognise it... . I will tell you

6   In the discussion after the lecture, a member of the audience reminded me that the Birmingham Rep's founder, Sir Barry Jackson, with whom Drinkwater worked very closely throughout the War, was a pacifist with strong Quaker sympathies.

how the authorities may effect a fundamental rural reform. Let them use some of the money available for the purpose to send companies [of actors] into the villages to play Shakespeare, and the work of our other great and fine dramatists, and in less than a generation the people will require decent conditions, and as soon as they desire them they will have them.... When we have passed through this present calamity, social reorganisation will inevitably begin on a scale hitherto unknown.... . We must turn from the enunciation of moral principles to the fostering of man's spiritual activity.[7]

There are two important things to say about that: first, it exemplifies how important for Drinkwater was the influence of William Morris. Drinkwater actually wrote about Morris: one of his earliest non-poetry projects was to publish an essay on Morris and his significance. In a way, this idea about the importance of beauty, now seen through drama, echoes precisely the kind of William Morris aesthetic and ethic: 'Have nothing in your house that you do not know to be useful, or believe to be beautiful'. Secondly, then, there was for Drinkwater, right the way through his life, a profound sense that poetry — all art but particularly the spoken word — could contribute both to the beauty of human life and to its moral value. That description of Drinkwater in the *New York Herald Tribune* had talked about his being a poet of 'sincere moral imperative'. Here Drinkwater charts a progression from beauty to moral principles to spiritual activity.

This theme is central to Drinkwater's short play $x = o$, first performed in April 1917; a one-act play in an age when one-act plays were extremely popular. It formed the middle of an evening of three one-act plays at the Birmingham Rep. The first was a short domestic tragedy, then there was $x = o$, and finally a light comedy to finish off: $x = o$ was the jam in the middle of the sandwich. This play, subtitled 'A Night of the Trojan War', caused great controversy when first performed. In it, four characters, two Greek soldiers (Pronax and Salvius) and two Trojan soldiers (Capys and Ilus), debate in alternate scenes the folly of war: how bizarre it is that as young men of action, as would-be politicians, would-be social reformers, or as artists they are trained to do one thing very well, which is to kill. It would have been impossible in 1917 to write a play in which two English soldiers, one a poet and one a budding politician, and then two German soldiers, one a sculptor and one a man of action, debated in these terms. So the play is deliberately set in the distant past, the Trojan War. At the end, by an irony absolutely central to the moral paradox of $x = o$, Pronax has killed his opposite number Capys, and Ilus has killed his opposite number Salvius. They have cancelled each other out.

---

7   Speech reported in the *Birmingham Mail*, 8 August 1914.

When the play first appeared, it was reviewed extensively in the local papers. This is the *Birmingham Post*:

> John Drinkwater's short new play stands above all else he has written in its sad, disquieting beauty. It's a story of a night in the Trojan War. Its construction is very simple; a studied parallelism. Salvius, the poet, and his friend Pronax, the man of action, are the Grecian counterparts of the Trojans, Capys the sculptor and Ilus the man of action. In all its essentials Drinkwater's night of the Trojan War is a night of the European war, of any war. Capys and Salvius are eternal types of the artist, the creator whose strength is turned towards destruction; Pronax and Ilus are types of the man of action, the social reformer, whose strength is turned to aggression — and they have in them all the qualities which make a good soldier — daring, resource, and above all workmanlike, orderly precision which distinguishes the professional soldier... . Mr. Drinkwater's play is not, as it may seem to some, a homily against war. But it is an exhortation to those who sit beside their hearths to remember the great renunciation and sacrifice that youth must make in a just cause. Its imagery is English, with the rich peaceful beauty of the English countryside. Its birth is passionate, varied and musical, and the poetry was spoken purely and tenderly by the players.

This reviewer is perfectly clear what the play is saying. Interestingly, he reviews the play again, two months later:

> This tragedy $x = o$ is Mr. Drinkwater's masterpiece, which at first seeing we declared not a homily against war, but an exhortation to those who sit beside their hearths to remember the great renunciation and sacrifice that youth must make in a just cause. Since then it has received the public and private benediction of pacifists, of anti-militarists, and conscientious objectors. Isolated from the patriotic poems Mr. Drinkwater wrote in the early days, when he was full of fervour in the cause of Belgium, there is enough in the play to justify a recantation, especially remembering the Quakerism of 'The God of Quiet'. Yet perhaps this isolation would be unfair to Mr. Drinkwater. (*Birmingham Post*, 13 June 1917)

It's useful to have those references to other poems by Drinkwater, written at the start of the war. Certainly that reference to Belgium is one that we can pick up, because in his volume *Swords and Ploughshares* there is a poem called 'England to Belgium':

> Not lusting for a brief renown
>   Nor apt in any vain dispute
> You throw the scythes of autumn down,

> And leave your dues of autumn fruit
> Unharvested, and dare the wrong
>   Of death's immitigable wing,
> And on your banners burn a song
>   That God's unrisen and yet shall sing.

This is hardly the voice of the conscientious objector:

> Because your Belgian fields are dear,
>   And now they suffer black despite
> Because your womanhood can hear
>   The menace on the lips of night,
> Because you are a little clan
>   Of brothers, and because there comes
> The thief among you, to a man
>   You take the challenge of your drums.

Here is the high rhetoric of 1914; and it is as if, by the time he comes to write *x = o* in 1917, Drinkwater has realised that the language he had been using was inappropriate to his later purpose. But not all the reviewers who saw *x = o* shared the enthusiastic view of the *Birmingham Post*. Indeed some felt Drinkwater had betrayed his earlier patriotic, nationalistic voice, exemplified in 'England to Belgium'. Here's the *Birmingham Mail*, reviewing the first performance. This reviewer puts the play in the context of what he sees happening to English poetry generally during war:

> The growing divorce between our poets and the nation is a very disquieting sign of the times. It's a comparatively modern development. Looking back on history and literature through all our great phases we have generally had a poet, at least, to express our national ideals; to voice the spiritual vicissitudes of his countrymen in the mass, to mirror England's mood of the moment, great or small... . But today, there seems a gap, a gap all the more incomprehensible because for two and half years the world has been passing through a period of spiritual surge unequalled since the French Revolution. For two and half years England has been seething with the tremendous emotions which make great poetry, yet our poets seem untouched... . Even the German poets, however lamentable their output in quality, have been sound nationally. But our singers have failed to produce any considerable work, except Mr. Masefield's prose epic on Gallipoli — inspired by England at war. This divorce was made all the more apparent locally on Saturday night when Mr. Drinkwater produced a war play at the Repertory. "X = 0: a night of the Trojan War" is the best play Mr. Drinkwater has given us

yet. The simplicity, the directness, the economy of both verse and action makes the tragedy a little masterpiece, yet this very perfection makes its production all the more deplorable. Mr. Drinkwater has plainly been deeply stirred by the war, but out of all the glories and horrors of the last two-and-a-half years the one impression made upon his mind is that war means that young poets, artists, dreamers, heroes of both sides shall mutually exterminate one another in a conflict in which they have no real interest over a paltry quarrel long since lost sight of. He is apparently oblivious of all that England went to war for; all the great ideals or the great crimes which seem fitting theme for the poet's pen he passes by.[8]

There is much more in the same vein. Finally the reviewer laments:

It only shows that Mr. Drinkwater is not the national poet he might have been had he used the same skill as he deploys here on some theme in tune with the national spirit.

I suspect that for some people this moment marked the turning point in their perception of Drinkwater as a poet: the idea that somehow he had let the national side down. I'm not suggesting this became a universal view, but it's interesting that here in print somebody goes to such lengths to say that Drinkwater has misjudged the national mood. The reviewer concludes:

A visit to the Front, especially the French sector, might convince Mr. Drinkwater that X does not = 0, for if the sordidness of war prevented him from seeing the ethical glories he would surely realise it then as a very unpleasant but very necessary sanitary duty.

It is fascinating that $x = o$ is treated by two reviewers in such contrasting ways. One holds it up as a model of a new pacifism, while the other rejects the play and the playwright for having abandoned the kind of poetic destiny which this reviewer thought he ought to have fulfilled. It seems to me there is an argument for saying that, from this moment on perhaps, even Drinkwater himself realises poetry is not the direction in which all his energies should be channelled. On the strength of this play he begins writing full-length drama and within a year has completed *Abraham Lincoln*, the success of which will elevate his career to a completely different level.

The war, inevitably, remains a theme in his poetry. 'Inscription for a War Memorial Fountain' is a touching and neatly epigrammatic piece, in which the fountain itself speaks:

They nothing feared whose names I celebrate.
Greater than death they died; and their estate
Is here on Cotswold comradely to live
Upon your lips in every draught I give.

---

8   *Birmingham Mail*, 16 April 1917.

The next brief poem, 'To a Poet on His Epitaph for the Fallen' is a tribute to Lascelles Abercrombie's 'Inscriptions':

> Splendidly dying, yet their fame
> Had fallen to imperious time,
> But for the living lips that came
> To save their splendour in a rhyme.

Abercrombie and Drinkwater remained friends throughout their lives, and indeed it was Abercrombie who gave the memorial address when Drinkwater died so unexpectedly in 1937, only in his mid-fifties.

In his post-war poetry, Drinkwater's poems refer to the sense of betrayal the dead and their families feel. '1914–1918: The Dead Speak' is an interesting example:

> In the earth, in the seas, we remember;
>   We dead, we are awake;
> But bitterness we know not
>   Who died for beauty's sake;
> We have no need of honour,
>   No quarrel we recall,
> The lies, the little angers
>   We have forgiven all.
>
> In the earth, in the seas, we remember;
>   We dead, a myriad name;
> But not among our legions
>   Is any word of blame;
> We gave, and there an ending
>   Of covenants gone by,
> We ask no funeral splendour
>   Who were content to die.
>
> In the earth, in the seas, we remember;
>   We dead, your length of days;
> But still the stealth of darkness
>   Makes one of all delays —
> A year, or ten, or twenty,
>   How little then the cost —
> Fear not, we have forgiven
>   The little years we lost.
>
> In the earth, in the seas, we remember;
>   We dead, your daily debt;
> The old heart-break is over,

> But we remember yet —
> Is earth a sweeter temple
> Because we let you live?
> Or do you still betray us,
> That we may not forgive?

I have suggested that $x = o$ might have represented a turning point in his career, and interestingly, a few months after the reviewers recommended that Drinkwater should go to the Front to see the war for himself, there appeared in the *Birmingham Mail* the following announcement:

Mr John Drinkwater for France

We do not usually associate the entertainments at the Front with the "highbrow" type. Jollity, and popular and sentimental music, are what the average man enduring the hardships of soldiering wants…. But as the army now includes in its ranks a fair representation of all classes of mind, it's only fair that those who like the stimulation of poetry should get it. There is, indeed, a definite demand for this kind of entertainment, and at the request, I understand, of Miss Lena Ashwell, Mr. John Drinkwater is to go to France on 23rd of December for a month. During that time he has undertaken to read for an hour or so to those who wish it passages of English poetry from its beginning to the "Georgians", and no doubt he will not disregard the requests which he is sure to receive to read some of his own verse. He's undertaken a big task, and will need to travel with a very good representative selection of the poets to meet all demands. But he will go out to France with the knowledge that he will get sympathetic audiences, for many letters have been received by him from men out there expressing their appreciation of his work. This is quite a new venture I believe and Mr. Drinkwater's experiences as a pioneer should be interesting.[9]

And that is how John Drinkwater came to be in Buchy in January 1918. I began by saying that poets need friends. This is true both in their lifetimes, for poetry can be a lonely business, and after their deaths. When Drinkwater's last book, *English Poetry: An Unfinished History*, was published shortly after his death, the Irish dramatist St John Ervine, who had been a close friend of the poet, wrote this in the Preface about friendship and about Drinkwater, which sums up Drinkwater the man:

When I made friendship with him he'd already won great renown and fortune with his play *Abraham Lincoln*, and was beginning to experience the blasts of envy which blow about a man who has

---

9   *Birmingham Mail*, 10 December 1917.

committed the crime of success. I came to know him intimately, and I formed a great affection for him which wasn't diminished by the break in our encounters during the last year or two of his life. His detractors said of him that he was pompous, and they lost no opportunity of belittling his work, yet I never heard him say a single bitter word about his most implacable enemy.... . He might complain of a man's criticism but he did not complain of the man himself, nor did he, when angered by those who depreciated his work, attempt to revenge himself by depreciating theirs. He was incapable of anonymous assaults. That he had defects is indisputable, for he was a man and fallible like the rest of us. But meanness was not one of them, nor was spite. He wasn't envious of anyone's good fortune, but was eager to promote it. He leaves in my recollection the memory of a most generous nature and an affectionate and friendly disposition.[10]

I am pleased to have had this opportunity to talk about a neglected Dymock poet to the Friends of the Dymock Poets. I have tried to make the case for re-reading Drinkwater and to suggest that he deserves to be rediscovered for the pleasure he gave to many readers and audiences. To speak personally, he has been part of my experience of literature almost since before I could read. I myself was born in Birmingham, and the first pantomime I ever saw, at the Birmingham Rep, was Drinkwater's *Puss in Boots* (still performed to this day). So in conclusion I will only add that that the padre who looked after John Drinkwater in Buchy, and in whose notebook the poet inscribed one of his best-known poems as a gesture of friendship, was the Rev Edward Barlow, my grandfather.

---

10 John Drinkwater, *English Poetry: an Unfinished History* (London: Sidgwick and Jackson, 1933), Preface, p.x.

2.4 Literature *now*: the place of literature in contemporary British life

This lecture was delivered at the University of Cambridge International Summer School in July 2009. I had been invited to give an overview of the importance (or otherwise) of literature in contemporary Britain, to an audience of international students attending a wide variety of programmes on the Summer School in that year. This was one of a series of lectures in which speakers were invited to assess the current standing of their particular subject or discipline in British public life. By no means all the students attending the lecture were studying literary courses or indeed courses in the arts and humanities. The students in my audience — over two hundred of them — came from all over the world. For many of them this was their first visit to Cambridge; for a good number, especially those from China and Eastern Europe, this was their first visit to the UK.

I wanted the lecture to be as topical as possible, and so illustrated it from news stories and literary publications current at the time I was speaking. I have chosen not to update the text of the lecture: my views about the strengths and weaknesses of the place of literature in public life in Britain today have not changed since this lecture was delivered, even though the illustrations presented to support those views belong to a particular time and place.

'Literature' in the celebrated words of the American poet Ezra Pound, 'is news that stays news' — a good headline grabbing, as well as headline defining — slogan. More prosaically, literature has been defined by Roland Barthes simply as 'what gets studied'. In this lecture I hope to embrace each of these definitions, but also to investigate some aspects of literature both as a cultural phenomenon and as a cultural enrichment. In terms of a cultural phenomenon, I want to explore the impact that books and authors have on public life here in Britain; but in terms of a cultural enrichment, I want to ask whether or not there is a special role for literature in the arts and what sort of contribution it can make to society, to academic life ('what gets studied') and to individuals at this present time. Hence the first part of my title, 'Literature now.'

The second part of my title, 'the place of literature in contemporary British life' also needs unpacking. It may seem strange to say so, but these days any combination of the words 'English', 'British' and 'literature' calls for comment. What is English literature? Is it literature written in English — in which case it can embrace American, Australian, Indian, African and many other literatures — or is it literature produced by British writers alone? Or, more specifically still, is it literature written by those who live (or anyway were born) within the strict borders of England — i.e. not Welsh, not Scots, not northern and certainly not southern Irish. Some years ago, Penguin Books published an anthology of what they called 'New British Poetry' in which the most prominently represented poet was Seamus Heaney. At a time when relations between Britain and Ireland (both north and south) were particularly strained Heaney found himself embarrassed at being labelled a British poet (in spite of the fact that his publisher, Faber and Faber, is one of the most respected of English, London-based publishers). In a famous statement which now gets quoted whenever the Nobel prize-winning poet's nationality is mentioned, Heaney declared, 'Be advised, my passport's green / No glass of ours was ever raised / To toast the Queen'.

The situation is not any more straightforward if one speaks of writers born in Scotland. At one time, if you simply referred to 'the Bard' the chances are people knew at once you were speaking of Shakespeare — indeed, the word 'bardolatry' was coined by the playwright George Bernard Shaw to describe the excessive adulation of Shakespeare as a playwright whose every word was perfect. But go north of the border and you'll find a quite different poet is known to all Scotsmen and women as 'the Bard': from Edinburgh to Elgin and from Arbroath to Aberdeen the Bard can only refer to their national poet Robert Burns. Indeed, a best selling new biography of Burns, published only this year, is simply entitled, *The Bard*.[1]

If you go into Wales, the word 'Bard' has another and equally powerful significance. Here it does not refer to a single pre-eminent writer from a distant past: it refers to the winner of the national poetry competition held each year at a national festival of poetry and music called by many Welsh enthusiasts simply 'the National' but officially the Eisteddfod Genedlaethol Cymru, the National Eisteddfod (assembly) of Wales. This is a spectacular annual celebration of Welsh language and culture, where everything is conducted in the medium of Welsh and where the two winning poets, chosen as a result of an anonymous poetry competition, are crowned or chaired in ceremonies which bizarrely combine elements of pagan druidism, freemasonry and non-conformist Christianity. Actually, I think there is something wholly admirable about a country which

---

1   Robert Crawford, *The Bard* (Princeton NJ: Princeton University Press, 2009).

can put such a high value on literature and on poets; but it has nothing at all to do with English literature. Indeed, there is a quite separate literary tradition in Wales of what is known, rather awkwardly, as Anglo-Welsh poetry.

You will have gathered already from what I have just described that it is impossible, even today, to keep the idea of literature separate at some level from the idea of national identity. This is one reason, even if unacknowledged by many people much of the time, why literature does always occupy an important place in the life of any country. It may also be why, when literature ceases to be highly valued by it, society may appear to lack confidence, or cohesion, or even a sense of its own identity. Is it a coincidence, for example, that two of the most recent winners of the Booker Prize have been Indian writers more concerned with American-Indian cross-cultural themes than with British experience? Or that the 2008 Orange Prize for Fiction was won by a British writer, Rose Tremain with a marvellous novel[2] about an Eastern European migrant worker trying unsuccessfully to make sense of his life as an outsider in London? The image of British life in the twenty-first century painted in this novel is neither flattering nor reassuring. It is certainly not an image of a society at ease with itself.

Suppose, to start with, we measure literature, very crudely, in terms of books published and sold, then literature is a very large industry which makes a significant contribution to the British economy: 1.3bn books of all kinds are sold each year, to a total value of £3.3 billion. 45% of all sales are for export.[3] I'm no economist, but these are big figures. It's worth remembering, though, that much of British publishing is now controlled by big-name multinational companies: Random House, for instance, Time Warner or News Corporation.

Are there other ways in which we can measure the standing or the impact of literature in contemporary British life? Suppose we put the spotlight on writers themselves rather than on the books they write. J.K. Rowling, author of the Harry Potter novels, was declared to be a dollar billionaire as long ago as 2004,[4] and current estimates (guesses, presumably) suggest that she may earn £3 million every day — £5 per second. How about public esteem or official recognition? A knighthood is the highest and most visible honour that most British or Commonwealth authors receive, and such awards can generate a great deal of publicity or controversy — as when in 2007 Salman Rushdie became Sir Salman.

---

2   Rose Tremain, *The Road Home* (London: Chatto and Windus, 2007).

3   Source: http://www.lboro.ac.uk/departments/ls/lisu/lampost08/stock08. html#publstock. (accessed 13 July 2009).

4   Source: http://www.forbes.com/2004/02/26/cx_jw_0226rowlingbill04.html (accessed 13 July 2009).

Actually, it is often more revealing to discover who has *declined* a knighthood than who has accepted the honour: among living authors, Alan Bennett and Michael Frayn have turned down the offer of a knighthood and they join a distinguished list of literary refusers, including Joseph Conrad, E.M. Forster, Rudyard Kipling and W.B. Yeats. But there is a higher honour than a knighthood, the Order of Merit, an award which is the personal gift of the Queen and which is limited to 24 people at any one time. Among previous literary holders of this (very discreet) honour are Thomas Hardy, Henry James, E.M. Forster and T.S. Eliot but the only writer among the current 24 OMs is Tom Stoppard, the playwright.

I must immediately qualify that statement. You'll have spotted that the names I have just been citing are all distinctly 'literary' — novelists, poets, playwrights. In other words I have narrowed down dramatically the definition of literature which I was using just now when talking about sales of books. There I was using literature to mean 'anything published in book format'. Now I am limiting my definition of 'writers' to those who work within a clearly 'literary' field.

Let me return to the list of current holders of the Order of Merit and see if the definition could, or should, be widened. Certainly it *could*: the most senior member of the Order (apart from Prince Philip) is Professor Owen Chadwick, the theological historian, former Master of Selwyn College and quondam Vice-Chancellor of this University. He is not the only historian on the list for Sir Michael Howard, a distinguished military historian, is also an OM. Should I be including historians among my categories of 'literary' writers? Is history a literary subject? In many ways, the answer should clearly be 'yes' and historians from Bede onwards have made defining contributions to literature and to the literary heritage of this country. I should say that this contribution continues and that it deserves fuller recognition. Indeed it is a remarkable, and welcome, fact that this week the number one best-seller in the hardback non-fiction category is Anthony Beevor's book *D-Day: The Battle for Normandy*.[5] This book has outsold all but one of the top ten hardback works of fiction in the past week. Beevor is a distinguished historian whose books on twentieth century war have always been praised for the quality of their writing as well as for their history, and he joins a distinguished list of authors — among whom are Thomas Carlyle and Lord Macaulay — who have been celebrated in their time both as writers and as historians.

Even 'historians' may be too narrow a category. This year sees the 200 anniversary of the death of Thomas Paine, one of the most significant of all British writers in terms of the impact his books such as *Common Sense*, *Rights of Man* and *The Age of Reason*, had on individual readers worldwide

---

5   *Guardian Review*, 11 July 2009, p.21.

and on political events — notably the American War of Independence and the French Revolution. Paine defined his own field as 'political literature' and his work is today as much in need of literary as well as political and historical revaluation. I doubt whether there is an English Faculty in any British University where Paine is studied and yet his books are key texts in the development of English literary, as well as English political, writing.

Categories therefore are dangerous, but for the rest of this lecture I shall adopt a definition that limits literature not only to the written word but also to writing which would wish to be placed within a literary tradition, though not necessarily only in a literary tradition. One way of identifying such writing is to look at literary journals and magazines, publications that proclaim themselves to be concerned with literature. Some, of course, limit themselves to particular categories of writing, *The Poetry Review*, for instance; others declare a broader interest: The *London Review of Books* or *The Literary Review*. I'd like to look particularly at two such journals, both of which are closely and explicitly linked with newspaper journalism and are published weekly, but which clearly signal that they are concerned with 'Literature' (capital L). These are *The Times Literary Supplement*, always abbreviated to the *TLS*, and the *Guardian's* weekly *Review*, published every Saturday.

The *TLS* is an avowedly scholarly but not purely academic journal. Its range is wide: it covers science and philosophy, film and fashion, occasionally even sport. Its Classics editor is Mary Beard, professor of Classics here in Cambridge and one of the best known media dons in Britain. As well as editing the Classics pages of the *TLS*, she writes a regular blog for the *TLS* which is apparently one of the most widely read literary blogs in the world. Her recent book on Pompeii[6] has just won the 2009 Wolfson Prize, a prize awarded annually to the two best history books written in a style that is scholarly but accessible to the general reader.

'Scholarly but accessible to the general reader' actually describes the style of the *TLS* rather well. Its reviewers these days are usually, though by no means always, academics but their readers are not assumed to be only fellow academics: perhaps the 'interested and knowledgeable layman' would best sum up the intended readership. This week's edition, for example, carries as its leading feature a review of a new translation of Chaucer's *Canterbury Tales* by Colin Wilcockson, emeritus fellow of Pembroke College, Cambridge. The review is by Dr Carolyne Larrington, Fellow in English at St John's College, Oxford. So far, so academic; but the review combines a summary of recent Chaucerian scholarship, a not un-critical but still enthusiastic review of Wilcockson's translation with an equally enthusiastic review of a new 're-telling' of Chaucer's Tales by the novelist and biographer Peter Ackroyd. This

6   Mary Beard, *Pompeii: the Life of a Roman Town* (London: Profile Books, 2008).

is very definitely a non-academic book but it is discussed fully and respectfully by Carolyne Larrington, who even manages to discuss these books in the context of recent productions of Chaucer by the Royal Shakespeare Company and a performance on YouTube of the *Rap Canterbury Tales* by the Canadian rapper Baba Brinkman.

Larrington's review, about 5000 words in length, is an example of contemporary literary discussion at its best: it is serious but not stuffy, open-minded without being populist. Here, to give a flavour of the review, is her concluding paragraph:

> Whether in Wilcockson's clear translation, Ackroyd's imaginative retelling, or in the numerous popular versions of Chaucerian Tales, Chaucer's plots continue to fascinate and to attract new audiences. On the Internet, even troubling Tales, like that of the Physician, which tells how the Roman Virginius executes his daughter to save her honour from a lecherous city governor, find fresh interpretation. These four-minute retellings are often dramatically updated ("Hey, you freakin' out?", the Clerk asks Walter, who staunchly insists on his right to choose his own wife) but there are also lively demonstrations of the affinities in rhythm, rhyme and alliteration between hip hop and Chaucer's English. He may not be as central to English culture as Shakespeare, but Chaucer's language, characters and stories are both holding their own in high culture and inspiring new kinds of creative responses in more popular media.[7]

This review by Larrington seems to me exemplary: it is 'scholarly but accessible' and makes serious efforts to build bridges between academic and non-academic approaches to Chaucer, and it is not only in the narrowly defined field of English Studies that we find such a concern. Alongside Larrington's Chaucer review sits a review of a new book of popular history, *Summer of Blood: the Peasants' Revolt of 1381*. The reviewer welcomes the appearance of a new book, aimed at the general reader, covering a nowadays neglected period of English history. He is scathing, however, about the poor quality of research and the poorer quality of writing exhibited by Dan Jones, the author of this book:

> In resorting to this dreadful prose, Jones is doing his readers a disservice. It is not just that he is debasing his story, oversimplifying it by eliminating any shades of grey from a narrative coloured entirely in black and white; worse still, he is insulting his readers by supposing that they cannot cope with anything more subtle or sophisticated.[8]

---

7   Carolyne Larrington, 'Talkin' Cock', *TLS* 10 July 2009, pp.7–9.

8   Nigel Saul, 'Souped Up', *TLS* 10 July 2009, p.9.

The reviewer is equally dismayed that the publishers should think there is a market for a book of such low quality, and if they are right, he argues, then:

> There is something terribly wrong with history publishing in Britain today. The production of superficial pulp of this ilk runs the risk of displacing substantial, well-written studies which do not treat their readers as idiots. Jones is absolutely right to maintain that there is a demand for lively, enjoyable books about our pre-1485 past. The fact that apparently not enough of such books are available is largely due to the reluctance of academics, absorbed in turning out indigestible prose read only by their fellows, to engage with the needs of the wider public.[9]

'Academic history' concludes the reviewer, 'is in danger of cutting itself off through the sheer folly of its self-absorption.'

The author of this swingeing attack is himself a distinguished academic: Nigel Saul, Professor of Medieval History at Royal Holloway, University of London. I shall return later to what he has defined here as 'the reluctance of academics to engage with the needs of the wider public' because it is crucial to my analysis of the place, and the perception, of literature in present-day British society. But I must pause to remark that this review was of a book dealing with the Peasants' Revolt of 1381, a key event in the life of Geoffrey Chaucer. The books being reviewed in this edition of the *TLS* — Wilcockson's translation of the *Canterbury Tales*, Peter Ackroyd's re-telling of the Chaucer stories, and even the book so savaged by Saul, have all been published by publishers who have made their commercial calculations and believe there is an appetite for writing from, and about, the fourteenth century. This is heartening in one sense, and I believe strongly that a sense of 'the pastness of the past, as well as of its presence' (to borrow T.S. Eliot's famous phrase[10]) is as vital for a literary intelligence as for an historical one. On the other hand, it is a sad fact that when Cambridge University Press tried to launch a Schools' Chaucer series to match its highly successful Schools' Shakespeare, the project had to be abandoned because of poor sales and lack of interest. Too few teachers, apparently, want to teach Chaucer these days, or they fear he will be too demanding for their students. I suspect, too, that too few teachers have themselves studied Chaucer either at school or even at university, to feel any desire or need to teach him when other texts and other authors may seem more appealing and more accessible. However, if the books by Wilcockson and Ackroyd can do anything to reverse this trend, that can only be good for literature in Britain tomorrow, if not today.

---

9   *ibid.*
10 T.S. Eliot, 'Tradition and the Individual Talent' (1922), in *Selected Essays*, (London: Faber and Faber, 1999) p.14.

It is when stimulating debate of this kind, and when defending the need for scholarship not to lose sight of its commitment to the wider public, that the *TLS* is at its strongest and makes its best contribution to British literary culture today. It has a circulation of about 35,000 and perhaps a worldwide readership of about 100,000;[11] however, it is heavily underwritten by Rupert Murdoch's company, News Corporation, which produces it. From time to time there are dire warnings in the press that Murdoch might soon turn off the tap of subsidy, forcing it to become literally a supplement to *The Times*, a pull-out section printed on Saturdays, in which case it would lose, I suspect, some of its academic seriousness and would have to go head-to-head with the other literary journal I want to mention, *The Guardian Review*, published as a supplement to the *Guardian* newspaper every Saturday.

This *Review* manages very successfully to combine interesting and challenging reviews with a much less 'academic' tenor to the writing — though a number of writers who can be found in the *TLS* also appear regularly in T*he Guardian Review* — Mary Beard not least among them. It does not usually cover such a wide range of books as the *TLS*, nor in such depth, but it is proof that good discussion of literature is still to be found in the national newspapers, and its style combines a measure of high seriousness with a more frankly populist touch than the *TLS*. In Saturday's issue, for example, the leading article was by the playwright David Edgar on 'The inner workings of plays'. In an extended piece exploring how apparently very different dramas can share the same architecture, Edgar begins by producing six brief plot summaries including this one:

> With her father's encouragement, a young woman allows herself to be wooed and wed by a prince. Her brother moves a long way away. The prince behaves peculiarly, and, shortly after the death of the woman's father, leaves on board ship. The woman goes mad, alarms the royal family, gives everybody flowers, escapes from her minders, and dies in a suspicious accident. The brother returns, angry, at the head of a popular army. There is a contest over the funeral arrangements between family, church and state. The prince returns and he and the brother end up fighting over the coffin.[12]

No prizes for spotting that this summary is about both *Hamlet* and the death of Princess Diana, but the whole point of the article is to explore what Shakespeare, and Brecht, Marlowe and Pinter — yes, and the soap operas on television today — have in common as drama. It is a fascinating and

---

11 Source: http://entertainment.timesonline.co.uk/tol/arts_and_entertainment/ the_tls/article2446901.ece (accessed 13 July 2009).

12 David Edgar 'Making a Drama', Guardian Review 11 July 2009, p.2.

thought-provoking piece, but written very definitely from the point of view of a practising playwright, not (as it would probably have been in the *TLS*) of an academic specialising in the history of the theatre.

Indeed, the *Guardian Review* places a higher value on writers themselves than the *TLS* does, perhaps because it knows that its weekend readership is more eager to glimpse behind the scenes, to listen to writers talking about themselves rather than about their work. There is a very popular weekly feature, Writers' Rooms, in which, alongside a carefully posed photograph of a room with a desk (or occasionally just a bed) a writer talks about the room in which he or she writes novels, or poems or plays — just so long as they are not writing short pieces for the *Guardian Review*, presumably.[13]

I don't want to make the *Guardian Review* sound frivolous, however; simply to point to the broader readership at which it is aiming. Maybe though I should define it as the slightly younger members of the *TLS* readership relaxing a little at the weekend but still wanting to be informed and provoked about books and writers. A good example of this is a weekly column by John Mullan, professor of English at University College London. Every month he selects a recent novel, discusses aspects of the novel for the first two weeks, then in week three gets the writer himself or herself to talk about the book, and finally in week four reports on a meeting between the novelist and Guardian readers who have attended a discussion in London, chaired by Mullan himself. It's a kind of newspaper book club and indeed when these articles first appeared they were described, somewhat condescendingly I thought, as 'a service to book clubs'.

It was nevertheless a shrewd marketing ploy to adopt this type of approach because book clubs have become one of the most striking phenomena of the British literary scene in the past decade. In fact, the Government is now, rather pathetically, offering financial support for this kind of 'informal' or 'lifestyle' learning as a way of disguising the damage it has done to extramural higher education. Here is clear evidence of damage being done to the literary health of the nation. Some estimates claim that over a million part-time adult students have been lost to the system in the past five years — and a high proportion of these were taking courses in literature.

I began this lecture by quoting Ezra Pound's dictum that literature is news that stays news. Sometimes, of course, literature and the literary world can itself make news. Cambridge is not immune from this and only this month was able to harvest a lot of news coverage when it announced a £1.25 million appeal to purchase an archive of papers and diaries belonging to the First World War poet Siegfried Sassoon. On the whole this coverage has so far been mostly benign,

---

13 This feature was subsequently replaced by *Artists' Rooms*, and then dropped in favour of *My Hero*.

though one or two voices in the wilderness have dared to question whether the money could not be better spent elsewhere. At any rate Cambridge has fared a good deal better than Oxford when a media frenzy broke out over the election of a new Professor of Poetry a couple of months ago.

I want to dwell briefly on this episode, not out of any sense of *schadenfreude* at the discomfiture of 'the other place' but because it exemplifies some of the problems facing literature in Britain today. The Oxford Professor of Poetry is one of the two most highly esteemed posts available to poets in this country. The other is of course the post of Poet Laureate, and earlier this year a new Poet Laureate, Carol Ann Duffy, was appointed to succeed Andrew Motion, who had resigned after ten years in the post. The Poet Laureate has few responsibilities and only a small income: approximately £300 and a butt of canary wine. His job (it has always been held by a man, up until this year) is traditionally held to involve writing poems for state occasions — royal weddings and the like — but Andrew Motion to his credit saw the job as to act as an ambassador for poetry, making it accessible and raising its profile. He launched National Poetry Day and was instrumental in the establishment of the Poetry Archive, the world's largest online collection of poets reading their own verse. The earliest item is Tennyson reading 'The Charge of the Light Brigade'. The choice of Carol Ann Duffy as Motion's successor gave the Press a field-day: not only the first woman Poet Laureate, but the first lesbian Poet Laureate. Some newspapers seemed hardly to know whether to let excitement or outrage colour their reaction.

By contrast, the Oxford Professorship of Poetry looked like being a rather staid affair, not likely to cause much excitement. Unlike the appointment of the Poet Laureate, who is chosen by the Prime Minister and the Queen, taking advice from civil servants and anyone else they choose to consult, the Professor of Poetry is elected by as many Oxford graduates with the degree of Master of Arts as care to turn up in Oxford and vote. No postal votes are allowed. It is a five-year post, and carries with it the obligation to give three lectures a year. Previous holders have usually been poets, but occasionally they have also been academics; indeed the last holder of the professorship was Professor Christopher Ricks.

At the start of this year, Dr Sally Mapstone, Head of the English Faculty at Oxford, said she hoped that graduates would want to elect a professor 'who sees poetry as culturally central to modern society as well as one who values its traditions and history'. It is a worthy aim, and normally an election such as this gives poetry a few days of media coverage and culminates in the election of a new Professor who (everyone agrees) will be 'good for poetry'. Whether their lectures prove to be interesting or memorable is less likely to be recorded by the press. This year there were two main contenders, the Nobel prize-winning Caribbean poet, Derek Walcott, and the British poet and author of books about poetry, Ruth Padel.

At first the election proceeded quietly enough, though the appointment of a woman Poet Laureate turned the spotlight on Ruth Padel, who numbered Carol Ann Duffy among her supporters; but then (shock-horror) Derek Walcott suddenly withdrew from the contest. It was revealed that a number of Oxford academics had received anonymous letters through the post reminding them that Walcott had been accused of sexual harassment by a student back in the early 1980s. Announcing his resignation from the contest, Walcott said,

> I withdraw from the election to be Professor of Poetry at Oxford. I am disappointed that such low tactics have been used in this election and I do not want to get into a race for a post where it causes embarrassment to those who have chosen to support me for the role or to myself.... I already have a great many work commitments and while I was happy to be put forward for the post, if it has degenerated into a low and degrading attempt at character assassination, I do not want to be part of it.[14]

Ruth Padel was thus left as the front-runner in the contest, and was duly elected on 16 May, giving the media plenty of opportunity to herald a new era for poetry when two such articulate women as Duffy and Padel were installed at the top of the profession. No doubt everyone in Oxford hoped that Padel's election would quickly lay to rest the embarrassing story of the Nobel Prize winner being forced out of the contest by a dirty tricks campaign. But then, only nine days after her election, the new Oxford Professor of Poetry herself resigned, admitting that she too had circulated a couple of emails mentioning the past allegations against Walcott. Speaking at the Hay Festival (one of the leading literary festivals — and these flourishing festivals, I should say in passing, are one of the more positive signs of the health of literature in Britain today) Padel made the following statement:

> I passed on in good faith the concerns of students. They felt the concerns had been brushed under the carpet by Walcott's supporters. The details were not news — they were in the public domain and as such were subject of concern to the students.[15]

She went on to admit that this was, in her own words, 'naïve and silly of me — a bad error of judgement' but she denied that she had had anything to do with the smear campaign that had been conducted anonymously against Derek Walcott. And as far as I know, no one has discovered who was behind that campaign. The upshot of this was that Oxford still does not have a Professor of Poetry and the Press had a good deal of fun at the expense

14 'Smears drive Walcott from Guardian poetry professor race', *Guardian* 12 May 2009.

15 'Padel admits "silly" error in Oxford Poetry election' *Guardian* 26 May 2009.

of poets. *The Daily Telegraph* for example led with a story headed 'Poetry's always been a rotten business' and listed all the poets it could think of whose morals and beliefs — sexual, political or racial — would have made them ineligible for the Professorship in today's climate of prurient Puritanism: Dylan Thomas, T.S. Eliot, Philip Larkin, W.B. Yeats, Ezra Pound, W.H. Auden (who was in fact Oxford Professor of Poetry in the late 1950s) — all were ritually denounced, as were Coleridge and Byron, thrown in for good measure. The article concluded:

> So no, poets are not always terribly salubrious. If the University wants someone who not only knows their ways around a rhyming couplet but is also morally spotless, it'll probably find that the sole candidate is Rupert the Bear.[16]

This whole saga demonstrates to my mind just how vulnerable literature is in the media and in British life today. It is so much easier and more amusing to focus on personalities and on scandal than on literature — whether to be enjoyed for itself or as a subject of intellectual importance to be taken seriously and studied professionally. Ruth Padel is a good poet: her latest book, *Darwin, a Life in Poetry*, is both timely (in this Darwin anniversary year)[17] and impressive in its own right. Her books about poetry are 'scholarly and accessible', to revisit the phrase I quoted earlier from the Wolfson prize for History. I hope her reputation will quickly recover, just as I hope that Walcott's is too secure to have been much damaged by the Oxford debacle. It is poetry and literature that have suffered, particularly on this occasion literature in an academic context.

I want to conclude by saying something about literature in this academic context, because English literature, and Literary Studies generally, are among the four or five most popular subjects studied in British universities today: only subjects with a more or less vocational slant come ahead of it: Medicine, Law, Management Studies, for example. This means that English Faculties and departments send a very high number of graduates out into the world, at no small cost to the taxpayer. What do these students contribute to society that is special because their special subject has been literature?

A great deal is made these days of 'transferable skills' and yes English graduates should certainly be articulate, thoughtful, analytical, incisive and insightful — all these things — but so should History graduates and psychologists and scientists. A great deal is made, too, of 'knowledge transfer': defined as organising, creating, capturing or distributing knowledge to ensure its availability for future users. I think that English faculties are generally very good at this, up to a point. I think this knowledge transfer as it applies to the study of literature works well within the academy (that is, within Higher

---

16 Michael Deacon, 'Poetry's always been a rotten business', *Daily Telegraph* 27 May 09.
17 Charles Darwin 1809–1882.

Education): scholarship is at a very high level, research is genuinely opening up the subject in ways that were unthought of fifty years ago when F.R. Leavis cast a long shadow across Cambridge and across the whole of English literary criticism. What I am less confident in saying is that enough thought and attention are given to putting literature to work productively for the benefit of society and for individuals.

I should like to see this work in a number of ways. First, I think it is essential that more students should be encouraged to become teachers of English in secondary schools. This may seem a dull thing to ask for but it is a matter of historical record that Cambridge in the Nineteen-Forties, Fifties and Sixties produced three generations of teachers who had an almost missionary sense of the value of literature and of the value of the subject to society. I was myself lucky enough to be taught by teachers who had this sense of mission, but these teachers have now retired and are not being replaced. It is a sobering fact that only one in five teachers teaching English at A level in Britain today possesses an English degree or any qualification in the subject at all.[18]

Secondly, and more broadly, I should like to see English faculties doing more to promote the value of reading in and to the community. There is an excellent scheme run by the English Faculty at Liverpool University, which has set up a charity called The Reader Organisation, designed to promote the value and the pleasure of reading in the community, in schools, hospitals and elsewhere. Here is its own description of its aims and purpose:

> We find people who are not readers or who have lost their connection with literature, people who are isolated, lonely, or who could otherwise benefit from reading books, and bring them together for the simple pleasure of reading aloud and discussing the thoughts and feelings that are evoked. Over time, people build up a confidence that enables them to tell their own stories, as well as to forge close relationships with fellow readers.[19]

The organisation publishes its own journal, *The Reader*, and encourages undergraduate students to take part in its outreach activities. What's more it is encouraging graduate students to undertake research into the benefits — social, cultural, personal and mental — that reading can produce. The poet and biographer Blake Morrison has said of the scheme that

> In the presence of books, it's as if a hand has reached out and taken our own. That's the hand The Reader Organisation is trying to extend.[20]

---

18 Government data cited by William Stewart 'No degree? No problem' *Times Educational Supplement*, 16 February 2007, p.18.

19 The Reader Organisation: http://thereader.org.uk/about-us/what-we-do/ (accessed 30.08.2011).

20 Blake Morrison, The Reading Cure', *Guardian* 5 January 2008.

This image of the hand reaching out and taking our own, is not Morrison's own. In the article he acknowledges that it comes from a character in Alan Bennett's play *The History Boys*. The whole passage is worth hearing:

> Books don't always save lives: writing about the Holocaust didn't prevent Primo Levi from ultimately committing suicide; and the reading — or perverse misreading — of *The Satanic Verses* led to the deaths of innocent people. But literature's power to heal and console outweighs its power to do damage. Hector, in Alan Bennett's *The History Boys*, puts it beautifully when he describes how, in the presence of great literature, it's as if a hand has reached out and taken our own.[21]

I would want to argue that literature has a further role to play in a healthy society, and here I think it is important to pay attention to what writers themselves, and not only critics and scholars, have to say about the value of their special field. Here, for example, is Susan Sontag:

> Serious fiction writers think about moral problems practically. They tell stories. They narrate. They evoke our common humanity in narratives with which we can identify, even though their lives may be remote from our own. They stimulate our imagination. The stories they tell enlarge and complicate — and, therefore, improve — our sympathies. They educate our capacity for moral judgement.[22]

Sontag was not herself an academic in the strict sense, but she was in the fullest sense of the word an 'intellectual' — a term with which we in Britain, certainly in England, are traditionally thought to have some difficulty. Back in 2002, a year after he retired as Merton Professor of English at Oxford, John Carey published a controversial polemic, *The Intellectuals and the Masses: Pride and Prejudice among the Literary Intelligentsia*. In this book Carey argued vigorously against the elitist and inwardly-facing approach to literary scholarship that he had encountered in his career. Three years later, he published a second polemic, *What Good are the Arts?*, in which he sets out his view of the value of literature and literary study. Since Carey's views closely echo my own, and since he speaks with an authority and from a position I cannot claim for myself, I shall end with his own claims for literature:

> Let me be clear what I am claiming. I am not suggesting that literature makes you more moral. It may do, but such evidence as I have come across suggests that it would be unwise to depend on this. Envy and ill-will are, I should say, at least as common in the literature departments of universities as outside. Faculty members

---

21 *ibid*.
22 Susan Sontag, *At the Same Time* (London: Hamish Hamilton 2007) p.213.

seem especially prone to 'a sense of injured merit', which is another characteristic of Milton's Satan... . My claim is different. It is that literature gives you ideas to think with. It stocks your mind. It does not indoctrinate, because diversity, counter-argument, reappraisal and qualification are its essence. But it supplies the material for thought. Also, because it is the only art capable of criticism, it encourages questioning, and self-questioning.[23]

If literature can really do these things, and if faculties of English can produce students capable of practising these virtues and sharing them when they leave university, then I think the place of literature in contemporary British life (or, not to be insular) in life generally, should be right at the centre.

I'm aware that this is a rather tentative, conditional, note on which to end. I actually believe that the first decade of the twenty-first century has been a very good decade for English literature: I think that novels by Ian McEwan and Rose Tremain, plays by Alan Bennett and David Hare, poetry by Carol Ann Duffy, Wendy Cope and Jo Shapcott all have a good chance of being still read and admired in the last decade of the century. What I'm less sure about is whether, in the era of iPod culture, we can still be confident that literature really is news that stays news.

---

23 John Carey, *What Good are the Arts?* (London: Faber and Faber 2005), p.208.

2.5 Alan Bennett and The Habit of Art

I have always believed that teachers of literature should be prepared to teach very new, as well as very canonical, texts. Indeed, teaching students of any age how to read new texts seems to me important: new books deserve an informed critical welcome. One of the purposes of teaching literature in adult education is precisely this: to deepen students' enjoyment of reading by teaching them how to read critically.

In November 2009, the National Theatre (NT) in London launched a new play by Alan Bennett, The Habit of Art, *which centres on an imagined reunion, late in their lives, between the poet W.H. Auden and the composer Benjamin Britten. The play was very well received and early in 2010 the NT announced that it would beam a live performance from the Lyttleton Theatre to screens and theatres around the world. Among the venues in Britain were to be Bury St Edmunds in Suffolk, Guernsey in the Channel Islands and Cambridge.*

At this time the States of Guernsey and the Institute of Continuing Education (ICE) at Cambridge had just established an agreement that ICE should provide occasional Higher Education courses at St Peter Port, and I was invited to give an inaugural lecture to launch this scheme. It was agreed that a lecture to introduce Bennett's new play in advance of the screening would be popular, especially since the background to the play would not be familiar to most of the audience.

Having agreed to give this lecture, I decided also to offer it both in Cambridge and in nearby Bury St. Edmunds. The lecture was to be free, both as a gesture of public engagement between the University and the regional community and as a means of reaching new audiences to promote the programmes offered by the Institute.

I much enjoyed preparing this lecture, especially since in the previous term I had been teaching a Diploma course on W.H. Auden's later poetry and had also previously given a lecture on 'Auden, Britten and St. Cecilia'. However, just as I was about embark on the mini lecture tour, an eruption of Icelandic volcanic ash brought all air traffic across Europe to a standstill. I was trapped in Italy where I had been on holiday, so I could not give the lecture in Bury St. Edmunds; all flights to Guernsey were cancelled anyway and I only just managed to return (overland) from Italy to Cambridge in time to give the final lecture, at Madingley Hall itself.

The Habit of Art at the National Theatre is set in the National Theatre itself. It is a comedy about actors rehearsing a play that seems to have something to do with Shakespeare's *Tempest*, (it's called *Caliban's Day*) but turns out to be about many other things and several other people instead. And when on 22 April the National Theatre beams an actual performance of Alan Bennett's play to screens in over 200 cinemas and theatres across Europe and beyond, it's likely that *The Habit of Art* will enter the record books for winning the largest audience ever to watch, simultaneously, a live stage play performance.

Ironically, the play nearly didn't happen. It was due to be launched in October 2008, but earlier that year Alan Bennett was taken ill and the production was postponed. When he recovered, Bennett decided to rewrite the play almost entirely, but in the process nearly fell out with his Director, Nicholas Hytner. However, in 2009 it finally went into rehearsal with Michael Gambon and Alex Jennings in the lead roles as W.H. Auden and Benjamin Britten. Publicity photos had been taken and posters were ready to go up, when Gambon withdrew and his role was taken over at very short notice by Richard Griffiths, who had played the lead as Hector in Bennett's previous play, *The History Boys*.

At first glance *The Habit of Art* seems an unlikely choice for world-wide transmission: a play about old men behaving badly; it starts with an elderly gay poet lamenting his loss of inspiration, arguing with his would-be biographer about his career, and waiting impatiently for a rent boy who fails to understand what he really wants; this poet then receives an unexpected visit from an old friend, a composer he has not seen for thirty years but who has come for reassurance about his latest opera project. They talk, and very soon nearly fall out while arguing about their sexual and emotional hang-ups. The rent boy returns just as the composer is leaving, and after a discussion about the value of art and what the rent boy really wants out of life and whether he is likely to get it, the play ends inconclusively with the actors finishing their rehearsal and going their separate ways.

It hardly sounds like a gripping evening's theatre, and yet Alan Bennett's play has been the great success of the season, with the National Theatre packed for every performance. The audience laugh, and occasionally roar with laughter, at an intelligent play which is by turns challenging, uncomfortable, crude, civilised, witty and sad.

So why this play of all plays? Why this playwright of all playwrights? What does such a choice tell us about the state of theatre in Britain today? I have called this lecture 'An introduction to Alan Bennett's play', but if it is to deliver what it says on the tin, I must also ask these questions — indeed, I need to start with them.

The ten years between 1929 and the outbreak of the Second World War may have been, as W.H. Auden defined it, 'a low dishonest decade' but it produced a remarkable generation of British playwrights. John Osborne was born in 1929, Harold Pinter the following year; Arnold Wesker was born in 1932, Alan Bennett in 1934, Tom Stoppard in 1937 and Alan Ayckbourn in 1939.

Osborne and Pinter are both dead but of the others remaining, only Alan Bennett is still regularly producing new work that provokes serious critical discussion, while filling theatres every night. In Box Office terms his last two plays have been his most successful, making a significant contribution to keeping British subsidised theatre afloat. Nicholas Hytner, not just Bennett's chosen Director but Director of the National Theatre, has admitted that the National 'was better off by about £5 million by the time *The History Boys* finally closed'.[1]

It's worth remembering what a long and varied career Bennett has had. With Jonathan Miller, Peter Cook and Dudley Moore, he made his first appearance at the Edinburgh Festival in 1960. Before that time he had been teaching history quietly at Oxford, but once *Beyond the Fringe* had moved from Edinburgh to London and then to New York, it was clear his future would not lie as an academic. Characteristically, he now claims he was not much good as either a student or a teacher anyway:

> I must have been a dull pupil to teach, tutorials tentative and awkward affairs, punctuated by long silences — exactly the kind of tutorials I was later to give myself.[2]

I find this a revealing statement, for two reasons. First, its piling up of phrases to enlarge the main sentence idea — that he was a dull pupil — is a very characteristic Bennett device. He takes a literally dull statement ('I must have been a dull pupil to teach') and then dramatises it by sketching, in fewer than ten words, a scene that illustrates precisely *why* he must have been a dull pupil to teach. And notice, secondly, how he undersells himself: the tutorials may have been 'tentative and awkward affairs' but those two adjectives are epithets that perfectly fit the persona he has so successfully created. Don't forget, in one of his first TV roles he played the Dormouse to Peter Cook's Mad Hatter in Jonathan Miller's 1966 adaptation of *Alice in Wonderland*.

It's tempting to say that Bennett has had a lucky career, and as I have suggested he himself is expert at the role of backing shyly into the limelight. But luck is the least ingredient of his reputation, and a key question he asks in *The Habit of Art* is what drives a writer to go on writing. As the elderly poet W.H. Auden, the central character in the play, cries out in frustration:

1   Nicholas Hytner, 'A Director's Notes', *Areté*, Issue 30, Winter 2009, p.55.
2   Alan Bennett, *The Habit of Art*, (London: Faber 2009), Introduction, p.vi.

I am no longer employable. I am venerated, monumental, shackled by
my reputation. And I need to work or who am I?[3]

The Habit of Art is certainly about the poet W.H. Auden. It is also about the
composer Benjamin Britten. It is about their friendship in the past, during the
1930s and at the start of the Second World War; but the central action of the
play revolves around an imagined reunion between them at Oxford in 1972,
the last year of Auden's life. Then, as I said at the start, it's about many other
things and people as well. For instance, it's about the biographer, Humphrey
Carpenter, who wrote biographies of both Auden and Britten: he features as a
character in the play that is being rehearsed throughout the *Habit of Art* and
his presence gives the cast and through them, Auden and Britten, the chance to
discuss whether or not biography and art are compatible. You may remember
that Auden himself was famously averse to biography or to anything that might
expose the writer's life to public view. As he says at one point in the play:

AUDEN   Why poets should be interviewed I can't think. A writer is not
               a man of action. His private life is or should be of no concern
               to anyone except himself, his family and his friends. The rest is
               impertinence.[4]

So Bennett's play, set in a rehearsal room of the National Theatre itself, is
about a group of (fictional) National Theatre actors, trying to rehearse this
new play which has the title *Caliban's Day*. We know it is a new play, because
the author is also there, and he is not happy with the way the Director is
making changes to the script and cutting the text as the rehearsals develop.

Is this author, as portrayed in *The Habit of Art*, really Alan Bennett himself?
Hardly at all, for he is a younger, and much more evidently abrasive character
called Neil who puts the actors off simply by being there and by complaining
about the way his play is being cut: he feels its whole point is in danger of
being lost. But he can't have this out with the Director, because the Director
is absent from the rehearsal, having gone to give a lecture in Leeds on the
relevance of theatre in the provinces. Leeds, famously, is where Alan Bennett
comes from, and so this is a neat reminder of Bennett's own provincialism:
although he lives in London, he is something of a professional Yorkshireman.

What I have been describing so far — a play in which a playwright appears
worrying about his play — indicates that *The Habit of Art* is a metadrama,
a drama about drama. It is, importantly, a play which has another play
contained inside it: the outer play is Bennett's, *The Habit of Art* itself, the play
we the audience have paid to come and watch, and the inner play is *Caliban's*

---

3   *The Habit of Art*, p.25 [Subsequent references to the play will be given thus:
    Habit, p.25].
4   *Habit*, p.9.

Day, the play about Auden and Britten, which is under rehearsal. Critically, though, as metadrama it is a play which self-reflexively explores both the problems of acting and being an actor, and the relationship between theatre and real life, especially when actors have to portray real people. In doing this, *The Habit of Art* reflects on the very concept of theatre as a magical space in which illusions are created and then broken.

This idea of metadrama is fundamental to Bennett's play, so I should like to explain it more clearly by drawing a parallel with Shakespeare. In *A Midsummer Night's Dream* some of the characters (the 'rude mechanicals' led by Bottom the weaver) rehearse and then perform the story of Pyramus and Thisbe in front of Duke Theseus at his wedding feast. As audience, we watch the rehearsals, and we are made only too aware of the underlying contrivance which goes into creating the illusion: when Peter Quince, the Director of the play, realises that somehow they are going to need a wall with a hole in it through which Pyramus can whisper to his beloved Thisbe, it is Bottom who explains how they can get over the difficulty:

BOTTOM: Some man or other must present Wall; and let him have some plaster, or some loam, or some rough-cast about him, to signify wall; and let him hold his fingers thus, and through that cranny shall Pyramus and Thisby whisper.[5]

All this parallels the situation in *The Habit of Art* quite closely. The characters in Bennett's play adopt other roles when they rehearse the play within a play, and they too have great difficulty with the mask of illusion — literally so, because the character Fitz, played by Richard Griffiths, is only too aware that he does not physically resemble the poet Auden, and has actually ordered a very lifelike mask to wear in the hope of creating a better illusion for the audience. But when he puts the mask on the opposite is true: not only is it very hot and uncomfortable for the actor, but it obscures his voice so that the audience can't hear him properly. He, and we, are relieved when he takes it off and throws it down.

'It's been said,' says Auden during the play, 'that nowadays my face resembles a scrotum.'[6] Shortly afterwards Humphrey Carpenter, the biographer of Auden, refers to 'his famously fissured face and its congregation of wrinkles'. This is the cue for one of the oddest interludes in the play, when two of the back-stage characters bring on a large blown-up photograph of Auden and begin a zany conversation between two of the poet's wrinkles, Wrinkle 1 and Wrinkle 2, in which while Wrinkle 1 explains that Auden was actually suffering from a condition known as Touraine-Solente-Golé Syndrome, Wrinkle 2 complains about Auden's failure to wash properly. As he puts it:

---

5   *Midsummer Night's Dream* II.ii.60ff.
6   *Habit*, p.41.

WRINKLE 2   The crud in our cracks goes uncolonised and uncleansed and all we
represent is a Q-tip's missed opportunity and a challenge to Botox.[7]

This surreal snatch of dialogue perhaps harks back to Bennett's apprenticeship
as a writer of revue sketches, but it helps to cover the hiatus while Auden is waiting
for Benjamin Britten (played by Alex Jennings) to arrive. Britten was younger
than Auden, but they had both been at the same boarding school, Gresham's
in Norfolk, and later, in the Thirties, they had collaborated on a number of
documentary films produced by the GPO Film Unit. In these films, Auden wrote
verse commentaries and Britten produced the music — most famously, of course,
in *Night Mail*. Later, shortly before the outbreak of the Second World War, they
met again in New York, where Britten had arrived with his companion Peter
Pears, and Auden had just met and fallen in love with Chester Kallman.

This was the period of their closest collaboration, when Auden wrote the
libretto for Britten's first attempt at opera, *Paul Bunyan*. It wasn't a critical
success but it brought them close, though Britten always complained that
Auden treated him like a schoolboy. He was right, of course, for that is how
Auden treated most people. More importantly, though, Auden saw in Britten
a Peter Pan figure, someone who never wanted to grow up and whose interest
in young boys could be explained as a succession of attempts to recapture
the innocence of childhood. They collaborated on a work which came to be
the *Song for St Cecilia's Day*, the words of which Auden dedicated to Britten,
even though they were extremely critical of him. In the second section, for
instance, Auden wrote a passage in which a Peter Pan character sings:

> I cannot grow;
> I have no shadow
> To run away from.
> I only play.[8]

Auden was critical of Britten's decision to return to England in 1942: he
saw it as a flight back to the cosy comfort of home and a cowardly refusal to
take the risks with life that might turn him into a really great artist. In a letter,
from which Bennett quotes in *The Habit of Art*, Auden wrote to Britten:

> Wherever you go you are and probably always will be surrounded by
> people who adore you, nurse you, and praise everything you do.... Up
> to a point this is fine for you, but beware. You see, Bengy dear, you are
> always tempted to make things too easy for yourself in this way, i.e. to
> build yourself a warm nest of love (of course when you get it, you find
> it a little stifling) by playing the lovable talented little boy.

7   Habit, p.43.
8   W.H. Auden, 'Song for St. Cecilia's Day', *Selected Poems* (ed.) Edward Mendelson
    (London: Faber and Faber, 1979) p.97.

If you are really to develop your full stature, you will have, I think, to suffer, and make others suffer, in ways which are totally strange to you at present, and against every conscious value that you have; i.e. you will have to be able to say what you never yet have had the right to say — God, I'm a shit.[9]

It's no coincidence, I'm sure, that in an interview with the scholar Duncan Wu, Bennett himself has said, 'The writer's inner life is always nasty, it seems to me, writers are shits.'[10] In the play, Britten comes to visit Auden to talk to him about his new, final opera, *Death in Venice*. He knows it will be his last because, like Aschenbach the hero of Thomas Mann's novella, he is dying, but he is worried that people are already disapproving of his choice of story:

BRITTEN   I've only mentioned it to a select few, but word gets round. 'Here we go again,' is what they're saying. '*Peter Grimes, Billy Budd, The Turn of the Screw*. Britten's perennial theme of innocence corrupted'.[11]

When Britten first arrives, Auden is full of admiration that he is still working on new and exciting projects, while he nowadays only works out of habit, producing writing nobody thinks is as good as his early poetry. At once he offers to write the libretto for Britten's opera, ignoring the fact that he's been told Myfanwy Piper has already written one. It doesn't take long, though, for them to start arguing. Auden grabs the Piper libretto and begins crossing large sections out. He refuses to accept Britten's contention that in *Death in Venice* Aschenbach, the old man, is actually the innocent, seduced by a vision of beauty, the young boy Tadzio. 'Where does innocence come into it?' demands Auden. Neither of them are innocent. It's not corruption. It's collaboration.'[12]

This is too much for Britten. 'Constraint' he shouts at Auden, 'that's what you've never appreciated. You don't believe in restraint. I do. I always have.' Auden's reply is worth listening to carefully:

AUDEN   This is England talking, isn't it, Ben? This is taste, modesty, self-restraint.... Lovable, sought after, beautifully mannered.[13]

Here Auden paints Britten as in every way the antithesis of himself, and the thing I find interesting about this is that the playwright puts into Auden's mouth words that could apply as well to Bennett himself as to Britten:

9   W.H. Auden: letter to Benjamin Britten dated 31 January 1942; in David Matthews, *Britten* (London: Haus Publishing, 2003) p.65.
10 Duncan Wu, 'An Interview with Alan Bennett', *Areté*, Issue Thirty Winter 2009, p.16.
11 *Habit*, p.64.
12 *Habit*, p.67.
13 *Habit*, p.67.

modest, lovable, self-restrained Alan Bennett. We recognize him at once, and Bennett actually admits this in his Introduction to the play:

> Though in some ways I find Britten unsympathetic he, much more than Auden, is the character I identify with.[14]

And yet, Bennett is also close to Auden: part of him admires people who throw away restraint, and who don't have the middle England mentality that people assume is part of his persona. Two of his personal heroes, about whom he wrote affectionately in *Writing Home*, are Russell Harty and the film director Lindsay Anderson. Of Harty, Bennett has said:

> Russell never made any secret of his homosexuality even in those unliberated days when he was an undergraduate. He didn't look on it as an affliction, but he was never one for a crusade either. He just got on with it.[15]

He could just as well be speaking there of Auden.

Auden, it is clear, is Bennett's touchstone, someone who has been central to his writing and to his thinking about art for a very long time — ever since he was an undergraduate, in fact, and went to hear Auden's inaugural lecture as Oxford Professor of Poetry. And anyone who assumes that *The Habit of Art* is the first time Bennett has written about Auden in a play is forgetting *The Old Country* (1984). In this play, people assumed that the central character, yearning for home while in self-imposed exile, was the spy Kim Philby, but Bennett has explained that

> If I'd had anyone in mind ... it was not Philby but W.H. Auden, the play seeming to me to be about exile, a subject that does interest me, rather than about espionage, which interests me not a bit.[16]

Here, I think, one can see a fundamental problem emerging for the author of *The Habit of Art*. If it is true that Bennett admits to identifying in part with Britten, yet finds Britten unsympathetic, the same is even more true of his identification with Auden: for though he admired Auden he also came to dislike, even to disapprove of, him:

> Auden was wise to want no biography written. The more one reads about him, the harder it is to see round him to the poetry beyond, and he grows increasingly hard to like... . He didn't care much for fame, for instance, or go in for self-advertisement, was careless about his reputation, and was unmoved by criticism. So much about him

---

14 *Habit*, p.x.
15 Alan Bennett, 'Russell Harty 1934–1988' *Writing Home* (London: Faber 1994) p.68.
16 Alan Bennett, 'An Englishman Abroad', *Writing Home*, p.329.

is mature and admirable, he seems a bigger baby for what is not… . 'You're not the only pebble on the beach,' one wants to say. 'Grow up.' Grow up, or don't grow old.[17]

This ambiguity in Bennett's attitude to both his central characters, Auden and Britten, is (I suggest) never resolved. And the lack of resolution is reflected in the on-stage relationship between poet and composer, though Bennett, with a carefully placed image and a deft piece of stage business, shows that they realise their relationship is damaged beyond repair. After their great argument, Auden says plaintively:

AUDEN   I've failed the test, haven't I?

To which Britten replies

BRITTEN   There was no test. I needed a hand. Not with the writing. Someone to say, 'Go on, Go on.' You used to be good at that.[18]

'I needed a hand.' Britten had hoped his former friend would offer him some moral support, but none was forthcoming. When Britten comes to leave, Auden (trying to make amends) asks him 'Hold my hand a second'. Here, Bennett's stage directions, usually very explicit, are silent as to whether Britten does or does not respond to Auden's invitation. In the text of the play, Bennett simply says, 'Britten having gone out, Auden thinks of something and runs to the top of the stairs.' He calls after him, 'Ben. Go on,' by now it's too late: Britten is out of the door and half way down the stairs. At this critical moment in the play, when the metonymic gesture of the proffered hand is literally centre-stage, Bennett leaves it to the Director to decide whether or not Britten should accept this offer of reconciliation.

****

It's time I explained fully who else is who in *The Habit of Art*, but as you may already have gathered, this is not always easy. Just as there is an outer and an inner play, so there is an outer and an inner set of characters. Some only exist in the outer play; others exist in both outer and inner plays and therefore move between the outer set, literally the rehearsal room, the set of the inner play, the one called *Caliban's Day*.

To make the point that the action of *The Habit of Art* is taking place during an afternoon, Bennett has one character who actually only appears during the interval. This is an actor called Brian, who should have been playing the part of Boyle, the college servant with the unenviable task of cleaning W.H. Auden's room. However, Brian isn't able to take part in the rehearsal because he is performing in a matinée of a Chekhov play next door in the Olivier

---

17 Alan Bennett, 'The wrong blond', *Writing Home*, p.514.
18 *Habit*, p.69.

theatre. During the interval of his Chekhov play, however, he wanders back in to the rehearsal room to chat to his friends rehearsing *Caliban's Day*. This is why during the interval of the play we are watching in the Lyttleton theatre a man dressed in Russian peasant costume wanders onto our stage and is seen quite happily chatting to the other members of the cast and backstage crew.

There are some other characters whom we see onstage but who never speak: one is Joan, a motherly woman whose role is to act as chaperone to the child playing Charlie. Charlie is a choirboy being auditioned by Benjamin Britten for a part in his forthcoming opera, *Death in Venice*: he might or might not end up singing the role of Tadzio, the young boy who lures the elderly, famous writer, Aschenbach, to his death. There is Ralph, the dresser, who looks after the actors' costumes — though since this is a rehearsal and they are mostly not in costume, he has very little to do. There is also Matt, the sound technician who sits against the wall of the rehearsal room behind a bank of sound equipment, and occasionally chats to Tom, the rehearsal pianist.

Tom does not speak, but (unlike Brian, Joan, Matt and Ralph) he has a significant and visible role to perform. Music is an important theme in the play, and it is an important element in the performance too. Both Britten and Auden play a piano at different points in the action, and the actors simply mime this, while the actual sound of the piano being played is created by Tom on a keyboard, next to the bank of sound equipment at the side of the outer stage. All this we see; as we are meant to — for *The Habit of Art* is very much a play about the breaking down of illusions. As I've mentioned, no curtain rises or falls, the lights never go down, the actors wander on and off stage and sometimes switch in mid-sentence between one character and another: themselves as actors and themselves as the characters they are representing.

Anyone who has ever watched a play by Bertolt Brecht — *The Threepenny Opera* for example or *The Caucasian Chalk Circle* — will recognize from what I've just described that Bennett is adopting Brecht's famous Alienation Technique, or *Verfremdungseffekt*. This 'distancing effect', to give it a literal translation, is designed to prevent the audience from passively accepting the illusion aimed at in realist theatre — i.e. that the characters are 'real' people and that the sets represent real places. This deliberate distancing and breaking down of the theatrical illusion is of course another ingredient of metadrama; the self-reflexive questioning of what theatre is all about — how it works and why it matters — which, as I have already suggested, is fundamental to our understanding of Bennett's play.

Two other members of the backstage crew play important roles in *The Habit of Art*: George, the young ASM or Assistant Stage Manager, and Kay, the Stage Manager herself, played by Frances de la Tour. These two are a constant presence: they keep the rehearsal under way; they stand in for actors like Brian who are unable to be present; and they are clearly actors *manqués*, who would rather be front stage than back. Indeed, at the end of the rehearsal, Kay has to explain to Neil, the author, what acting is all about:

KAY   To act is to be frightened. When I used to do it I was always frightened. Threw up before every performance.

AUTHOR   I didn't know you acted.

KAY   Yes. I loved it.

AUTHOR   What happened?

KAY   Nothing. That was the trouble.[19]

This is one of the most poignant moments in the play.

Neil, the author, talking here to Kay, both is and isn't Alan Bennett. I've already suggested that he is difficult and defensive, and this is because he feels he must stand up for his play as he intended it, yet knows he and his play are at the mercy of the Director and the actors. The former cuts his play without consulting him and adds in stage business of which he disapproves, while the latter resent having him at the rehearsal at all and complain about how their characters are portrayed, about the amount of sex in the play and even about the ending. Bennett uses him as a device to fill in some of the background the audience needs to know. When for example Fitz, the actor playing Auden, asks why the play doesn't end with Auden reciting one of his most powerful poems, he says to Neil:

FITZ   I still don't see what's wrong with what we've got. It's a nice dying fall. It's in the poet's own words. What's the matter with that?

Neil, the author, replies:

AUTHOR   It was something Auden himself said — which is in the play, or was, till you cut it out — how he felt that he end of *The Tempest* really won't do, that it's all very neat but that there's more to be said. And so he lets Caliban speak. That's why the play is called *Caliban's Day*. Auden and Britten are dead, Carpenter died in 2005, the only survivor the boy — which is Caliban again.[20]

I fear something rather contrived is going on here. Bennett himself admits in the Introduction to the play, that the idea of the play-within-a-play only came to him at a late stage (as late as 2008 or even 2009) when 'it occurred to me,' he says,

---

19 *Habit,* p.87.
20 *Habit,* p.81.

that the business of conveying the facts could be largely solved if a frame were put around the play by setting it in a rehearsal room. Queries about the text and any objections to it could then be put in the mouths of the actors who (along with the audience) would have their questions answered in the course of the rehearsal.[21]

This is not just a technical device; it turns Neil, the author himself, into a device rather than a fully realised character. He is not the only one, either. Donald, the actor playing Humphrey Carpenter, feels his part has not been properly written: half the time he doesn't know whether he should even be on stage. When Neil tries to massage his ego by telling him that he is 'the story-teller', Donald replies tartly:

DONALD   Mr Know-All. I just feel I irritate. I'm in the way. I just feel ... I just feel I'm ... *a device*.[22]

No one could have called the real life Humphrey Carpenter a device, but Bennett's Carpenter (played by Adrian Scarborough) is a misfit, looking for a role. At the start of Act 2, he appears ludicrously in drag, singing 'I'm Doris the Goddess of Wind' and trying unsuccessfully to accompany himself on the tuba. His absurd justification for this is that since the real Humphrey Carpenter had been a good musician, this might help the audience to understand more about the character he is trying to play. And when, as the play ends, he asks the Stage Manager, 'Did the music thing help?' it's a question Kay is too kind-hearted to answer: according to the stage directions she simply 'makes an equivocal gesture'. But Donald is not to be deflected. He says,

DONAL   It's hard because to me, you see, Carpenter is the centre of the play. Its heart.[23]

and wanders off, muttering to himself 'I wonder if I should have worn a wig' and bumping in to the author as he leaves. Neil and Carpenter, in fact, are two of a kind, neither of them believing they are properly valued and both of them resented by the actors. As the author exclaims in exasperation at Donald's lament that he is nothing but a device:

AUTHOR   Of course he's a fucking device. And what's more, he should be grateful. Actors. Why can't they just say the words? Why does a play always have to be such a performance?[24]

If the author and the biographer are largely caricatured by Bennett, the same is not true of Stuart, the rent boy. Auden has rung up an escort agency

21 *Habit*, p.xi.
22 *Habit*, p.39.
23 *Habit*, p.86.
24 *Habit*, p.40.

to ask for a boy to come round and when instead Carpenter appears, Auden assumes that he is the rent boy; so when Great Tom, the famous Christ Church bell, strikes the half hour and Auden realises that he's only got 30 minutes before it's time for cocktails, he launches into one of the most comical moments of the play: 'Here we go,' says Auden. 'Take off your trousers.' 'What for?' demands the astonished Carpenter. 'What do you think?' says Auden impatiently. 'Come along, it's half past.'

CARPENTER   What am I being asked to do?

AUDEN   You aren't being asked to do anything. You're being paid. This is
            a transaction. I'm going to suck you off.[25]

To which the astonished Carpenter can only reply, in a voice expressing outrage and anxiety in equal measure, 'But I'm with the BBC.'

Stuart, by contrast, is treated by Bennett entirely seriously. Although the College servant, Boyle, recognises him as someone seen soliciting at Gloucester Green Bus Station, Stuart himself is moved by the more academic clients he services in Norham Road and North Oxford. One client in particular:

STUART   The guy I go and see, he'll open the door and there are books
            everywhere, books in the hall, books on the landing, books and
            pictures... . And he's sitting there under the lamp in front of
            the fire and the clock's ticking and the sherry's poured. And he's
            playing classical music on what he calls his radiogram ... It's
            just lovely.[26]

This is not just Stuart the rent boy being sentimental; this is Bennett the playwright sentimentalising Stuart. Bennett has admitted in *Untold Stories* that he recognises in his plays how often there is a character who evinces a deep uneasiness about learning and in particular about books. This wasn't, says Bennett,

> something I had been especially aware of when writing but I found
> quite late in the day that I had been writing and rewriting the same
> scene for half my life. In this set-up someone stands looking at a
> bookcase, baffled and dismayed by what one is expected to assimilate
> and despairing of ever doing so ... And the thought is always the same:
> 'How will I ever catch up?' ... me, as a boy or an undergraduate,
> baffled by the world of words.[27]

25 *Habit*, p.19.
26 *Habit*, p.74.
27 Alan Bennett, *Untold Stories*, pp.550–1.

It's almost as if, in fact, Bennett has created Stuart to illustrate this thesis and he goes as far as to identify him as Caliban to Auden's Prospero. Stuart is the one who gets left behind; the one Auden thinks should be allowed the last word after the others have left. And in the play within a play, *Caliban's Island*, he very nearly gets it. That play ends with Auden, like Prospero at the end of *The Tempest*, addressing us directly. But when he says, 'So once more Caliban prepares to address the audience', Stuart's speech takes us by surprise:

STUART   No, not Caliban, whoever he was. And not in the language of Henry James, or any other tosser. No. Me. Us. Here. Now. When do we figure and get to say our say? The great men's lives are neatly parcelled for posterity, but what about us. When do we take our bow? … Because if nothing else, we at least contributed. We were in attendance, we boys of art. And though there's the odd photograph, nobody remembers who they're of: uncaptioned or 'with an unidentified friend', unnamed girls, unnameable boys, the flings, the tricks, the fodder of art.[28]

For the second time, I have to admit to seeing a weakness in the play. Here I do not think Bennett has really resolved who and what Stuart is to represent: if, for instance, Stuart has never heard of Caliban, then he certainly won't know the very recondite fact that when Auden gave Caliban the last word in *The Sea and the Mirror*, he allowed him to deliver a lengthy monologue in a style that was a pastiche of Henry James, the novelist.

I'm interested in two linguistic features of Stuart's speech, however, which illuminate what Bennett is trying, consciously or otherwise, to do here. First of all, notice that trio of negative adjectives, created by the repeated prefix, 'un' : 'uncaptioned', 'unidentified', 'unnamed'. This is a habitual trick of Bennett's and one which he acknowledges obliquely in *The History Boys* where Hector, the old-fashioned schoolmaster, explains to his pupil, Posner, that it's a device used by Thomas Hardy and later adopted by Philip Larkin — two writers Bennett has identified as major influences on his own writing. And of course, it's a stylistic trick which helps to confirm the reader or the audience in their view of Bennett as a timid figure, 'tentative and awkward', defined more by what is not said and not done, than by what is.

The second linguistic feature I want to mention comes when Bennett gives Stuart two phrases, the 'boys of art' and 'the fodder of art', which resonate against the three-times repeated phrase 'the habit of art'. The habit of art is what Auden says he has — indeed what he claims he now lives by. By contrast Stuart feels that he and his kind are used by art, by artists, but are ultimately excluded and rejected by them. In his final speech he turns on Auden and Britten, complaining bitterly to Carpenter:

---

28 *Habit*, p.84.

STUART   I want to figure. He goes on about stuff being cosy, England and that. But it's not England that's cosy. It's art, literature, him, you, the lot of you. Because there's always someone left out.... I want to get in. I want to join. I want to know.[29]

Auden rejects this: 'We can't help you' are his final words to Stuart, and as he leaves, Auden and Carpenter stare fixedly ahead; Britten gives him a brief glance but then he too turns away. That is how *Caliban's Day*, the play within a play, ends. No wonder Henry, the actor playing Britten, describes this ending as bleak, and suggests that perhaps Britten should take Stuart's hand. But the author, Neil, does not want his play ending with this gesture of comfort.

I find this significant, and I want to sum up this introduction to *The Habit of Art* by explaining why I think the ambiguous gesture of the proffered hand tells us so much about the play, and about Alan Bennett himself. Once again my point of reference is that scene in *The History Boys* where Hector, having taken Posner through Thomas Hardy's poem, 'Drummer Hodge', and pointed out the negatives — 'unknown', 'uncoffined' etc — describes the effect of great literature as being like a hand that stretches out and takes one's own. Although that play is only six years old, this scene and this statement about art has already become a defining utterance. Here for example is the writer Blake Morrison giving his own account of the importance of literature:

> Books don't always save lives: writing about the Holocaust didn't prevent Primo Levi from ultimately committing suicide; and the reading — or perverse misreading — of *The Satanic Verses* led to the deaths of innocent people. But literature's power to heal and console outweighs its power to do damage. Hector, in Alan Bennett's *The History Boys*, puts it beautifully when he describes how, in the presence of great literature, it's as if a hand has reached out and taken our own.[30]

The links to Auden, and to *The Habit of Art* in what Morrison says here, are important. First of all, it became an article of faith with Auden later in his career that, as he puts it in the play, 'Art is small beer'[31] and that 'nothing I ever wrote in the thirties saved one Jew from extinction or shortened the war by five seconds'.[32] Secondly, however, Morrison's reference to *The History Boys* reminds us that, immediately after Hector has likened the impact of great literature to a hand reaching out to take our own, it looks as though Hector

29 *Habit*, p.84.
30 Blake Morrison, 'The Reading Cure', *Guardian* 5 January 2008.
31 *Habit*, p.28
32 *Habit*, p.20

himself is about to take the boy's hand, but he finally and fatally desists from doing so. Poor Posner longs to be one of Hector's favourites, and his life is blighted because of that rejection. So too, in *The Habit of Art*, the image of hands and the trope of offering — and not taking — someone's proffered hand runs throughout the play. Near the start, when Boyle is cleaning Auden's room, and points out Auden's habit of peeing in the washbasin, he asks indignantly:

BOYLE   What I'd like to know is where does he wash his hands after he's washed his hands.[33]

Then, near the end, when Britten is leaving, Auden comes back from having a pee and says:

AUDEN   Are you going, Benjie? Hold my hand for a second.[34]

But Britten (as I've previously explained), remembering where that hand has just been, is reluctant to make this last gesture — his fastidiousness almost getting the better of his friendship.

If, finally, I am right that there is something of Bennett in Stuart the rent boy, something of him also in Auden and in Britten too, then these interlinking gestures of hands proffered or withheld, accepted or not taken, reflect Bennett's own unwillingness to let anyone — himself included — have the last word. That seems an unresolved, uncomfortable way to bring down the curtain on both *Caliban's Day* and *The Habit of Art*, but I think the point of the play and the appeal of Alan Bennett's work, lie precisely in a shared recognition, that in art as in life there are no easy answers. Nicholas Hytner, director of *The History Boys* and of *The Habit of Art*, sees the reaching out of the hand as the defining image of Bennett's relationship with his audience. I will leave the final word to him: Much of Alan Bennett's popularity, he suggests:

> seems to me the consequence not so much on his insistence on the essential loneliness of every human journey, as on his acknowledgment that the communal recognition of it, in the theatre, makes it tolerable. His audiences probably buy tickets first of all for the laughs, but they know that behind the jokes is a hand they want to take.[35]

---

33 *Habit*, p.12.
34 *Habit*, p.78.
35 Nicholas Hytner, *Areté*, p.58.

2.6 Mistaking Magdalen for the Menin Gate: Edmund Blunden's 'November 1, 1931'

Edmund Blunden's writing has played an important part in my career. Undertones of War was the first memoir of 1914-1918 I ever read and it helped to define my interest in the literature of the Great War. I was later fortunate to get to know Blunden's widow, Claire, and when I was commissioned by Cambridge University Press to edit an anthology of First World War Poetry,[1] she advised me on the selection of Blunden's poetry. I was pleased therefore to be invited to contribute an article for a proposed new online Edmund Blunden Journal, and had been intrigued by his poem 'November 1, 1931', which I had not known until I found it by chance in a Cambridge second-hand bookshop a copy of Halfway House, an edition of poems published by Blunden in 1932. The following discussion of the poem was my contribution to the Journal, and was posted on the Edmund Blunden website.[2]

Edmund Blunden's first volume of Collected Poems (*Poems 1914–1930*) was published when he was only 33 — showing how early and how strongly he had established his reputation as a poet. Of course, the success of *Undertones of War* (1928) had helped: it had introduced a new generation of readers to Blunden, and some of his most famous poems had first appeared as the appendix (entitled 'Poetical Interpretations') to that prose account of the Great War.

His next book of poems, *Halfway House*, was published in 1932.[3] Its title is not at first obvious, since no poem is called 'Halfway House', but there is an immediate clue: Blunden chooses for an epigraph to the book the opening lines of Dante's *Inferno*, as translated by Cary:

---

1 Adrian Barlow (ed.) *Six Poets of the Great War* (Cambridge: Cambridge University Press, 1995).

2 www.edmundblunden.org.

3 Edmund Blunden *Halfway House, a miscellany of new poems* (London: Cobden-Sanderson 1932). All quotations from the poem 'November 1. 1931' are from this edition, pp.67–8.

In the mid way of this our mortal life,
I found me in a gloomy wood, astray.

This sense of being lost, half way through life, is at the heart of the key poem of *Halfway House*, 'November 1, 1931', which begins:

We talked of ghosts; and I was still alive;
And I that very day was thirty five.

In other words, Blunden memorialises the exact day on which he reaches the midpoint of his 'three score years and ten': he had been born on All Saints Day, 1 November 1896. But with whom was he celebrating his 35 birthday? And who were the ghosts of whom they were speaking? Questions like these lead us into a complex and unsettling poem.

Despite the precise dating of its title, this poem (written unusually for Blunden in thirty eight rhyming couplets) nevertheless appears to be looking back from some vague point in the future: if the poet had been 'still alive' in 1931, his state now, as he writes, is indeterminate. He is not only 'Here and elsewhere' but also 'Baffled in time'. Like Dante, in fact, he is 'astray'. In part, he can see the absurdity of this: living now in Oxford (Blunden had taken up a fellowship at his old college, Merton, in 1931) he can laugh at himself for behaving like an old man, getting his dates wrong and muddling up landmarks from his past and present life. He does not need a conversation ('transmortal talk') with a ghost to teach him that the war he survived has in a sense turned him into a ghost — 'War had ended my sublunar walk'. Nevertheless, he still wants 'some kind ghost' to come and explain to him why, even now (after the publication of *Undertones of War*) he continues to write compulsively ('why I drove my pen so late'). More than this, he needs an explanation of what the war and his surviving of it really means: he 'yearned to catch' what he should say when the time came for him to explain 'What my gross late appearance was about'.

Blunden's simile of a man on an important secret mission who is kidnapped by bandits and 'long delayed' well expresses the poet's feeling of bewilderment and frustration, his sense of existing perhaps in a halfway house between being alive and being dead. It is an image we might understand today in terms of a hostage captured in the Middle East. This bewilderment is also reflected in the speaker's need to ask forgiveness both of his former comrades, now dead, and of his 'sweet, red-smiling love'. He is afraid that to the former — his 'dear, honoured and saintly friends' — his inability to enjoy or justify the life that was spared to him must seem like a betrayal of what they died for. And when he tries to explain his feelings to the woman he has loved he understands neither why their relationship has failed nor whether he or she is to blame:

> from my silences your kindness grew,
> And I surrendered for the time to you,
> And still I hold you glorious and my own,
> I'd take your hands, your lips; but I'm alone.
> So I was forced elsewhere.

The restless changing of tenses in these five lines — past, past, present, future subjunctive or past imperfect, present, past — and the movement from active to passive again reflect the speaker's sense of hovering in a kind of limbo. He isn't even sure 'If this is life', as he murmurs to the woman, parenthetically and apologetically.

'November 1, 1931' is thus a disturbing poem, sometimes uncertain in tone, occasionally unconvincing in its couplets, necessarily inconclusive and downbeat. It is, after all, about the consequences of something that did not happen:

> No ghost was granted me; and I must face
> Uncoached the masters of that Time and Space
> And there with downcast murmurings set out
> What my gross late appearance was about.

It would, though, be a mistake to underestimate this poem and the significance of its 'survivor-as-ghost' trope, which of course is a recurring feature of the literary expression of post traumatic stress. No one in the 1930s would have been more familiar than Blunden with Charles Lamb's poem 'The Old Familiar Faces', in which Lamb (1775–1834) struggled to come to terms with the shock and consequences of his mother's death at the hand of his sister Mary. In this poem, Lamb reflected on how this tragedy separated him from his past life and from his closest friends:

> Ghost-like I paced round the haunts of my childhood,
> Earth seem'd a desert I was bound to traverse,
> Seeking to find the old familiar faces.[4]

Blunden too represents himself as endlessly searching. 'I must go over the ground again', he had said in *Undertones of War*; and here in 'November 1, 1931' he is 'always on the bivouac ... for ever changing ground'. His mental clumsiness ('Baffled ... fumbling') is like that of an old man, and this is a reminder that those who survived the War characteristically thought of themselves as old before their time. Richard Aldington's poem 'Epilogue to *Death of a Hero*' (1929) begins:

---

4   Charles Lamb 'The Old Familiar Faces' in Francis Palgrave (ed.) *The Golden Treasury* (Oxford: OUP World's Classics series new ed. 1924) p.220.

Eleven years after the fall of Troy,
We, the old men — some of us nearly forty —
Met and talked on the sunny rampart.

          …

Some spoke of intolerable sufferings,
The brightness gone from their eyes
And the grey already thick in their hair.[5]

For the speaker in 'November 1, 1931' premature old age is both a cause and a consequence of this apparently futile and so far fruitless seeking; but 'Mistaking Magdalen for the Menin Gate' — the only line in the whole poem with a triple alliteration — is not so much a wry smile at a senior moment as an inexcusable error for which he must ask forgiveness from the very people, his dead friends, whose names are engraved on the walls of the Menin Gate in Ypres. And just as Blunden knew intimately the work of Charles Lamb, so in 1931 he would also have known Sassoon's recent poem, 'On Passing the New Menin Gate':

Well might the Dead who struggled in the slime
Rise and deride this sepulchre of crime.[6]

For Blunden, as for Sassoon, this memorial was no laughing matter. Sassoon's reference in the same poem to the 'intolerably nameless names' expressed clearly enough the reaction of the survivors, left to look for the names of their former comrades on the walls of this ponderous memorial: the Menin Gate, despite being designed on an overbearing scale by Sir Reginald Blomfield, proved still too small to hold the names of all the missing of the Ypres Salient.

However, important as these echoes of other poems may be, they do not sufficiently reflect the significance of 'November 1, 1931', this account in rhyming couplets of waiting for a ghost (who doesn't appear) to give the poet a justification (which he has not yet heard) for what he has endured and why he has survived it. In the Preface to *Halfway House* Blunden states that he intends to 'still haunt the earth at certain seasons "waiting for the spark from heaven to fall"'. Characterising himself here as already a ghost, he waits for the Arnoldian 'spark'[7] of poetic inspiration to bring him back to life both as a person and as a poet. What should he say and do next?

---

5   Richard Aldington, 'Epilogue to Death of a Hero' in *Complete Poems* (London: Allen Wingate 1948) p.303.

6   Siegfried Sassoon, 'On Passing the New Menin Gate', in *The Heart's Journey* (London: Wm Heinemann Ltd 1931) p.31.

7   'Waiting for the spark from heaven to fall' is a quotation from Matthew Arnold's poem, *The Scholar-Gipsy* (1853).

It is this question, and not the answer to it, that Blunden's birthday poem is fundamentally about. His poetry of direct experience of war has been written and collected in *Poems 1914–1930*; his edition of Wilfred Owen's poetry (1931) has just been published; his present poetry, in *Halfway House*, is of uncertainty and unfocused foreboding, hovering between the past and the to come. What he doesn't yet know (though it will shortly become clear) is that, with Europe moving rapidly towards another war, his job will be to adopt in the poetry he has yet to write the stance adopted by Wilfred Owen back in 1918: 'All a poet can do today is warn'. To understand therefore why 'November 1, 1931' is itself a half-way house in Blunden's poetic output, one should read it alongside 'Another Journey from Bethune to Cuinchy' (published 1928) and 'To WO and his Kind' (published 1939). When read in sequence with these other two poems about conversations with the dead, 'November 1, 1931' demonstrates how, by the end of the Thirties, Blunden was certain that his responsibility as a poet was to warn against a repeat of 1914–18. And Owen, whom Blunden had never met but whose friendship he most missed ("Would you were not dust!" he exclaims in 'To WO and his Kind'), was the friendly ghost — Virgil to his Dante — who would guide him through the 'gloomy wood'. It was to be Owen who would make his future poetic direction clear to him and, as the Second World War began, Blunden acknowledged this in 'To Wilfred Owen (killed in action November 4th, 1918)'. The poem begins:

> Where does your spirit walk, kind soldier, now,
> In this deep winter, bright with ready guns?
> And have you found new poems in this war?

It ends

> And I, dream-following you, reading your eyes,
> Your veteran youthful eyes, discover fair
> Some further hope, which did not formerly rise.
> Smiling you fade, the future meets you there.[8]

---

8   Edmund Blunden, *Overtones of War* ed. Martin Taylor (London: Duckworth 1996) p.197.

2.7 From Stage to Page: the Marlowe Dramatic Society and Cambridge English

This review of Tim Cribb's history of the Marlowe Dramatic Society: Bloomsbury & British Theatre: The Marlowe Story[1] *was first published in the Newsletter of the Rupert Brooke Society 2008. Because it was commissioned by the Rupert Brooke Society, the focus of the article was necessarily more on Brooke than it might otherwise have been. Nevertheless, Rupert Brooke (like Edmund Blunden) played an early and important part in my developing interest in literature and literary study. I had read his* Collected Poems, *edited and with a Memoir by Edward Marsh, and Christopher Hassall's 1964 biography of him by the time I left school. Through these books I became aware of the reach of literature beyond and behind the words on the page, and this awareness has always helped to give focus to my teaching.*

I have found Brooke a valuable writer to use with adult students at Cambridge, not simply because of his local connections but because of the lack of consensus about his reputation and standing as a poet and as a prominent figure in early twentieth century literary history. Both this and the succeeding review (of Jill Dawson's novel The Great Lover*) attempt to see Brooke in a broader context than that in which he is most often placed.*

The Marlowe Dramatic Society is a Cambridge student drama society which in 2007 celebrated the centenary of its first production, *Doctor Faustus*. Any such society that reaches a century has surely earned a history, but Tim Cribb's fascinating book is far more than just a dutiful chronicle of the society's first hundred years, trawling through minute books, production notes, programmes and reviews. There is inevitably a good deal of this, but the book is an attempt to show how, from the start, the Marlowe was intimately connected to the ideals and personalities of the Bloomsbury Group. Even more than this,

---

1   Tim Cribb, *Bloomsbury and British Theatre: the Marlowe Story* (Cambridge: Salt Publishing 2007).

Cribb sets out to demonstrate both that theatre is a neglected aspect of the Bloomsbury story and that the influence of Bloomsbury, as manifested in the productions of this influential but sometimes eccentric society, contributed directly to the way English as a subject was developed and taught in Cambridge during the first half of the twentieth century. He goes further still, arguing that Bloomsbury — through the Marlowe — has even influenced British theatre from the post-war period up to the present day. It is an ambitious task.

Early on, Tim Cribb describes his book as a ghost story:

> Anyone who has ventured into an empty theatre, especially onto a deserted stage set, will have felt the peculiar atmosphere that haunts the place. There is something existential about it, a sense of having just missed something intensely significant or delightful, a feeling that some god has just left the temple.

He is right, of course, and even the cover illustrations of *Bloomsbury and British Theatre* make the point. On the back is a splendidly evocative photograph of a deserted, almost a derelict, theatre. It looks as if it might once have been a music hall or, conversely, a temperance hall. Just visible through the flaking paintwork on the wall is the slogan 'PREPARE to meet THY GOD'. In the well of the empty auditorium, the seating stacked against the walls, sits an old man in a centrally positioned armchair. He is carefully dressed: polished brown shoes, brown tie and lovat jacket; elegant fingers clasp the handle of a walking stick. His eyes are tightly closed as if he is trying to remember something from a long time past. At first glance, indeed, he looks like Gielgud performing in Harold Pinter's play *No Man's Land*.

This photograph first appeared in *The Times* in 1994, and the old man is Dadie Rylands, for over sixty years the presiding genius of the Marlowe (Dadie *ex Machina* as he was known — waspishly or affectionately). Rylands is inevitably the central figure in Cribb's book and appropriately appears also on the front cover where he is photographed some time in the 1920s in his rooms in King's College. Beside him sits Virginia Woolf, cigarette to her lips, her eyes gazing away from the camera. She seems a good deal more relaxed than the young Dadie: he is wearing a chalk-stripe double-breasted suit and fiddles nervously with a pipe. He looks tense, his brow is furrowed. It is as if, still in his twenties, he hasn't quite got used to the mantle that is being placed on his shoulders. Virginia Woolf herself wrote of him (in a letter to Jacques Raverat):

> At King's they are all reminded of Rupert — partly his yellow hair – partly his poetry, which is not as good as Rupert's. He is a very charming spoilt boy … but at heart he is uncorrupted (so I think — others disagree) and all young and oldish men, like Eddie Marsh and so on, fall in love with him.

Dadie Rylands, the reincarnation of Rupert Brooke? No wonder he looked nervous. Did he relish such praise and such comparisons? Interestingly, on p.58 of the book there is another photograph, presumably taken on the same occasion (same room, same chair, same suit, same pipe) but with Virginia Woolf nowhere to be seen. In this photograph Rylands seems much more relaxed. There is plenty in this book to suggest that Dadie's attitude to Bloomsbury could be rather ambivalent.

But before Dadie came on the scene there was Rupert, who played the part of Mephistophilis in that inaugural *Doctor Faustus*, but who was not the actual founder of the Marlowe. This distinction belonged to his namesake Justin Brooke, who had had the original idea of starting a society 'specifically for the performance of plays by Shakespeare's contemporaries'. It is perhaps hard today to imagine a world in which the plays of Marlowe, Webster and other Elizabethan and Jacobean playwrights were simply never performed. Such, however, was the situation in Edwardian England and Cribb is very good at sketching the highly conservative atmosphere of this era when performing plays in Cambridge at all was fraught with difficulty if you were an undergraduate: the Vice-Chancellor had statutory powers to act as censor, and was not afraid to use them. In 1914, the V-C was the Provost of King's, M.R. James — now best remembered for his Ghost Stories — who made such swingeing cuts to Ben Jonson's comedy *The Alchemist* that the cast pronounced him to be anathema. Other difficulties were more fundamental: women were not allowed to act during term-time, so the early Marlowe Society tried to establish a routine of one play during term-time with an all-male cast, and one during the vacation in which women could act. From the start, however, the Society's constitution had called for the Committee to be 'bisexual' (*scilicet* consisting of men and women) though the first woman committee member, Margaret Drabble, was not appointed until 1960.

Not that women weren't involved early on; in addition to the support of the formidable Jane Harrison of Newnham College, the Society was able to call on the artist Gwen Darwin (later Gwen Raverat) as scene painter and poster designer: her advertisement for a 1911 production of *The Knight of the Burning Pestle* contained the first woodcut she ever published. Gwen, together with her husband Jacques, and the Cornford family (Francis Cornford was the Society's first Senior Treasurer — a post currently held by Tim Cribb himself) were part of the inner circle of Rupert Brooke's friends. Add to that list the names of Lytton Strachey and Virginia Woolf, Geoffrey Keynes (who had been a friend of Brooke's at Rugby, and who shortly became Secretary of the Marlowe), his brother Maynard and E.M. Forster, and it will be clear that listing the Marlowe's early friends, supporters and officers is like taking a roll call of the Bloomsbury clan.

And support they did. Sometimes this was financial, when the Society got into difficulties if a production made a loss. Later on such help was more far-reaching: Maynard Keynes was responsible both for the creation of the Arts Theatre in Cambridge and for establishing an endowment intended to ensure its financial stability. This last point is important because it would be wrong to suggest that the Marlowe alone was, and remains, the heart of dramatic life in Cambridge. Keynes's vision for the Arts Theatre went well beyond simply providing a home for the Society, since from the start there were already other theatres (the New, the Festival and the student-run ADC) and other acting groups, not least the Mummers and those who performed in the triennial Greek play. By the same token, today the Arts Theatre itself has to compete with the growing number of theatres belonging to the colleges themselves, and the Marlowe Society may be said to have been partly upstaged by the Cambridge Footlights. But back in 1908 it was with the Society's tercentenary production of Milton's masque *Comus* that a strongly Bloomsbury aesthetic began to define the Marlowe's productions, and perhaps to lay the groundwork for the approach to English as a discipline of study that came to be known as 'Cambridge English'.

Rupert Brooke was the producer of *Comus*; he also played the attendant spirit. Astonishingly, the invited audience included not only the Vice-Chancellors of both Oxford and Cambridge but also a first-division team of poets, novelists and biographers, among them the Poet Laureate, Alfred Austin, as well as Thomas Hardy, Robert Bridges, Edmund Gosse and Sidney Lee. The performance was reviewed in *The Spectator* by Lytton Strachey who attacked Milton's poem for its lack of dramatic quality but praised the performers for their speaking of the verse, which he recognised as the result of 'technical study and hard work'. Much of this had come first from Brooke himself, who had prepared for the production by making a detailed study of the text in facsimile and by paying particular attention to the versification. It was this which Strachey perceptively spotted as the key to the actors' achievement, and it was this, too, which anticipated the later emphasis on close reading that would be associated with Cambridge English and the teaching of I.A. Richards, William Empson and F.R. Leavis. From this time on, the Marlowe's style became synonymous with effective verse speaking, in strong reaction against the prevailing style of performance in London and provincial theatres. Strachey, in his review, had summed up the situation:

> The hideous and barbaric utterance with which, in our ordinary theatres, actors attempt to reproduce the poetry of Shakespeare is nothing short of a disgrace to the stage.... The existence of such a body of able and enthusiastic lovers of poetry and the drama [i.e. the actors in Brooke's production of *Comus*] must be welcomed as at least an augury of a better state of things.

Two points follow from these trenchant remarks, with their focus on the poetry of Shakespeare and on 'enthusiastic lovers of poetry and drama'. First, the early years of the Marlowe Society coincide with a growing interest in performable contemporary verse drama. Brooke himself wrote a verse play, *Lithuania*; and the newly established Birmingham Rep, founded by Barry Jackson and managed by Brooke's friend and fellow Dymock poet, John Drinkwater, gave a platform to new verse plays throughout the First World War. But the Marlowe remained true (more or less) to its principles of performing earlier drama, not tackling a modern verse play until Dadie Rylands produced T.S. Eliot's *The Family Reunion* at the Arts Theatre in 1952.

Secondly, it is important to note the emphasis on Shakespeare's plays as dramatic poems rather than simply as dramas that happened to be written in verse. This looks back, on the one hand, to the criticism of Charles Lamb, whose groundbreaking work in rescuing and editing forgotten plays by Shakespeare's contemporaries was published under the title *Specimens of the Dramatic Poets* (1808). On the other it looks forward to the attack on A.C. Bradley, led by young critics such as L.C. Knights with his polemical 1933 essay 'How Many Children Had Lady Macbeth?' Knights argued that *Macbeth* had more in common with *The Waste Land* than with *A Doll's House*. Attention to the language of the play, Knights argued, revealed that Shakespeare's *Macbeth*, like Eliot's seminal poem, was concerned with themes such as the reversal of values, unnatural disorder and deceitful appearance. Consequently, the way to understand the plays was to approach them as dramatic poems rather than as performance. Language first, and only afterwards any Bradleyan focus on psychological characterisation.

Later in his book, Cribb rightly praises Dadie Rylands for his 'attention to minute verbal detail and his acutely sensitive ear', suggesting that no Director before him would have been able to spot the ironic echo in two widely separated lines in *Antony and Cleopatra*: 'That I might hear thee call great Caesar ass / Unpolicied' and 'Now boast thee, death, in thy possession lies / A lass unparallel'd'. He goes further, however, and claims that:

> Under Ryland's direction the Marlowe Dramatic Society extends into
> the practical laboratory of theatre the work of the new Cambridge
> Faculty of English, with a pronouncedly Bloomsbury inflection.

If this is true, then the Bloomsbury inflection can presumably be traced back to Brooke's production, and Strachey's review, of *Comus* in 1908.

Some readers may find the discussion of Cambridge English and its links with the Marlowe rather arcane. However, Tim Cribb, as a fellow of Churchill College and a member of the English Faculty, is generally adept at untangling its mysteries, though a statement such as 'Q had a Chair without a Tripos to support it', might pose a challenge to anyone who was not a

Cambridge insider. (It actually means: Sir Arthur Quiller-Couch was Edward VII Professor of English Literature but at that time, pre-1917, it was not yet possible to take a degree in English Literature at Cambridge.) Sometimes, too, it is difficult to be sure what the author really thinks of Dadie Rylands and of his work in the theatre; though he is quite happy to praise 'Rylands at his incomparable best', he nevertheless reaches the rather revealing conclusion — picking up a phrase from a Lytton Strachey letter — that:

> One of the limits of Bloomsbury and of the Marlowe productions under Dadie could perhaps ... be described as a certain absence of semen.

Does this mean that Rylands's style of production, beautifully articulated as the verse would always have been, was ultimately lacking in life? It is certainly true that many school teachers in the days of long playing records were grateful for the clear speaking in the Argo recordings of Shakespeare's plays, masterminded by Rylands. At the same time, though, they were often frustrated by the lack of dynamic variation in pace and characterisation in the performances; so that it wasn't long before the LPs were relegated to the back of the staff room cupboard, to be replaced by taped recordings of Shakespeare performed on BBC Radio. Nevertheless, it is right that Cribb should devote a chapter to the Argo project, its importance highlighted by a comment from J.C. Trewin in 1958 when the recordings first appeared: 'Here is the word, and only the word: it is extraordinarily satisfying, the perfect listening edition.' The recordings used past and present members of the Marlowe and provided young actors and directors such as Ian McKellan and Trevor Nunn with the chance to perform alongside older actors like Donald Beves and Miles Malleson. The full fifteen-year project to record all Shakespeare's plays was only completed when Rylands had reached his seventieth birthday, and Cribb is fully justified in saying that this was 'a significant chapter in the history of recording'. It may though be stretching a point to say that these recordings 'remain the nearest we can get to the ghost of theatre in its Marlovian manifestation under Rylands, which is to say, the ghost of Bloomsbury.'

This ghost seems sometimes rather faint in the closing chapters of *Bloomsbury & British Theatre*. As the author's attention turns to the dominating figures of the RSC, John Barton, Peter Hall and Trevor Nunn, though with help from reviewers such as Harold Hobson, Cribb is able to justify his argument that the new generation of English actors, graduates both of the Marlowe and of Cambridge, remained true to the distinctive principles established by Brooke and Strachey and then carried forward by Rylands. Reviewing a key performance of the two parts of *Henry IV* (1959), Hobson praised the anonymous actor — Marlowe performances were still anonymous at this time — playing Falstaff:

There was no laborious effort made to be realistic, or to surround the man with the aura of the stews. He listened attentively to every word that was said to him.... This Falstaff actually appeared to believe that the words which Shakespeare had written for him were witty.... He exaggerated nothing.... The result was astonishing.

Hobson concluded, 'The virtue of the Marlowe, seen especially in Falstaff ... was intelligent speaking.' This production was by the young John Barton, but Cribb is quick to point out that 'in it the spirit of Rylands was visibly at work, and behind him we can discern the ghosts of Lytton Strachey and ultimately Justin Brooke', the founder of the Marlowe Society.

This is the essence of the book's argument, and in developing it Tim Cribb has done an excellent job for the Marlowe Society, for Bloomsbury addicts and for students of Cambridge English and of English theatre alike. Members of the Rupert Brooke Society will forgive him for locating Brooke's burial place on Lemnos rather than Skyros, but Margaret Drabble may be less forgiving of the caption to a photograph on p.74. The picture shows a rather over-furnished sitting room, and the caption reads, 'One of Ryland's rooms in King's College, where he entertained Virginia Woolf and Margaret Drabble writhed upon the hearth-rug'. She did, but only because (as she herself explains much later in the book) in 1960 she was rehearsing for the role of Imogen in *Cymbeline* and 'writhing in despair by an imaginary headless corpse on Dadie Rylands's carpet in front of a painted fireplace that I now know to be the work of Carrington'. There's simply no getting away from Bloomsbury.

2.8 Punting from the Cambridge End: The Great Lover

When Jill Dawson's novel[1] about Rupert Brooke appeared early in 2009, critical reaction and the largely adverse attitude to Brooke himself were revealing. Here for example is the opening to the *Daily Telegraph* review (by Lorna Bradbury):

> Rupert Brooke might seem at first glance an unappealing subject for a novel. Apart from a handful of notable exceptions, his poems were mediocre, and his life didn't amount to much, cut short as it was at the age of 27 when he died from septicemia, contracted from a mosquito bite early in the First World War.

Frances Spalding, in *The Independent*, was quick to identify Brooke's 'inner dissolution' while others expressed their irritation with the whole pre-Great War Cambridge era exemplified by the 'half-cocked paganism, Fabianism … naked swimming and class politics' of Brooke and his friends (Joanna Briscoe in *The Guardian*).

In terms of *The Great Lover* itself, there was greater admiration for Dawson's recreation of life in Grantchester and at The Orchard than for her portrayal of Brooke himself. This was chiefly because the strongest element of the novel is the entirely fictional character Nell Golightly, a young Fenland girl who comes to work as a maid for Mrs Stevenson at the The Orchard. The narrative is shared between Nellie and Brooke, and the girl is more convincingly drawn than the man she finds so infuriating but lovable. This is in part because Dawson has set herself to interweave Brooke's own words into his own narrative (mainly from letters, occasionally from the diaries and correspondence of others) to lend authenticity and interest to the character. This device, though, often has the opposite effect, only making Brooke seem more brittle and self-

---

1 Jill Dawson, *The Great Lover* (London: Sceptre 2009).

regarding than ever, while nobody could describe Dawson's fictional maidservant as either brittle or self-regarding. Early in the novel she rescues Rupert from being attacked by a swarm of bees; as she dabs a salve of honey onto the single sting he has suffered, proleptically, on his lip, Nellie says to herself:

> Well, I'm not one of his Cambridge girls who knows only her books and bicycles; he needn't think he can take liberties with me! The bees showed him that. Nell Golightly might be just a maid from Prickwillow, but she can face facts and she won't be anybody's fool.

The ease with which she moves from first to third person here introduces an important narrative strategy. In her Acknowledgements at the back of the book, Jill Dawson reminds her readers:

> This is a novel. I have made things up. Nell and her family are made up, as are the other maids. Of course I made Rupert up, too, and he is 'my' Rupert Brooke, a figure from my imagination, fused from his poetry, his letters, his travel writing and essays, photographs, guesswork, the things I know about his life blended with my own dreams of him, and impressions.

This suggests that Nell's dreams of Rupert might in some ways be a projection of the author's own (and Dawson herself lives in the village of Prickwillow), but she is careful to use a distancing device to enable her heroine and herself to stand back from the object of their dreams. Not only can Nell think of herself in the third person; at certain moments in her own narrative, she suddenly detaches herself from the events in which she is involved and is able to become an observer of herself and Rupert. It's a disturbing but effective device. In a scene one night when Rupert has persuaded Nellie to accompany him for a midnight swim, he unexpectedly admits to a sense of failure and self-contempt as a poet. Nellie, surprised by his outburst, begins to answer, ('"Well," I venture,') but suddenly,

> One minute I'm standing next to Rupert in a wood, by a river, late at night, the next I'm somewhere else — I don't know where — watching. A chill passes over me and I observe only two figures talking: one tall, troubled; the other wearing a coat over her shoulders and looking up to the man with a shining face.
>
> It lasts only a moment, then I'm back at the river, back in my body, with my heart hammering and the scent of river garlic floating round me, and I'm talking.

And when Rupert cries out to Nell ('Help me, he says') she simply replies, 'Why write, then? No one is making you'.

There have been several other novels in the past few years based on Brooke's contemporaries — for example, Helen Dunmore's *Zennor in Darkness*, about D.H. Lawrence and Katherine Mansfield, C.K. Stead's *Mansfield*, and Michael Cunningham's *The Hours*, about Virginia Woolf. Jill Dawson's novel goes further than these in creating a wholly fictional character as a foil to the historical hero. Thus her novel begins and ends with a tease: it opens with a letter sent in 1982 by a Mrs Arlice Rapoto, Brooke's alleged illegitimate daughter by his Tahitian mistress, Taatamata. This letter asks for information about the father Arlice never knew and is answered by the now ninety-year-old Nell, still living in Grantchester and the only person there who remembers Brooke first-hand. This is of course essentially a device to unlock Nell's memories (Arlice does not feature again in the story) but at the end of the novel, Jill Dawson drops the intriguing fictional hint that if Brooke did father a child, then the mother might not have been Taatamata but Nell herself.

The Great Lover is full of fascinating detail and unexpected insight: Nell, for example, inherits her father's genius for bee-keeping; indeed, her artistry as an apiarist, the novel suggests, is actually greater than Brooke's as a poet. Revealingly, in writing to Arlice, ninety-year-old Nell says that 'Many English people forget that he wrote prose, knowing only his poetry' but, she adds, 'to my mind it contained the best of him'. Those who have read with care Brooke's posthumous *Letters from America* may well agree with Nell on this point. Not all the details or the insights, however, are as convincing or as accurate as the bees or Nell's critical opinions. It's pushing literal attention to the last line of 'The Old Vicarage Grantchester' a bit far, to deduce that Brooke was fanatical about honey, though this perhaps provides a slightly forced justification for making Nell such an expert with the bees. We hear too much of Brooke's onanistic penchant for 'pumping ship'; and his lovemaking with everyone — except of course with Nell, for one night only — is a messy, brutal, embarrassing business. The current modish phrase 'punting from the Cambridge end' aptly describes the way Brooke loses his virginity in the novel.

Punts and punting pose a problem for Jill Dawson who, unchracteristically, gets her facts wrong: even allowing for Brooke's tendency to exaggerate, one does not have to drag a punt for 'a few hundred yards over the wooden rollers' (p.32) to avoid the weir at Laundress Green. And undergraduates certainly did not go punting up to Grantchester as early as 1899 (p.19) — pleasure punts for hire or belonging to the colleges were not seen on the Granta before the turn of the century. Gwen Raverat (née Darwin) in *Period Piece*, her memoir of a late Victorian Cambridge childhood, notes that the Darwin family 'grew up knowing how to manage boats by instinct: row-boats and canoes; but not punts, for there were then none on the Cam.' F. Scudamore, founder of the boat building and boat hiring company, opened for business in 1906.

The Great Lover may have its problems, but it is still an important, appealing achievement of this book to have presented both a 1909 and a 2009 perspective on 'the handsomest man in England'. Nell's insight is at times almost a second sight, anticipating the ambivalence with which Brooke is viewed today. Jill Dawson's success is due to the skill with which she has fashioned her narrator Nell to be simultaneously in the story and at odds with it. Sometimes, as this resourceful and resilient girl explains, 'The world simply stops. I do not belong. I am separate, outside, looking on.'

Part 3

3.1 About Madingley

For many people, 'Madingley' is synonymous with the Institute of Continuing Education (ICE) in Cambridge. Madingley Hall is indeed the headquarters of ICE, its administrative centre, and now also the location of most of the Institute's teaching. When I began to write a regular blog, 'World and time', part of its purpose was to make people more aware of Madingley as a place and to advertise the range of courses offered there. I also wanted to describe and reflect upon my own work at Madingley, teaching literature and architectural history.

'Posthumus, alas!' describes my first experience of Madingley, as a student. 'In a green shade' and 'Woodman, spare the axe!' pay tribute to the gardens and to the work of the Madingley gardeners. 'The Line of Beauty' discusses the great arch at Madingley and the link it provides, architecturally and symbolically, with the University. I hope the research I did for that article would have appealed to Carola Hicks, who formerly taught Art and Architectural History at ICE and whom I recall in 'Carola, Kempe and the King's Glass'. Finally, 'At Madingley' attempts to capture the atmosphere of a typical Madingley weekend.

Posthumus, alas!
4 January 2010

Eheu fugaces, Postume, Postume,
Labuntur anni nec pietas moram
  rugis et instanti senectae
    adferet indomitaeque morti.   (Horace, *Odes*, II. xiv).

('Alas, Posthumus, O Posthumus, the fugitive years hasten away and mere piety can delay neither wrinkles nor the onset of old age and indomitable death.')

I must confess it wasn't Anglican piety that drew me to Ely Cathedral on New Year's Day, but the need to take some photographs for a series of lectures on Cambridge architecture I've been asked to give to the Guild of Cambridge Guides. I wanted pictures to demonstrate the links between the Bishop's Palace at Ely and the Gatehouse of Jesus College, and between the Wren Library at Trinity and the north transept of the cathedral. I wanted, too, to re-photograph the interior of the second finest cathedral in England on a day when the clear winter sunlight made flashlight unnecessary.

It was very cold in the cathedral, and even the formidable Gurney Stoves in the aisles were offering barely local warmth. These great ribbed cylinders, each surmounted by a Queen Victoria-style crown, must be terrific gas-guzzlers, but they used to be coal-fired. I have a clear memory of being in the cathedral on a bleak and gloomy winter afternoon many years ago and seeing an aged verger pushing a trolley laden with buckets of anthracite from one Gurney to the next. It was like a moment from an M.R. James ghost story — 'The Stalls of Barchester Cathedral', perhaps, for which I suspect Ely may have been the setting. In the half-light, there was something sinister about the glow of the red-hot stoves.

However long ago was that? I found myself murmuring a barely-remembered line of Horace: '*Eheu fugaces, Postume, Postume*'. To my surprise, I could recall the exact date: 1 January 1975 — thirty-five years ago to the very day. What's more, I could remember exactly why I was there. I had been attending a course at Madingley Hall (my first), which ran from 28 December over the New Year until 2 January. On the last afternoon, one of the students announced she was going to drive over to Ely Cathedral, which she had never visited before, and asked if anyone would like to join her. In those days I had no car and was only too happy for the chance to re-visit the first intact medieval cathedral I'd ever seen.

(Why say 'intact'? Why 'medieval'? Because I was born in Birmingham: so the first cathedral I ever entered was St Philip's, a fine Georgian building, and the first medieval cathedral in which I set foot was the ruined shell of Coventry. Then, when I was six, we moved from the Midlands to the Fens, and Ely in those pre-Beeching days was just a short train journey from Wisbech.)

The Madingley course was on Shakespeare's late plays. It was run by John Andrew and Leo Salingar, and one of the guest lecturers was Richard Luckett, then a junior fellow at St Catharine's but for many years now the Pepys Librarian at Magdalene. We were only a small group — not more than fifteen or so. Several of us were young teachers, but one student was the recently retired Agnes Latham, shortly to publish her Arden Shakespeare *As You Like It*.

For me it was a memorable course in every way. I would not be working for the Institute now, would not be writing this blog, if I had not spent those six days at Madingley. And I remember the exhilaration of the classes, held in the Hickson Room. Leo Salingar, the distinguished scholar of Elizabethan and Jacobean drama, was developing his theory that Shakespeare's profoundest insights were found in the comedies, not the tragedies. His book *Shakespeare and the Traditions of Comedy* (still in print) was to appear in 1976 and contained chapters elaborating the ideas he teased out with us on that course.

He and John Andrew sparred cheerfully, Leo defending *Cymbeline* against John's tongue-in-cheek charge that the play was almost unactable and all but unreadable. 'Why should Shakespeare have sent poor Imogen all the way to Milford Haven, for goodness sake?' asked John. Leo, of course, had the answer. 'Is there any scene in Shakespeare more absurd,' demanded John, 'than the moment when the hapless Imogen wakes from her drugged sleep to discover a headless corpse beside her, which she promptly mistakes for her beloved Posthumus?' (It actually belongs to the treacherous Cloten.) 'It doesn't have to be absurd,' argued Leo. 'Act it and see.'

And we did. On New Year's Eve, in the Saloon, we rehearsed and then acted scenes from the late plays. Anne, a drama teacher from Solihull, gave a performance as Imogen that won great applause, and no one laughed when she reached the lines:

> O Posthumus, alas,
> Where is thy head? Where's that?[1]

People said Susan Fleetwood, playing Imogen that year for the RSC, could not have done better. My performance too was praised. I was the headless corpse.

In a green shade
27 May 2010

> No white nor red was ever seen
> So am'rous as this lovely green.   (Andrew Marvell, 'The Garden'.)

Celebrations at Madingley Hall this week: a reception to congratulate Faye Steer, our deputy Head Gardener, on becoming Young Horticulturist of the Year. Faye secured the title after winning a series of local and regional heats that led to the national finals at Kew Gardens. It's a great achievement, and a good opportunity to celebrate both Faye's success and the gardens themselves.

Where else in Cambridge can you stand looking out across a landscape (the meadows and trees in front of the Hall) that is quintessential Capability Brown: rolling grassland fringed with trees, glimpse of lake, raised bank beyond to obscure the road etc? Then turn left and take the steps down to the north terrace and discover a garden that is formal, almost Italianate, with its

---

1   *Cymbeline*, IV.ii.320-1.

croquet lawn, hedges and avenue of bushes manicured to within an inch of their lives? Or tread the gravel path that enfolds the whole meadow — still unmown at this time of year to allow the wild flowers full rein? If you sit patiently on John's Seat at this time of year, especially in the early morning, you won't have long to wait before a deer lopes into view (I've seen one hurdle over the fence and into the garden to admire the bust of Socrates) or a hare pricks its ears as it skips out from the woods.

Trees dominate the lower garden: the cedars, the copper beeches, the horse chestnut avenue in all its magnificence right now, and the giant sequoia — only this week, with the light in just the right place, I noticed a succession of circular indentations dotting its trunk to quite a height. This old tree is still the tallest at Madingley even though its crown got struck by lightning a few years ago; pock-marked like this, it now looks as if had once been caught in the cross fire of some unrecorded Civil War siege of Madingley Hall. I asked Faye what had caused the holes: woodpeckers, she said, which peck enthusiastically through the spongy outer bark only to give up in despair when their beaks strike the very hard wood beneath. I should have worked that out for myself: we often see woodpeckers at Madingley, along with pheasants, herons, treecreepers, wagtails — all creatures great and small.

Back to the north terrace, and a friendly nod at the Buddha who sits, meditative as ever, in his little aedicule above the pond. He is guarded by two dragon heads peering out from the wall. (Actually they are gargoyles probably looted from a church in Histon, but that's another story). After my first visit to Madingley, over thirty-five years ago, I wrote a poem which began here:

> The Buddha sits and smiles at the trees
> Lord of the old wall
> Immemorial
> Above the pool, pebbles in his lap.

No pebbles there now alas: frosts have bitten off half the hand which held them.

I agree with Gertrude Jekyll that a good garden should be like a succession of rooms. Madingley's garden is full of rooms and, like the rooms in the Hall itself, some are grand and formal, others small and comfortable. There's the dog cemetery, which every spring is blanketed with snowdrops; the topiary garden, peopled with strange shapes, walled by a marvellous hornbeam hedge and guarded by four venerable terracotta urns; the little lawn between the Wayper Building and the Game Shed; the sunken garden, the circular lawn, the Hazel Walk and more and more. Even now, I sometimes pinch myself to realise that I actually work here:

What wond'rous life is this I lead!
Ripe apples drop about my head;
The Luscious Clusters of the Vine
Upon my mouth do crush their Wine;
The Nectaren, and curious Peach,
Into my hands themselves do reach.[2]

No peaches grow in the garden now, but they did once. Into my hand has come a little piece of Madingley history: a battered piece of lead, a garden label, still with the nails that must once have pinned it to a south-facing wall. Laboriously, one of the gardeners of the early nineteenth century (predecessors of Richard Gant and Faye and our present garden team) had punched the following, letter by letter:

1816

Royol

Kinsington

pech

He evidently could not find an 's', and perhaps the 'a' was missing too. Robert Hogg in *The Fruit Manual* (1884) tells us that the Royal Kensington peach is a variety of the Grosse Mignonne, introduced from abroad into the royal gardens at Kensington in 1784.

Gradually, a number of these garden labels are being unearthed (sometimes literally). Faye Steer is recording them and after a day of meetings — strategic plans, five-year forecasts, risk registers and key point indicators — it is a blessed thing to be able to stagger out into the garden of Madingley which puts all such necessary but mind-numbing stuff into a different and (as Marvell perfectly puts it in 'The Garden') better perspective:

Annihilating all that's made
To a green thought in a green shade.

Woodman, spare the axe!
19 November 2009

An email to Institute staff from our Head Gardener at Madingley Hall, Richard Gant, offering Yuletide logs for sale: the logs are from the last remaining poplar tree planted on the estate after the war and originally grown to be sold for matchwood. It was felled last year.

The trees of Madingley are one of the glories of the gardens, but no tree lasts for ever. All the same, I can't help recalling how often poets lament the felling of poplars. Here's Gerard Manley Hopkins, writing in 'Binsey Poplars':

---

2   Andrew Marvell, from 'The Garden' (1652).

> O if we but knew what we do
> When we delve or hew—
> Hack and rack the growing green!

And here is William Cowper, from 'The Poplar-Field':

> The poplars are fell'd, farewell to the shade
> And the whispering sound of the cool colonnade,
> The winds play no longer, and sing in the leaves,
> Nor Ouse on his bosom their image receives.
>
> Twelve years have elaps'd since I first took a view
> Of my favourite field and the bank where they grew,
> And now in the grass behold they are laid,
> And the tree is my seat that once lent me a shade.

Who now reads Cowper? His gentle melancholy once had wide appeal (he was Jane Austen's favourite poet) but today he isn't widely read. Does this matter? I think so. Poets need friends; certainly poets who are out of fashion need them, for who can say when their turn will come again? John Donne as a poet was out of fashion for two hundred and fifty years: famously dismissed by Dryden and Johnson, and condemned by Coleridge who complained that Donne's 'muse on dromedary trots', it needed the advocacy of T.S. Eliot really to ensure his rehabilitation. In literary terms, it was almost a miracle. But then, as Cowper memorably observed, God moves in a mysterious way / His wonders to perform.

Or who now reads Herrick, the seventeenth century poet and clergyman with a penchant for pretty girls called Julia, Anthea etc.? Check the index of your *Oxford Book of English Verse*, (1900) the one edited by 'Q' – Sir Arthur Quiller Couch: you'll find that Robert Herrick has twenty nine poems in the anthology, second only to Shakespeare and well ahead of Wordsworth. Contrast that with the number of poems by Robert Herrick appearing in the 1999 edition of the *Oxford Book of English Verse*, edited by Christopher Ricks. His fall from favour has been precipitate.

Does he deserve such a decline? One of his few remaining famous poems is 'To Julia':

> WHENAS in silks my Julia goes,
> Then, then, methinks, how sweetly flows
> That liquefaction of her clothes.
>
> Next, when I cast mine eyes and see
> That brave vibration each way free;
> O how that glittering taketh me !

Perhaps not surprisingly, Herrick has been treated severely by feminist critics. More recently his poems have been subject to radical reinterpretation: I remember reading essays by eager A level students who had all been encouraged to re-read the last line of the first verse above in the context of Monica Lewinski's dress. Yet in a way, Robert Herrick (a keen tree poet – read 'To Sycamores') was the John Betjeman of his day – loved for his engaging eccentricity as much as for his poetry, and a more serious poet than most people suspected.

Betjeman is the subject of a course at Madingley Hall this weekend, and it's a sell-out which is very encouraging news. Sadly, I doubt if a course on currently unpopular poets (e.g. Herrick, Cowper) would attract as many takers, and at the moment we cannot risk offering too many courses that won't enroll good numbers of students. But with weekends still to come on Coleridge, on War Poets, on Eliot and Auden, on early Christian poetry (no doubt including 'The Dream of the Rood' – one of the earliest tree poems in English), on Sylvia Plath and on Edward Thomas (author of perhaps the best of all poems about a fallen tree: 'As the Team's Head Brass') there is much to look forward to.

The line of beauty
10 June 2011

It's embarrassing to admit, but I have only recently discovered that William Hogarth coined the phrase 'the line of beauty'. Nor had I understood its significance. For Hogarth the serpentine, S-shaped line was an essential concept in his treatise on aesthetics, *The Analysis of Beauty*: the line of beauty, according to Hogarth, indicates liveliness and movement, by contrast with the straight lines and right angles which denote only stasis and lack of vitality. Straight away, I understand why I so much prefer Gothic to classical architecture.

It makes perfect sense, as you can see for yourself at Madingley, where Lancelot 'Capability' Brown adopted Hogarth's principle in his 1758 landscaping of the east approach to the Hall. As you come in through the gates you pass on your right the lake that Brown created from a much smaller, earlier fishpond. The lake itself curves away towards the woods, and its edge is indeed S-shaped. So, too, is the drive which snakes gently - serpentine almost the right adjective to describe its course - up the slope towards the great archway which is in its own way every bit as imposing as the Hall, to which it is attached by a curtain wall.

The story of this arch and of how it came to be at Madingley is striking. Originally, it stood at one end of University Street, a narrow lane (long since gone) linking Great St Mary's Church and the Old Schools, whose main entrance it once was. Then, in the 1750s, it was carefully dismantled when the new Palladian façade of the Old Schools was erected, and was stored in case a later use might be found for it. Along came Sir John Cotton of Madingley, who wanted something imposing to greet the eyes of visitors coming up his new driveway. He bought it on 17 October 1757 from the Vice-Chancellor, Dr Sumner, for the sum of 10 guineas and carried it home well pleased, no doubt, with his bargain.

Or at least, he was until he discovered it was too small.

As originally built, the arch wasn't freestanding at all: it had been an entrance into a building, a doorway rather than an archway. Now Sir John needed it to be both wide enough to allow carriages to reach his coach-house, and strong enough to support the weight of the heraldic devices that were part of the original design. The solution he came up with was as risky as it was ingenious. He converted what had been a depressed (i.e. low) 15th century arch into a magnificent depressed ogee by adding an extra, sharply upturned and cusped, central section. This made the arch both wider and higher, and gave it the distinctive double-S shape you can see today.

The effect of this transformation was dramatic, but it was structurally a nightmare, because ogee arches are notoriously weak; in fact they are usually decorative, not structural at all. John Ruskin, in *The Stones of Venice*, had described this problem in relation to the small ogee windows and arcades to be seen everywhere in later Gothic Venetian architecture:

> So long as an arch is pure circular or pointed, it does not matter how many joints or voussoirs you have, nor where the joints are; nay, you may joint your keystone itself, and make it two-pieced. But if the arch be of any bizarre form, especially ogee, the joints must be in particular places, and the masonry simple, or it will not be thoroughly good and secure.[3]

You could not call the masonry of Madingley's arch simple. If you stand behind it and look carefully at the joints between the sections, you'll see that they are held together by iron staples – without which the arch would no doubt have collapsed years ago. Indeed, I know of no other ogee arch in the world as wide as Madingley's – nor one that supports so much weight on top of it. If you see one, please let me know.

These reflections on the arch at Madingley have been prompted by two things. First, I came across this passage in Alan Hollingsworth's 2004 novel, *The Line of Beauty*:

> The ogee curve was pure expression, decorative, not structural: a structure could be made from it, but it supported nothing more than a boss or the cross that topped an onion dome …. The double curve was Hogarth's 'line of beauty', the snakelike flicker of an instinct, of two compulsions held in one unfolding movement.[4]

3   John Ruskin, *The Stones of Venice* (1853) Book I, Ch. XI, §xiv.
4   Alan Hollingsworth, *The Line of Beauty* (London: Picador 2004) p.200.

This is a good example of free indirect discourse. Are these the thoughts of the narrator, or of the novel's main character, Nick Guest, who at this moment is gazing at a different 'line of beauty' – the naked back of his lover, Wani? 'He didn't think Hogarth had illustrated this best example of it, the dip and swell – he had chosen harps and branches, bones rather than flesh.'

Second, the arch at Madingley illustrates powerfully the links, seen and unseen, between the University and its Institute of Continuing Education, with its home at Madingley Hall. So it's only right the arch should be on the cover of the brochure introducing our new Madingley Weekly Programme. The brochure is published this week, and you can also read it online. See for yourself.

Carola, Kempe and the King's Glass
5 July 2010

I first met Carola Hicks, not at Madingley while she was Staff Tutor in the History of Art, nor at Ely when she had been Director of the Stained Glass Museum, but in South Wales where she used to visit her family at Christmas time, and where she was introduced to me as someone who wanted to find out about the stained glass artist, Charles Eamer Kempe (1837-1907).

Kempe, in the late nineteen eighties, was a largely forgotten figure, though his stained glass fills over 4000 windows world-wide and his style is rich and distinctive. I had become interested in him because he had started his career working very closely with the architect George Frederick Bodley (1827-1907) who was my hero. Discovering that there was a wealth of Kempe glass, some of it very early, in Monmouthshire where I was then living, I had joined the fledgling Kempe Society, and had started to learn about, photograph, and record the art of stained glass and the artistry of Kempe. Which is how I came to meet Carola.

In 1995 the Kempe Society held its bi-annual Members' Weekend in Cambridge, at Selwyn College, and Carola was the guest speaker. At this time I still did not associate her with Madingley; so when two years later, having moved to Cambridge myself to work for the University of Cambridge Local Examinations Syndicate (UCLES in those days, Cambridge Assessment in these), I received an invitation from Carola to run a weekend course at Madingley on Bodley and Kempe, it came as a surprise. I taught that course in the summer of 1998 and thus began my career at ICE.

Carola's work as a teacher, as a curator and as a writer was all about sharing her research with an audience that spread well beyond the walls of the university. Her first best-selling book was an introduction to stained glass (1996) in the distinctly non-academic series of Shire Publications. She was a very good lecturer indeed, much in demand whenever a new book of hers appeared. After she left the Institute to concentrate on her Fellowship at Newnham, she began to publish books that won high praise from historians and reviewers. Look up the reviews of *The Bayeux Tapestry: the Life Story of a Masterpiece* (2006) or *The King's Glass* (2008) and you'll see I am not exaggerating.

The King's Glass is, I suspect, the book for which she will be remembered. It will certainly go on being sold in Heffers and the Fitzwilliam Museum, in shops along King's Parade and in King's College Chapel itself for years to come. Chosen by the BBC as its Book of the Week, it is subtitled 'A Story of Tudor Power and Secret Art' and manages to focus the unending public fascination with the Tudor age onto one of the most iconic buildings in Cambridge, Britain, Europe, the world. It is both scholarly and popular, written for the Common Reader, as Virginia Woolf, (echoing Samuel Johnson) defined the interested and intelligent but not necessarily academic readers at whom all serious writing should be aimed. I'd love to know whether her publisher, Chatto and Windus, entered it for the Wolfson History Prize, awarded annually for the best book of new historical research written for the general public. (It was won in 2008 by Carola's colleague at Newnham, Mary Beard, with her book *Pompeii*.)

The King's Glass is a reinterpretation of the stained glass of King's College Chapel in the light of Henry's VIII's political and matrimonial ambitions. But is it much more, of course: it opens with a startling evocation of 15th century Cambridge as 'a distant little town with a dreadful climate':

> Masterpieces can bloom in unexpected places: medieval Cambridge, on the edge of the awful fens, was an unprepossessing spot. Yet out of its mists and marshes, stench and squalor, rose the chapel whose walls of glass and soaring vault would make the town famous.[5]

It ends with a finale describing how MR James, the Provost of King's, best known today for his exemplary ghost stories, invited the leading stained glass designer of the late nineteenth century to advise on the restoration of the glass which after nearly 350 years was in a parlous condition. This part of Carola's book particularly appeals to me. No one understood better than she did the craftsmanship, as well as the art, that went into making and conserving stained glass; no one was better than she at communicating a sense of excitement about looking at glass and discovering the story behind the windows. Her account of the involvement of Charles Eamer Kempe (for it was he) in the saving of the windows at King's reminds me of my first conversation with her, in Monmouth many years ago, when she asked me to tell her what I knew about Kempe.

Carola last spoke at Madingley in 2008, giving a guest lecture at a special week-long course to celebrate the 60th anniversary of the University's association with Madingley Hall. She spoke not just about the windows of

5   Carola Hicks, *The King's Glass* (London: Chatto & Windus 2008) p.2.

King's but also about her life as a writer: she was giving up her role as Director of Studies at Newnham to concentrate on writing full-time. She was fulsome in praise of her editor, the biographer Jenny Uglow who, as she acknowledged in *The King's Glass*, 'brought order and lucidity to the windows' tangled and absorbing tale'. But Carola's lucidity as a writer and as a speaker was her own, and her skills were exactly those that make teaching in continuing education, in places like Madingley, so absolutely rewarding.

Carola Hicks died two weeks ago. She had almost finished a new book, a 'biography' of the Jan Van Eyck painting, *The Arnolfini Wedding*.

At Madingley
7 August 2011

At Madingley it's been a vintage weekend: the Hall has been at capacity and seven residential courses have been in full flow: courses on Marx and Engels, on the ancient Greeks in history, on memory and mental health, on Cambridge architecture, on art and propaganda in Nazi Germany, on creative writing and on Anglo-Norman castle building.

The weather has been excellent, the gardens admired; the food has been its usual high standard, the Bar well patronised. Everything has run smoothly. There are plenty of familiar faces among the students (some already on their fourth weekend, or more, of the year) but a good number of new and younger faces too. At dinner people swap notes about speakers and courses: which course will you come to next? Which tutor should you not miss next time?

Students have many reasons for coming to Madingley. 'I think of Madingley as my college,' one says to me, 'and it's the only one I've had.' Another tells me that for her, Madingley is an academic retreat, and more: 'It's a lifeline, it keeps me sane.' Some students always choose courses on their favourite or specialist subjects; others follow a particular tutor: they will sign up for whatever he or she is teaching next time. I admire those students who deliberately opt for a topic they know little or nothing about, or who want to discover a subject that has always sounded interesting but outside their experience. 'The older I get the more I learn how little I know,' I overhear a student say during a coffee break. 'That's not a bad definition of education,' replies her neighbour, 'and anyway, isn't most of the trouble in the world caused by people who think they know everything?'

My course, 'Exploring Cambridge Architecture', is one I have taught every summer for the past twelve years. Usually it has been held in the first week of September, when Cambridge is a bit quieter. This year, as our party makes its way up Bridge Street and turns right by the Round Church heading for St. John's, I realise why a Saturday afternoon in central Cambridge in August is not the best time to be having an architecture field trip. Our group of twenty is overwhelmed (almost literally) by a tide of visiting schoolchildren 'doing' Cambridge in an afternoon. I remind myself they have as much right as we do to be there, but I'm thankful when we are able to cross the threshold of the College and enter the tranquillity of First Court.

One of the strands of our course this weekend has been the Victorian re-invention of Cambridge: the way the Victorians embarked on a building spree that attempted to re-imagine what a medieval university ought to look like in the nineteenth century. But Sir Gilbert Scott's new Chapel for St. John's, built during the 1860s, shows how they sometimes challenged, as well as re-imagined, the idea of Cambridge architecture. His Chapel, in the sunlight and with a visiting choir rehearsing for Evensong within, looks, feels and sounds awe-inspiring, but is still outrageously out of scale and out of keeping with the rest of the College buildings and with the winding streetscape outside.

Earlier, we had been talking about what Alec Clifton-Taylor used to call 'architectural good manners'. I had shown an image during my lecture on 'The anatomy of a Cambridge College' of the view of King's College Chapel seen from across the Backs (or the 'Kinge's back-sides' as they are labelled on Richard Lyne's 1574 map of Cambridge). It's probably one of the most photographed views in Europe, certainly in England, but also in a way one of the most shocking. The eighteenth century Gibbs Building, less than a cricket pitch's length apart from the Chapel, fights it in every way. The Chapel is stately Gothic, the Gibbs Building aggressively classical; the Chapel celebrates the Perpendicular, Gibbs' asserts the horizontal; the cold Portland stone of the latter offends the warmer Weldon stone of the former. In every way the design and positioning of the Gibbs ought to be condemned as architectural bad manners, crass insensitivity. But it isn't. 'One of the things age teaches us,' says another of my students back at Madingley, is that architectural forgiveness can be just as important as architectural good manners.'

As ever, one learns from one's students. 'Humility is endless,' T.S. Eliot reminds us in *Four Quartets*. I partly repent me of my intemperance about the Gibbs Building, but at least it has spurred the students into looking again at what they may have been taken for granted. Assumptions have been challenged, eyes opened, thresholds crossed. Once one has learned to see something differently, at whatever age, one cannot go back to thinking about it in the old ways: otherwise, like T.S. Eliot's Magi, one is 'no longer at ease here, in the old dispensation'.[6] Lifelong learning in action, and a good weekend to be at Madingley.

---

6   T.S. Eliot, 'Journey of the Magi', *Collected Poems* 1909-1962 (London: Faber and Faber, 1963) p.110.

3.2 On lit. crit. and teaching literature

All the pieces in this section focus on the job of literature – on the one hand, what it means to study literature and why one does it; on the other, why and how one teaches it in continuing education. 'What is the use of literature?' takes as its starting point a seminar of that title arranged by the Royal Society of Literature (RSL) and concludes by illustrating how a newly published novel presents me with opportunities for answering through my teaching the question posed by the RSL. 'End-of-term report' illustrates the work done by one of my groups of students and is a tribute to their commitment and to the way they had worked with me in evening classes on challenging literary texts and topics throughout an academic year.

It is impossible to teach literature in Cambridge and not be aware of the legacy of I.A. Richards, F.R. Leavis and their successors. But the man who actually established a School of English in Cambridge, Sir Arthur Quiller-Couch, is these days too readily dismissed as an Edwardian belles-lettristic *amateur. He deserves better, and 'On Q' was written as I prepared to introduce him to my students at the start of a course on 'Cambridge Critics and Cambridge Criticism'. The tensions between literary criticism and literary theory have existed in Cambridge as strongly as anywhere and 'Lit. Crit.' was my grateful response to a review article by Stefan Collini, Professor of English Literature and Intellectual History at Cambridge, restating the value and importance of literary criticism. 'Romeo and Radiohead' started with a chance overhearing of a song in a pub but led to an exercise in something I should like to spend more time doing: close reading in Shakespeare. Close reading is also the subject of 'To Sycamores', my account of a class in which we wrestled with the ambiguities behind the title and the text of a poem by Robert Herrick. Finally, 'Life in the Cosmos' began with the launch of the Madingley Lectures in 2010 and ended with my revisiting an author I have long enjoyed but too rarely taught, Geoffrey Chaucer.*

'What is the use of literature?'
30 June 2011

A colleague of mine, a geographer, was dining on High Table recently. 'So tell me,' said her neighbour, 'What use are geographers to mankind?' All along the table, eyes and ears turned towards my colleague. 'Well,' she replied, 'we make good travelling companions: we understand the weather, and we seldom get lost.' Neat answer. It made me wonder (not for the first time) how would I have replied, about English?

I thought of this last week when invited to a Royal Society of Literature seminar with the provocative title, 'What is the use of Literature?' The panel of speakers included the great and/or good – Polly Toynbee as Chair, Sir Andrew Motion – plus writers and academics from King's College London (where the seminar was held) and Cambridge.

For me, the most interesting speaker was the Scottish-African novelist, Aminatta Forna. "If you want to know a country," Forna has written, "read its writers." It seemed good advice and, knowing little about Sierra Leone other than its place on the map and that it has endured a bloody civil war, I immediately went out and bought her novel, *The Memory of Love* (2010). It's a longish book (445 pages) but I have spent a lot of time in the last few days on long train journeys – Cambridge > Grenoble > Paris – and have now read and re-read it, three times. It's been a remarkable experience.

For a start, this is the first novel I've ever read whose central character is called Adrian. Has not every Emma at some time measured herself against Jane Austen's eponymous heroine? Or Flaubert's? How often does an Adrian get the chance to do likewise? This is not a trivial point, and I have found myself wondering how far my reactions to this weak but well-intentioned character have been affected by our shared forename.

Adrian Lockheart is a psychologist, seconded to work as a psychotherapist in Sierra Leone after its Civil War. Gradually, through his patients, he comes to understand something of the War and its effects on the lives of those who survived it. But where he sees signs of a whole population suffering different forms of Post Traumatic Stress Disorder, those who have lived through the war see it differently. Dr Attila, director of the local mental hospital, tells him bluntly, 'You call it a disorder, my friend. We call it *life*.' Everyone has their own reasons to grieve or to keep silent, and the scars of war – the physical and the emotional, the amputations and the nightmares – are all too present. Nowhere more so than in a hospital: much of the novel's action takes place in and around the emergency operating theatre or in the mental hospital's locked wards where the patients are chained to their beds and former enemies lie side by side.

Adrian has come to Africa to prove to himself that he can make a long-term difference to people's lives *('So tell me, Mr Lockheart, what use are psychotherapists to mankind?')* and at first he believes 'that since arriving here his life has seemed more charged with meaning than it ever had in London.' He befriends a young orthopaedic surgeon, Kai, who has become expert at repairing the savagely damaged limbs of those he treats. 'C' on a patient's hospital notes stands for 'cleaver attack'.

Kai is an insomniac, partly because of the ceaseless demands of his work at the hospital, partly because of the appalling nightmares he has. Dreams and nightmares, sleep and sleeplessness, are a crucial thread running throughout the book. For Kai, the tragedy of the Civil War is compounded by his own private tragedy: his girlfriend, Nenebah, disappeared during it, and he has found no trace of her: his memories of her 'come at unguarded moments, when he cannot sleep.' When he treats patients with severed limbs and hears how they complain of 'feeling pain in the lost limbs, the aching ghost of a hewn hand or foot', he knows it's a trick of the mind: 'the nerves continued to transmit signals between the brain and the ghost limb. The pain is real, yes, but it is a memory of pain.' Now he makes the crucial connection:

> When he wakes from dreaming of her, is it not the same for him? The hollowness in his chest, the tense yearning, the loneliness he braces himself against every morning until he can immerse himself in work and forget. Not love. Something else, something with a power that endures. Not love, but a memory of love.[1]

Meanwhile Adrian has fallen for Mamakay, a girl who plays the clarinet and seems to have a past so strange he cannot at first comprehend it or her. But it's Mamakay who has the clearest view of what is happening in post-war Sierra Leone:

> People are blotting out what happened, fiddling with the truth, creating their own version of events to fill in the blanks. A version of the truth which puts them in a good light, that wipes out whatever they did or failed to do and makes certain none of them will be blamed. They're all doing it … .[2]

She challenges Adrian's belief in the value of what he does and doubts his commitment to staying and helping the people he treats as patients:

> Whatever you say, you will go away from here, you will publish your papers and give talks, and every time you do so you will make their version of events the more real, until it becomes indelible.[3]

The Memory of Love is an important and beautifully written novel. It's a book I want to teach, because it's a book that teaches its readers. It teaches you how easy and dangerous it is to rewrite history, while paradoxically fiction may show you truths history never can. With this book I hope I could persuade anyone that literature is self-evidently useful. No, more than that: essential.

---

1   Aminatta Forna, *The Memory of Love* (London: Bloomsbury 2010) p.185.
2   *ibid.*, p.351.
3   *ibid.*

End-of-term report
1 August 2010

Coming back to Cambridge from a meeting in London last week, I fell asleep on the train and woke up at Ely. It could have been worse: I might have slept until King's Lynn. All the same it was both embarrassing and a nuisance. It meant I was late getting to Madingley Hall for an end-of-course class with the students who have been completing a project module as part of the Diploma of Higher Education in Modern English Literature. The students were very forbearing.

There were two parts to the evening's discussion. First, each student spoke in turn about his or her project. The range of topics was exhilarating: Shaz, who has been commuting from Wolverhampton each week this year for his classes, chose 'Waiting as a theme in Beckett's *Waiting for Godot* and Chekhov's *Three Sisters*'; Tamsin also chose Beckett, writing about the dramatic impact of a play 'in which nothing happens, twice', as the *Irish Times* reviewer, Vivian Mercier, so aptly summarised the plot. Beckett and Pinter had been the two key authors studied in the Lent Term course, and part of the point of the Project Module is to enable students to extend their exploration of the authors, texts and topics studied earlier in the year.

Jim explored the poetry of Marianne Moore, Diana wrote about the kaleidoscopic construction of a late novel by Elizabeth Bowen, *Eva Trout*. Eileen devoted her project to a detailed analysis of Virginia Woolf's stream of consciousness technique in *To the Lighthouse,* while Molly contrasted the way Seamus Heaney has written about childhood in his early and his late poetry, and explored the significant differences between published versions of poems such as 'The Aerodrome'; Emily, also returning to Heaney (one of the key authors — the other was Auden — whose later poetry was the subject of last Michaelmas Term's course) explored his appropriation of classical texts and myths in his late poetry and drama.

Anil, too, wrote about Heaney, but from a different perspective. He took an unflinching look at Philip Larkin's unflinching poem about death, 'Aubade':

> An only life can take so long to climb
> Clear of its wrong beginnings, and may never.[4]

Anil argued that even such a poem as this proved poetry was an affirmative art; and, in doing so, he reproved Heaney for his rather reductive and disappointed reading of the poem.

---

4   Philip Larkin, 'Aubade', *Collected Poems* (London: The Marvell Press and Faber and Faber, rev. ed. 1990) p.208.

Everyone agreed with Anil, in the second part of our discussion, that one of the things they had learned from researching and writing these project essays was the importance of having the courage to challenge other people's critical views, no matter how eminent the critic. Literary criticism, after all, is a debate. It should have the qualities that mark out effective debating: sharp thinking, clear argument, conviction. Professor Rachel Falconer has put this very well:

> Literature — not to mention film, theatre and the visual arts — is a tool to think with, and the business of literary criticism should be to make sure that that thinking is clearer, sharper and more penetrating than it otherwise might be.[5]

There is plenty of evidence of sharp and penetrating thinking in the project essays I am now marking, but more (and even more important) than that is the sense of enjoyment engaging with serious writers can bring. Larkin himself has said that:

> at bottom poetry, like all art, is inextricably bound up with giving pleasure, and if a poet loses his pleasure-seeking audience he has lost the only audience worth having, for which the dutiful mob that signs on every September is no substitute.[6]

The students I have been teaching on this Diploma programme could hardly be described as a 'dutiful mob': they are cheerfully stroppy and independently-minded to a fault. They've even started their own informal literary society. They keep those of us who teach them permanently on our toes. But all of them are at the same time fully paid-up members of Larkin's pleasure-seeking audience. I hope they will indeed be signing on for more of the same next term.

On Q
17 January 2011

Once upon a time, anyone glancing at my title, 'On Q', might well have said, 'Aha, you're blogging about Sir Arthur Quiller-Couch!' Indeed I am. 'Q' was both his pen name and his nickname. Look at the cover of the old *Oxford Book of English Verse* (1900), which he edited and which still sits on many shelves: there under the title is the single letter, Q. Friends, students, (enemies, too, no doubt) all called him Q, and his rooms in Jesus College (C staircase, First Court) were known as the Q-bicle.

---

5   Rachel Falconer, quoted in Matthew Reisz, 'Style Points', *Times Higher Education*, 15 July 2010, p39.

6   Philip Larkin, *Required Writing*, (London: Faber and Faber, 1983) p.82.

Sir Arthur Quiller-Couch (1863–1944): Cornishman, man of letters, writer of novels and books for children, poet and anthologist, academic, lecturer, founding father of the School of English (*sc.* the Faculty) at Cambridge; I hope I have listed these attributes in an order he'd have approved. He was first in a line of idiosyncratic Cornish writers who flourished through most of the twentieth century: Daphne du Maurier, A.L. Rowse (possibly), Charles Causley, John Betjeman (by adoption and burial). He liked to let people know he was Cornish. In 'The Commerce of Thought', a lecture he delivered at the Royal Institution in London, he lamented the passing of the three- and four-masted sailing ships, 'these beautiful things that used to wing it home, five months without sighting land, and anchor under my garden' — the garden of his house, The Haven, opening on to the estuary at Fowey.

He was sent as a boy to Clifton College — for the rest of his life he was fond of referring to 'our great public schools' — and thence to Trinity College, Oxford, where he read Greats and achieved a reputation as a poet. But he believed passionately in the importance of a liberal education for all — not just for the privileged. He was briefly a lecturer in Classics at Oxford, before taking up a career as a novelist, short story writer, editor, essayist, reviewer and independent scholar. He edited the New Cambridge Shakespeare series, had a passion for seventeenth century religious poets, and in 1912 became Edward VII Professor of English at Cambridge, where he stayed for the rest of his life. He was precise about places: on the same page of the lecture in which he referred to his garden in Cornwall, he began a sentence thus:

> For my pupils in Cambridge, the other day, I drew, as well as I could, in the New Lecture Theatre, the picture of an old Roman colonist in his villa in Britain.[7]

Q is mainly remembered today (if at all) for his anthologies and for a couple of books that used to be readily found in second-hand bookshops: *On The Art of Writing* (1916) and *On The Art of Reading* (1920). These contain lectures mostly delivered in Cambridge during the First World War: they sometimes give an unexpected insight into what the University was like in those days. In a lecture, 'Patriotism in English Literature', he recalls how in 1913 he saw:

> a cavalry troop of the C.U.O.T.C. [Cambridge University Officer Training Corps] clattering home over the bridge by Magdalene ... calling to one another, as they wheeled by St. John's, as if all Cambridge belonged to them — as now in retrospect one sees that it did. For these also were in their careless confident way preparing themselves.

---

7   Sir Arthur Quiller-Couch, *Studies in Literature* 1st. Series (Cambridge: Cambridge University Press, 1924) p.8.

They are gone. They have taken their cheerfulness out of Cambridge; and they have left us to an empty university, to dull streets, the short days, the long nights. And we who, by age or for other causes, must stay behind, must needs question our heavy thoughts.[8]

What were Q's heavy thoughts? I think he was someone who — in spite of his outward appearance of suave self-confidence — was not at ease in his own skin. He was a fervent believer that English Language and Literature were central to a liberal, humanistic tradition, and it was this belief that led to his campaign (ultimately successful) to establish a separate School of English at Cambridge; but he did not believe that English should be professionalised, and he hated the idea that it should be treated as a 'subject'. Although his love of the Classics underpinned all his teaching of English, he knew that the Classics were the preserve of the rich and, what was worse, that children who spent their schooldays learning Latin and Greek often knew very little of their own literature and — worse again — often could not write their own language well. He hated jargon, abstractions and pomposity (his lecture 'On jargon' should still be compulsory reading) and despaired of the way English Literature was taught in schools:

> I declare to you that Literature was *not* written for schoolmasters, nor for schoolmistresses. I would not exchange it for a wilderness of schoolmasters.[9]

(NB the echo of Shylock's anguish in that second sentence.) He was also acutely aware that he was teaching at a moment when the direction of Literature was taking a radical turn, the turn to modernism. He believed profoundly that the literature of the present day should be taught and that students should be taught (as I believe, too) how to read modern literature. Yet he knew that, temperamentally, his own love of literature and his own ear for language were steeped in the literature of the past, and that he had great difficulty in appreciating the T.S. Eliots and the Ezra Pounds who were beginning to steal his thunder. Nevertheless, it was his commitment to critical appraisal that led the way to the development of practical criticism as the key principle of Cambridge English, exemplified in the next generation by I.A. Richards, F.R. Leavis and, after them, by William Empson.

I find Sir Arthur Quiller-Couch a fascinating, contradictory and unduly neglected figure, and I shall begin my teaching this term (a course on Cambridge critics and Cambridge criticism) with him.

---

8   *ibid.*, pp.300-301.
9   Sir Arthur Quiller-Couch, *On the Art of Reading* (Cambridge: Cambridge University Press, 1924) p.104.

Lit. Crit.

3 April 2011

I was much taken by a piece in this weekend's *Guardian Review*. Stefan Collini was reviewing a new book, *The Good of the Novel*, edited by Liam McIlvanney and Ray Ryan and published by Faber. It sounded my kind of book: a collection of thirteen essays about recent novels, most of which I have read and some of which (J.M. Coetzee's *Disgrace*, for instance, and Colm Tóibín's *The Master*) I have also taught.

I admire Collini's writing. He is good at pithy, memorable statements. One that has stuck in my mind from a few years back and which I often quote is 'Close reading is inseparable from hard thinking'. Quite. Nearly eighteen months ago he wrote in the *Times Literary Supplement* a passionate polemic, defending the humanities in the face of what he saw as the absurd decision to assess the quality of academic research and scholarship in terms of its impact outside academia. The impact of impact has been a contentious issue ever since, and Collini's essay will be cited for years to come, I'm sure.

What struck me about his *Guardian* review on Saturday was, as it happens, also about the essay. He was talking about the value of a particular kind of writing:

> These thirteen essays together constitute something like a manifesto, speaking up for the continuing vitality of that traditional form, the critical essay, a discursive piece of writing which is longer than a journalistic review but more accessible than an academic article.[10]

Collini's enthusiasm for the critical essay is heartening indeed; even more so, his definition of literary criticism as an intellectual activity:

> Such criticism, at its best, involves a sustained attentiveness to how a work of literature achieves its effects plus a focused analysis of what kind of achievement it represents in the scale of things.

Some people might seize on that phrase 'at its best'. How and why, they might ask, should one presume to make such value judgments about literature — or about literary criticism, come to that? Isn't that simply intellectual snobbery? Collini is not a whit abashed:

> The best criticism involves being intelligent about the best writing, and the best writing involves being intelligent about living.

I'm delighted Collini has said this so emphatically, and said it just now. In a single sentence he has reasserted the importance of intelligent reading and writing and of the relationship between writer, text and reader. In doing so, he has summed up just why literature matters so much outside as well

---

10 Stefan Collini, 'The art of making it up', *Guardian Review*, 2 April 2011.

as inside the academy, and why studying it with students, whether eight, eighteen, forty-eight or eighty years old is so worthwhile.

I can't imagine a more rewarding job than teaching people who actually want to learn how to become critical readers of literature. As part of that work, I have been lucky in the past fourteen years to spend a lot of time working with teachers on new — and old — ways of teaching literature: helping (mainly) young people learn how to read critically and with respect both for what they read and for the writers who wrote what they read. I spent two days last week in Paris, with a group of fifty teachers from all over France, doing just that. And while I was there, a few lines by Susan Sontag about the importance of literature kept nagging away at the back of my mind. I couldn't quite remember them, but I've looked them up now that I am home again:

> Serious fiction writers think about moral problems practically. They tell stories. They narrate. They evoke our common humanity in narratives with which we can identify, even though the lives lived may be remote from our own. They stimulate our imagination. The stories they tell enlarge and complicate — and, therefore, improve — our sympathies. They educate our capacity for moral judgment.[11]

I hope Sefan Collini would agree with Sontag about this. Certainly her words resonate with what he wrote in his polemical *TLS* essay, and together they convince me that what I've been trying to do all these years has been fundamentally worthwhile:

> It is worth insisting that what we call 'the humanities' are a collection of ways of encountering the record of human activity in its greatest richness and diversity. To attempt to deepen our understanding of this or that aspect of that activity is a purposeful expression of human curiosity and is — insofar as the expression makes any sense in this context — an end in itself.[12]

Romeo and Radiohead
6 December 2010

I was having lunch on Sunday in one of my favourite pubs, The Rusty Bike in Exeter, when Radiohead's 'Exit Music (for a Film)' started to play. If you ever saw Baz Luhrman's film of *Romeo and Juliet* you'll remember this music: it accompanies the climax of the film when Romeo (Leonardo di Caprio, in one of his earliest movies) finds Juliet (Clare Danes) in the tomb and, assuming she is dead, drinks poison:

11 Susan Sontag, *At The Same Time*, London: Hamish Hamilton, 2007) p.213.
12 Stefan Collini, 'Impact on humanities', *Times Literary Supplement*, 13 November 2009.

> Come, bitter conduct, come, unsavoury guide!
> Thou desperate pilot, now at once run on
> The dashing rocks thy sea-sick weary bark.
> Here's to my love! [*Drinks*] O true apothecary!
> Thy drugs are quick. Thus with a kiss I die. [*Dies.*] [13]

Whereupon Juliet wakes up — the drug given to her by Friar Laurence (Pete Postlethwaite) having worn off — and, finding Romeo dead beside her, grabs his dagger, stabs herself and dies for real.

Romeo's dying speech is a good example of Shakespeare's way of lighting on an idea, creating an image from it and then seeing how far it can be pushed. Here Romeo begins with a literal adjective 'bitter' — the poison is bitter-tasting — which has also a metaphorical significance: the poison will lead Romeo to a bitter end. If it is going to lead him, then it is a 'conduct[or]', and Shakespeare immediately parallels the phrase 'bitter conduct' with another, 'unsavoury guide', where (as before) the adjective has both a literal and a metaphorical sense.

Next Romeo produces a third parallel phrase: 'Thou desperate pilot'. In these three phrases each signifier has become successively more sharply defined: 'conduct … guide … pilot'. By contrast, the adjectives have become vaguer — or at least more suggestive: 'bitter … unsavoury … desperate'. A pilot's job is to steer a ship to safety; so a desperate pilot is presumably one struggling to prevent the ship from going aground. But he might also be one who instils despair into his passengers, and here Romeo, seeing himself as the ship (the sea-sick weary bark), orders the pilot (the poison) to run the ship onto the 'dashing rocks' — that is, of course, to kill him. The transferred epithet 'dashing rocks' is another instance of Shakespeare's concentration of ideas: the rocks are not themselves dashing — but the ship (Romeo) will be dashed against them and destroyed as a consequence of the pilot's (the poison's) actions.

As he swallows the poison, Romeo offers a toast — 'Here's to my love!' Is this addressed to Juliet? Presumably, though it could also be aimed ironically not at her but rather at his love for her, the passion that has made him so sea-sick he longs to die. Immediately, the potion does its work, and Romeo's penultimate words are actually addressed to the 'true apothecary' who had sold him the poison in the first place: 'Thy drugs are quick'. Even here, Shakespeare plays on words for the drug which is killing him is 'quick' — that is, it contains life. As in 'the quick and the dead', the deathly poison is both itself and the opposite of itself.

It is characteristic of Shakespeare that Romeo's final line is simultaneously proleptic — it anticipates what is to happen — and analeptic: it looks back to

---

13 *Romeo and Juliet* V.iii.116-120.

what has already happened. 'Thus with a kiss I die' is a line we shall remember when Juliet wakes up, sees that Romeo has poisoned himself and kisses him in the hope that the poison still on his lips will still be potent enough to kill her too. But by then it is too late: the drug is no longer 'quick' and she has not been quick enough to return Romeo's kiss.

The line is analeptic in that it reminds the audience of Romeo's visit to the Apothecary. Remember: as soon as he is told (mistakenly) that Juliet is already dead, he resolves to abandon his exile, return to Verona, break into her tomb (the Capulet 'Monument') and die beside her. He recalls seeing a destitute-looking apothecary, and heads straight to his shop:

> Come, hither, man. I see that thou art poor;
> Hold, here is forty ducats: let me have
> A dram of poison; such soon-speeding gear
> As will disperse itself through all the veins,
> That the life-weary taker may fall dead,
> And that the trunk may be discharged of breath
> As violently as hasty powder fired
> Doth hurry from the fatal canon's womb.[14]

Romeo certainly got what he asked for, even if his (and Shakespeare's) grasp of what happens when a canon is fired was a bit tenuous: somehow, the image of 'hasty powder' hurrying from the 'fatal canon's womb' does less than justice to the idea of firing a canon — as the Globe theatre would one day find to its cost, when the wadding (not the powder) from a canon fired during a performance of *Henry VIII* set fire to the thatch and burnt the theatre down.

Analepsis is often defined these days as 'flashback' — a term introduced to describe a narrative technique in film rather than in theatre. It's rare on stage, though you could say that the dumb show in *Hamlet*, in which the death of Hamlet's father, re-enacted in mime by the Players at Elsinore, is a form of flashback. That scene, incidentally, is another example of quick-acting poison proving useful in a Shakespeare plot — as it also does, of course, in the final scene of the play where poisoned chalices and poisoned rapiers bring the play to a suitably bloody climax.

Come to think of it, if Baz Luhrman ever fancied having a go at filming *Hamlet*, Radiohead's 'Exit Music (for a Film)' would fit *Hamlet* even better than *Romeo and Juliet*. Actually, I didn't like the song much and I thought the words were rubbish compared with Shakespeare's — which they very effectively drowned. In any case, if you want to see how *Romeo and Juliet* should be filmed, watch Zeffirelli's 1968 movie.

---

14 *Romeo and Juliet* IV.iv.58-65.

'To Sycamores'
11 February 2011

Never underestimate titles.

We had been making heavy weather of Robert Herrick's poem 'To Sycamores'. The consensus among the class was that they did not much like it, but they weren't sure how to explain why:

> I'm sick of love; O let me lie
> Under your shades, to sleep or die!
> Either is welcome; so I have
> Or here my Bed, or here my Grave.
> Why do you sigh, and sob, and keep
> Time with the tears, that I do weep?
> Say, have you sense, or do you prove
> What *Crucifixions* are in Love?
> I know you do; and that's the why,
> You sigh for Love, as well as I.[15]

I had not divulged the name of the poet or the date of the poem, but I had (contrary to the instructions of I.A. Richards whose methods of Practical Criticism I was trying to illustrate) given away the title, because I believe that titles are important: they are like a label, giving a clue about how the poet wants you to approach the poem. Imagine John Donne's poem 'A Nocturnal upon St Lucie's Day' called simply 'December 13th', or Wordsworth's 'Daffodils' re-titled 'Walking round Ullswater'. Any change makes a difference to what we expect from a poem.

Sometimes, too, the title may be an integral part of the poem itself – Ezra Pound's haiku 'In a Station of the Metro' depends upon the title to provide the necessary context: without it the poem cannot really work. Eliot's poem 'The Love Song of J Alfred Prufrock' also leans heavily upon its title. Minus the pedantic name (with its initial initial and the insinuations of the surname: prudent? prudish? prurient? and 'frock' for goodness' sake? frock coat, let us hope) the poem would surely be diminished. What kind of 'love song' is it, after all?

So, we started (and finished) with the title. Herrick was fond of titles that told you to whom the poem was addressed. Lots of them are addressed 'To Julia', 'To Anthea' or to other (mythical?) mistresses. 'To Daffodils', 'To the Virgins, to Make Much of Time' are two textbook examples of *Carpe Diem* poetry. But is a speaker who addresses himself to a glade of trees, and announces that he is 'sick of love', to be taken seriously? And in any case, I asked, is being 'sick of love', in the sense of having had enough of love, the same thing as being love-sick?

---

15 Robert Herrick, 'To Sycamores' in F.W. Moorman (ed.), *The Poetical Works of Robert Herrick* (Oxford: Oxford University Press, 1921) p.157.

Among the class, opinion was divided. Ian McEwan's title *Enduring Love* was invoked. John thought the idiom 'to be sick of something' (i.e. 'to be fed up with') was probably later than 1640s, and Peter agreed. He was reluctant to believe that the poet could be saying anything so cheap: he must only mean that he is pining for love of someone. But, after the class, Emily emailed to say she'd looked up 'sick of' and found that it had indeed been used to mean 'fed up with' at the time Herrick was writing. John was unrepentant, pointing out that when Malvolio is accused by Olivia in *Twelfth Night* of being 'sick of self-love' she treats this as an illness: he tastes 'with a distemper'd appetite' because he is out of sorts. If any one is fed up it is those who have to put up with the moans of the person who complains of being sick of love.

So, we didn't agree about this – or about much else – but we had at least started to look at the words and the imagery with more care. In particular, the lines

> Say, have you sense, or do you prove
> What *Crucifixions* are in Love?

caused trouble. What did they actually mean? Should an Anglican clergyman, Jim asked (once I had revealed the author's identity and given a brief sketch of his career), be using a word like 'crucifixions' in a love poem anyway? Was this an acceptable profanity? Could the trees, the sycamores, really represent all those who have been tortured to death by love? Sarah argued that if this had been what Herrick meant, then in a sense it was primarily a religious poem, the plural word 'crucifixions' extending the notion of God's love for mankind.

I do not see the poem in this way myself, but I agreed that even if 'To Sycamores' was not exactly a love poem – it wasn't addressed to, or about, a particular person – it was certainly a poem about love, and about the experience of love. It was, I thought, a poem that simultaneously asked to be taken seriously and taken as a joke. The crucifixions image was at once witty, profane and heartfelt.

But why sycamores? I suggested that while it would have been more obvious to have addressed weeping willows, Herrick had chosen sycamores for several reasons. First, the poem is set in summer, for it is the leaves on the trees that supply the 'shade'. While the poet weeps, the sycamores 'sigh and sob', keeping time with the tears the poet himself is shedding. And this is not because they shed their leaves: it is because their distinctive, tear-shaped sycamore seeds keep helicoptering down, just as his tears keep falling.

Second, this idea of the trees sobbing in sympathy with the poet is both a conceit, (*scilicet* a concept, a neat and clever idea which underpins the argument of the poem) and an example of pathetic fallacy. But it is more than these, for the poem is controlled by the idea of the sycamores from the moment you read the title until you reach the last line:

> You sigh for Love, as well as I.

The sycamores, after all, embody a double pun – in the way that no other species of tree can do. Herrick was an admirer of the Latin poet Ovid, and especially of his collection of poems entitled *Amores*. So, turn the name of the trees into a Latin phrase – *Sic amores* ('thus loves') and you get a cheeky nod in the direction of Ovid. Then, lastly, as if to corroborate the idea of the poet fed up with the way he is treated by Love, the title offers a second pun: 'Sick *amours*'.

Never underestimate titles.

Life in the cosmos
11 January 2011

It would have been hard to imagine a more auspicious start to the Madingley Lectures: the Vice-Chancellor introducing the lecturer as 'the greatest scientist in Britain' and Lord Rees, the speaker, holding the audience in Madingley Hall's Saloon (and an overspill audience in the Board Room downstairs) spellbound with an illustrated lecture on 'Life in the cosmos', making an almost unimaginable subject tantalisingly imaginable.

It was good to learn, for instance, that if there is life elsewhere in the universe it/they will be composed of the same atoms of stardust as we are. Good, too, to hear Lord Rees declare that good science-fiction is better than second-rate science, and just as likely to be true. I was glad to hear him quote Woody Allen: 'Eternity is very long, especially towards the end.' But what struck me most was the Astronomer Royal's own personal model of the universe: a ring in the form of a great green snake devouring its own tail.

I found this immensely reassuring. In the end, despite the extraordinary achievements of astrophysics and the endeavours of manned and unmanned space exploration — all of which Lord Rees celebrated during the course of his lecture — we need metaphor to describe what we cannot fully comprehend. Literature always attempts to answer the question, *What is it like?* with the answer, *It is like this.*

There is a marvellous example of this in the Second Book of Chaucer's *House of Fame*. In a dream, the poet himself has been swept up into the sky by a giant eagle:

> Thus sone in a while he
> Was flowen from the ground so hye
> That al the world, as to myn yë

No more semed than a prikke;
Or elles was the air so thikke
That y ne myghte not discerne.[16]

Anyone who has ever looked out of the window of an aeroplane as it climbs towards its cruising height will recognise that Chaucer has imagined and described exactly *what it's like*.

Lord Rees had a lot to say about galaxies, and he showed an extraordinary simulation of the effect of plasma dynamics as two galaxies collided in space. Geoffrey Chaucer knew about galaxies, too: the same eagle (who calls him Geffrey, and provides a running commentary as he carries him up into space) tells him to 'turn upward thy face':

See yonder, loo, the Galaxie,
Which men clepeth the Milky Wey,
For it is whit (and somme, parfey,
Kallen hyt Watlynge Strete)
That ones was ybrent with hete.[17]

Look, see in the distance that Galaxy
which people call the Milky Way
because it is white (and some indeed
Call it Watling Street)
And was once burnt with heat [from the sun].

The idea that anyone ever called the Milky Way Watling Street was a new one on me. Luckily F.N. Robinson, the great editor of Chaucer (*The Works of Geoffrey Chaucer*, O.U.P. 1933) came to my rescue, suggesting that Watling Street (an ancient track long before the Romans paved it) may have been a corruption of Walsingham Way — a pilgrim route, therefore, to one of the most important shrines in medieval England. Robinson points out that in southern Europe the Milky Way was known as *la via di San Jacopo* (i.e. the road to Santiago de Compostella). I like the idea that people used to call the Milky Way, that great swathe of rather hazy light, after the pilgrim routes that, they hoped, might lead them — while still on earth — a little closer to heaven.

Chaucer took astronomy very seriously. Read his *Treatise on the Astrolabe*; or, if life is too short for that, *The Franklin's Tale*, where he also pokes some gentle fun at astrology. The model of the universe that Chaucer knew was the Aristotelian or Ptolomeic system: a geocentric universe, with the planets as a set of spheres, one outside the other (rather like the layers of an onion),

---

16 Geoffrey Chaucer, *The House of Fame* (ll.904–909.).
17 *The House of Fame*, ll.936-940.

revolving around the earth. Beyond the sphere of the last visible planet, Saturn, were the 'fixed stars' dotted all over the eighth sphere. At the end of his epic poem *Troilus and Criseyde*, Chaucer records how Troilus is slain by 'the fierse Achille':

> And whan that he was slayn in this manere
> His lighte goost ful blissfully is went
> Up to the holughnesse of the eighthe spere
>
> . . .
>
> And ther he saugh, with ful avysement,
> The erratic sterres, herkenyng armonye
> With sownes ful of hevenyssh melodie.[18]

> *And when he had been slain in this way,*
> *His spirit ascended blissfully*
> *Up to the hollowness of the eighth sphere*
> *And there he saw with perfect clarity ['observation']*
> *The wandering stars, hearing harmony [i.e. the music of the spheres]*
> *With sounds full of heavenly melody.*

As I listened, star-struck, to Lord Rees illustrating life in the cosmos in ways that I could (almost) understand, I remembered these passages from Chaucer, scarcely read since I was a student, and resolved to re-read them. I am glad I've been prompted to do so: across a gap of six hundred years — hardly a hiccup in the life of the universe — poet and scientist paint astonishingly similar pictures. At one point in his lecture Lord Rees explained how an alien, looking at 'the small blue dot which is our planet', would notice that, alone in our galaxy, the earth is covered with continents surrounded by oceans. As he said this, I remembered how Troilus, too, from the edge of space, is able to describe the world in exactly the same way: 'This litel spot of erthe,' he calls it, 'that with the se embraced is'.[19]

Chaucer, like Lord Rees, has the gift of looking at the cosmos, and teaching us *what it's like*. I'm grateful to them both.

---

18 Geoffrey Chaucer, *Troilus and Criseyde*, Bk. Vll.1807-1813.
19 *ibid.*, l.1815.

3.3 Concerning E.M. Forster

No writer has had a greater effect on my sense of the value of literature and of the importance of teaching it than E.M. Forster; and the discovery that he had in the earlier part of his career regularly taught for the University of Cambridge Extension Lectures (forerunner of the Board of Extramural Studies and hence of the Institute of Continuing Education) seemed confirmation of this. Then once I had rediscovered that Madingley itself had been a very significant place for Forster — its old chalk pit providing a key location not just for The Longest Journey *but recurring frequently in his writing — I could not resist talking about Forster and Madingley whenever I had the chance.*

'E.M. Forster and Madingley' introduces the Madingley Dell and its significance for Forster. 'E.M. Forster and the Sunday Times' is a rant against a sloppy and sensationalist article given undue prominence in a Sunday newspaper as a way of drumming up interest in a new biography of Forster. 'Rupert Brooke and E.M. Forster' argues that Forster himself is an identifiable presence in Brooke's famous poem 'The Old Vicarage, Grantchester'. (I'm not aware that anyone else has put forward this suggestion or indeed has explored Brooke's friendship with Forster.) A course that I taught on Forster for the University of Cambridge International Summer School is the starting point for 'Along Mill Lane', and the last book published by Frank Kermode, Concerning E.M. Forster (2009), *is reviewed in 'Frank Kermode's Creative Acts'. Finally, 'Berlin's Empty Shelves' revisits Forster's account of the 1933 Book Burning orchestrated by the Joseph Goebbels in the heart of the German capital.*

E.M. Forster and Madingley
25 September 2009

Every schoolchild knows — or would once have known — that the following lines

> And things are done you'd not believe
> At Madingley on Christmas Eve

come from 'The Old Vicarage, Grantchester'. But Rupert Brooke was not the only writer before the First World War to memorialise Madingley. I am re-reading the novels of E.M. Forster, and have just come across this half-remembered passage:

> A little this side of Madingley, to the left of the road, there is a secluded dell, paved with grass and planted with fir trees. It could not have been worth a visit twenty years ago, for then it was only a scar of chalk, and it is not worth a visit at the present day, for the trees have grown too thick and choked it.[1]

This dell is discovered by Rickie, a Cambridge student who is the central character of Forster's 1907 novel, *The Longest Journey*. It becomes for him a special place — somewhere he can escape to or take his friends: 'the dell became to him a kind of church — a church where indeed you could do anything you liked, but where anything you did would be transfigured.' Early on in the novel, Rickie takes his friends to see the dell and the chalk-pit which forms one side of it; later he comes there with his girl-friend, Agnes (they also visit Madingley Hall and Madingley Church). Agnes, writes Forster,

> sprang up the green bank that hid the entrance from the road. She stood for a moment looking at the view, for a few steps will increase a view in Cambridgeshire. The wind blew her dress against her.... Inside the dell it was neither June nor January, The chalk walls barred out the seasons, and the fir-trees did not seem to feel their passage. Only from time to time the odours of summer slipped in from the wood above, to comment on the waxing year.[2]

I thought I should see the dell for myself. It is just off the Cambridge road into Madingley, in the woods beyond the back entrance to the American Cemetery. Forster is right: a few steps will increase a view in Cambridgeshire. If you stand on the bank beside the road, or climb the half-dozen steps into the newly-established Cambridge 800 Wood, planted to commemorate the University's octo-centenary, you can clearly see the tower and lantern of Ely Cathedral. To follow Rickie and Agnes right into the dell today you would have to trespass: Madingley Wood, owned by the University, is now a designated site of special scientific interest (an SSI) and its flora and its archaeology have been studied and recorded for over 350 years. This makes it one of the oldest continuously-recorded woodland sites in Britain.

But you don't have to take Rickie's route over the gate (which wasn't there in Forster's day), and along the main ride through the wood before turning right to stand in the centre of the dell and feel yourself enclosed by a great

---

1   E.M. Forster, *The Longest Journey* (London: Penguin Classics, 2006) p.18.
2   *ibid.*, p.73.

wall of chalk: you can look down into it from the easternmost edge of the 800 Wood. Standing there, you are almost on the lip of the ancient and abandoned chalk pit (tread carefully: the fence is as precarious as the drop is precipitous) and you can glimpse the trees that have self-seeded or been planted there in recent years: poplar, ash and elm transplants from the old wood. The dell still has a strange atmosphere — a hidden world no one can enter, walled in chalk and only twenty yards from the road.

For Forster, chalk provided a *leitmotif* running through *The Longest Journey*. Later in the novel, for instance, Rickie is in Wiltshire, where 'chalk made the dust white, chalk made the water clear, chalk made the clean rolling outlines of the land, and favoured the grass and the distant coronals of trees.'[3] Forster sees the chalk formations that spread across southern and eastern England as veins and arteries running to and from the heart of the country and uniting the elements of his story. Indeed, at the defining moment of the novel, Rickie, standing on the edge of Salisbury Plain and learning a secret that will change his life for ever, 'was reminded for a moment of that chalk pit near Madingley'.[4]

I went to check Forster's geology with my colleague Gillian Sheail, who has taught the subject for the Institute for thirty nine years, inspiring students of all ages all over Cambs., Beds., Herts. and East Anglia. Her courses at Madingley Hall have always been a sell-out. She has been one of the Institute's great teachers. But Gillian wasn't there. She retired yesterday, and her desk was empty. She will be much missed. And I'll just have to take Forster's word about the chalk.

E.M. Forster and the Sunday Times
9 June 2010

Please forgive the indignant tone of what follows. I rarely read the Sunday papers, but by chance saw an article about E.M. Forster in last weekend's *Sunday Times*[5] which caught my eye and has made me very cross.

The article carries the alarming headline 'Sex led to Forster's end' (a laboured echo of 'Howards End'?). It is accompanied by two large photographs. One is a still from the 1985 Merchant-Ivory film of Forster's novel *A Room with a View*, showing Helena Bonham Carter looking virginal; the other shows a fifty-something Forster looking nervous, formally dressed (dark suit, white shirt with stiff collar), while a younger, less-formally dressed man (coloured shirt, soft collar — such distinctions used to matter) leans over his shoulder. The caption reads, 'E.M. Forster with his boyfriend, Bob Buckingham'. So far, so predictable.

3   *ibid.*, p.126.
4   *ibid.*, p.128.
5   'Richard Brooks, 'Sex led to Forster's end', *Sunday Times* (6 June 2010).

I'm about to teach a short course on Forster for the University's International Summer School; I'm also preparing Forster day schools to be taught in Cambridge and Stevenage next term, as well as a major course on Forster and his legacy for the Diploma of Higher Education in Modern English Literature. So, you can see, Forster is much on my mind at the moment, but when I read the lurid sub-heading of the *Sunday Times* article, I knew there would be trouble ahead:

A SECRET DIARY REVEALS HOW LOSING HIS VIRGINITY IN A GAY TRYST AT 38 CURBED THE CELEBRATED AUTHOR'S CREATIVE DRIVE.

The article is written by Richard Brooks. It begins:

> The enduring mystery of why E.M. Forster failed to write any novels beyond his mid-forties has been solved thanks to a secret cache of papers in which he confided his sexual desires.

With all due respect to the arts editor of a leading Sunday newspaper, this is tosh. There is no enduring mystery: it has been a commonplace of Forster criticism and biographical study since before the 1960s (when I studied *Howards End* for A level) that he gave up writing fiction once he felt he could no longer disguise the homosexual relationships, about which he wanted to write, behind the mask of the conventional fictional plots that led to marriage and a happy ending.

The 'secret cache of papers' is no more a secret than the fact that he had sex with a soldier on a beach in Alexandria in 1917. Here for instance, is the same encounter described by P.N. Furbank in his biography of Forster, and sounding anything but a 'gay tryst':

> In October he had a casual escapade with a soldier on the beach. It was his first full physical encounter, and he did not enjoy it greatly — not so much because he found it squalid, as because it was so anonymous.[6]

The 'secret cache of papers' resides among the Forster archive in King's College, and it is so unsecret that parts of it — including some extracts quoted by the *Sunday Times* — have already appeared in print: see *The Creator as Critic and Other Writings of E.M. Forster* (Toronto: Dundurn Press 2008, pp. 212ff) excellently edited by Jeffrey M. Heath.

Anyway, it's all too easy for critics and journalists to jeer at Forster's failure to write any more novels after *A Passage to India* (1924) and to write him off as a failure for not coming to terms in fiction with his homosexuality. Here is a good example:

---

6   P.N. Furbank, *E.M. Forster: a Life* (Oxford: Oxford University Press, vol.2, 1978) p.35.

Forster failed to make anything of his own homosexuality … and though he justified this failure on the grounds that his novels were to speak for all, not merely for a homosexual grouping, his liberalism prevented the emergence of anything more interesting and transgressive, kept him from a socialist vision and kept him from seeing the structure of oppression — class, race and gender-based — that he was part of.[7]

It seems only fair to hear what Forster himself had to say. In a BBC interview broadcast on his 79th birthday in 1958 he admitted:

> I would have been glad to write more novels after *Passage to India*. For one thing it sold so well, and I write for two reasons — partly to make money and partly to win the respect of people whom I respect. And novels, more novels, would have certainly made me better known. I somehow dried up after the *Passage*. I wanted to write but didn't want to write novels.[8]

What he did write were essays and broadcasts. His broadcasts for the BBC during the early years of the Second World War (published in *Two Cheers for Democracy*) constitute for me some of the most important writing of the mid-twentieth century. He went on to become an influential President of the National Council for Civil Liberties, and a committed advocate of free speech. No doubt, therefore, he'd have defended a newspaper's right to publish even an article as egregious as the one that caught my eye in Sunday's *Sunday Times* and which — without quite admitting it — is actually a puff for the new biography of Forster by Wendy Moffat, on sale in Heffers now.

I still think, though, that writers (especially dead writers) should themselves enjoy some civil liberties, including the right to be defended against stuff as disingenuous and prurient as 'Sex led to Forster's end'.

Rupert Brooke and E.M. Forster
4 November 2010

Thirteen months ago I wrote in *World and time* about E.M. Forster and Madingley — in particular about the Dell in Madingley Wood which featured so prominently in his novel *The Longest Journey*. Today, in the fiftieth *World and time* post, I want to revisit Forster's Dell.

Last Saturday I taught a day school on Cambridge Writers, and in preparing for it, I re-read Rupert Brooke's 1912 poem, 'The Old Vicarage, Grantchester'. I suppose it's a poem I have known for fifty years, but I had

---

7   Jeremy Tambling (ed.), E.M. Forster, *Contemporary Critical Essays* (London: Macmillan 1995) Introduction, p.11.

8   'E.M. Forster at Cambridge, 1958' in Jeffrey M. Heath (ed.) *The Creator as Critic* (Toronto: Dundurn Press, 2008) p.318.

forgotten how it is much more than just a nostalgic longing to be back in England by a love-sick, home-sick young poet stranded in Berlin:

> God! I will pack, and take a train,
> And get me to England once again! [9]

The poem is a roll call of famous Cambridge writers — both famous writers who have written about Cambridge, and famous writers who were once students in Cambridge. Brooke summons up the ghosts of Byron, Chaucer and Tennyson, for a start, before evoking all the nameless (mainly clerical) donnish figures who 'spectral dance, before the dawn' down the lawn of the Old Vicarage itself:

> Curates, long dust, will come and go
> On lissom, clerical, printless toe;
> And oft between the boughs is seen
> The sly shade of a Rural Dean ...
> Till, at a shiver in the skies,
> Vanishing with Satanic cries,
> The prim ecclesiastic rout
> Leaves but a startled sleeper-out.

The 'startled sleeper-out' is of course Brooke himself who famously liked to sleep out in the open air and to walk bare-foot and to swim naked (on one celebrated occasion he went skinny-dipping with Virginia Woolf) in Byron's Pool just above Grantchester:

> And I know
> How the May fields all golden show,
> And when the day is young and sweet,
> Gild gloriously the bare feet
> That run to bathe.

What I had missed, until I came back to the poem, was a reference to a contemporary writer whom Brooke had come to admire very much: a Cambridge man, a fellow King's man, indeed a fellow Apostle, that, is, a member of the élite Cambridge secret society, the Apostles. It is surely E.M. Forster himself Brooke has in mind when he claims that:

> Clever modern men have seen
> A Faun a-peeping through the green,
> And felt the Classics were not dead,
> To glimpse a Naiad's reedy head,
> Or hear the Goat-foot piping low.

---

9   'The Old Vicarage, Grantchester', *Collected Poems of Rupert Brooke* (London: Sidgwick and Jackson, 1920) pp.53-57.

Brooke admired Forster very much (though you would not think so to read Wendy Moffat's recent biography of Forster, *A Great Unrecorded History*, which makes no mention of their even knowing each other). Although Forster was a few years older than Brooke, he was still a familiar figure in and around Cambridge. He taught for the University's Extension Lectures, forerunner of the Board of Extramural Studies, precursor of the Institute of Continuing Education. He attended meetings of the Apostles whenever he could, he even stayed a few times as Brooke's guest at Grantchester. After one such visit, Brooke wrote to his mother, 'E.M. Forster the writer has been staying here two nights. He's a very charming person — an old King's man of 27 or 29. Get his new novel *Howard's* [sic] *End*. It would interest you.'[10]

It was, however, Forster's short stories as much as his novels that earned him his place in 'The Old Vicarage, Grantchester'. On one occasion, when the Apostles had a summer rendezvous on Salisbury Plain (a central location, of course, in *The Longest Journey*) Brooke carried a copy of Forster's latest short story in his pocket. Later, in 1914, when Brooke enlisted in the army, Forster gave him as a gift an expensive pair of field glasses, which he carried with him on his one experience of fighting, the Antwerp Raid. (It would be nice to think he was also carrying them with him on his last unfinished journey to the Dardanelles.)

But the clue which for me clinches the thought that Brooke includes a veiled and friendly reference to Forster in 'The Old Vicarage, Grantchester' appears in a letter Brooke wrote to Noel Olivier in 1909: 'You must read E.M. Forster's story in the English Review for July. It is *very* good.'[11] This is the story 'Other Kingdom', the genesis of which is described in *The Longest Journey*, when Rickie explains to his friend Agnes the story that he has been inspired to write by the Dell at Madingley. It is about a young woman who, to escape a man who wants to own and control her every thought and movement, runs into a wood and is turned into a Dryad: she becomes a tree. This is a marvellous proleptic and metafictional moment: Forster the novelist makes his fictional hero the author of a story that the novelist has himself not yet written but will one day publish.

I have been recommending 'Other Kingdom' as one of the most interesting of all Forster's short stories during my recent classes. What I have failed, however, to add is that the echoes in the story from Andrew Marvell's poem 'The Garden' are both irresistible and appropriate:

---

10 quoted in Christopher Hassall, *Rupert Brooke: a biography* (London: Faber and Faber 1964) p.240.

11 quoted in Pippa Harris (ed.) *Song of Love: the Letters of Rupert Brooke and Noel Olivier* (London: Bloomsbury, 1991) p.14.

Apollo hunted Daphne so
Only that she might laurel grow;
And Pan did after Syrinx speed,
Not as a nymph, but for a reed.[12]

Not only is 'the Naiad's reedy head' in 'The Old Vicarage, Grantchester'
Syrinx's, but the octosyllabic rhyming couplets of Brooke's poem are of course
borrowed directly from Marvell's.

Along Mill Lane
18 July 2010

Mill Lane runs from Trumpington Street down to the river. A convenient
thoroughfare it isn't: the pavements are too narrow, delivery vans and cars find
it hard to turn into or get out of. As with so many lanes in Cambridge, bicycles
fare best. But it is one of the most important locations in the city: from the Pitt
Building on one corner and the Board of Graduate Studies on the other, past
the Careers Service and all the way down to the University Centre in Granta
Place, there are probably more University officers hard at work in Mill Lane
than anywhere else in Cambridge except for the Old Schools.

I have been working there this past week, teaching for our International
Summer School in the Mill Lane Lecture Rooms. These are housed in an austere,
even daunting, 1930s building, but one with plenty of echoes and a few ghosts
– most of them friendly. Here F.R. Leavis used to lecture; here, these days, the
annual Clark Lectures are often delivered: in 2007 for instance Professor Sir Frank
Kermode spoke on E.M. Forster — as I have just been doing, for the Summer
School, in Room 7 on the top floor at the very back of the building.

Followers of 'World and time' will know that Forster looms large in
my reading, thinking and teaching. My course last week was entitled *E.M.
Forster and Cambridge* and the opening session was on 'Forster, Cambridge
and Madingley'. The link with which I began was a walk Forster took in
his first year as an undergraduate out to Madingley where he discovered an
abandoned chalk pit (now best located between the back entrance to the
American Cemetery and the Cambridge 800 Wood). This chalk pit, and the
dell in Madingley Wood of which it is part, meant a great deal to Forster.
As Elizabeth Heine points out in her excellent notes to the Penguin Classics
edition of *The Longest Journey*, Forster had written about it in his earliest
published Cambridge Essay: "a happy few find the little chalk pit this side of
the village where they may wander among the firs and undergrowth, folded
off from the outside world."[13]

---

12 Andrew Marvell, 'The Garden' 1654.
13 E.M. Forster, *The Longest Journey*, ed. Elizabeth Hine (London: Penguin Classics,
    2006) p.370.

(This chalk pit was actively quarried until at least the 16th century; indeed some of the last chalk taken from it was probably used as clunch in the building of Madingley Hall, 1543, by Sir John Hynde who owned Madingley Wood.)

In *The Longest Journey* Rickie, the most autobiographical of Forster's heroes, also discovers the dell in his second term at Cambridge. To him it becomes "a kind of church – a church where indeed you could do anything you liked, but where anything you did would become transfigured."[14] The place makes such an impact on Rickie (and on Forster) that he describes to his friends a short story that he would like to write about the wood; and indeed Forster himself was later to write just such a story, published as 'Other Kingdom'.

On Tuesday a student asked a question about Forster and D.H. Lawrence; I promised to answer her fully at the next session. To my astonishment, when I discovered Forster's obituary tribute to Lawrence (a BBC broadcast on 16 April 1930), I saw that he had chosen as an example of Lawrence's writing a passage from *The White Peacock* (1911) in which the novel's hero – walking in a Nottinghamshire wood with his girlfriend - discovers

A deep little dell, sharp sloping like a cup, and white sprinkling of flowers all the way down, with white flowers showing pale among the first inpouring of a shadow at the bottom ....[15]

I suspect Madingley Wood, and the dell within it, was one of the defining places in Forster's life. Certainly, after the success of *A Passage to India*, when he felt able to enter the property market for the first time, Forster went out and bought - not a house, but a wood.

I'm pleased to say the Summer School students shared my enthusiasm for Forster. They were a great group, by no means all of them English specialists. Their ages ranged from 20–80+ and they came from China, Pakistan, South Africa, Scandinavia, Italy, the Czech Republic, the United States and the UK: students, teachers, lawyers, scientists, journalists, the retired and the just beginning. Nina, a Norwegian, veteran of several summer schools, is about to start a full-time degree in Cambridge next term; Jason, a potential Gates Scholar, hopes to begin an MPhil here. Everyone has their own reason for coming, or coming back, to Cambridge.

I looked out of the window, half hoping to see the ghost of Forster pottering along Mill Lane. After all, Forster himself had once delivered a series of lectures entitled 'The Creator as Critic' here in the Mill Lane Lecture Rooms. But no, all I saw were the walls of Stuart House, a fine 1925 building in Queen Anne style with almost the most impressive pediment in Cambridge: the university's

---

14 *ibid.*, p.18.

15 Quoted by E.M. Forster in 'D.H. Lawrence', in *The Creator as Critic* ed. Jeffrey M. Heath (Toronto: Dundurn, 2008) p.224.

arms brilliantly blazoned and supported. Now the offices of the Careers Service, it is clearly a building of which the University was once proud. Rightly so: it was named after Professor James Stuart, originator of the idea that university teaching should formally extend beyond a university's walls, and it was built to house the University's then Board of Extramural Studies.

Frank Kermode's Creative Acts
19 August 2010

When Frank Kermode published his last book last year I reviewed it in the English Association *Newsletter*. This was the only time I had written about Kermode but I sensed then an era coming to an end, one which could justly be called The Kermode Era. For over fifty years his books, opinions and authority have helped define the temper of English criticism. His Arden edition of *The Tempest* (1955) offered the first post-colonial reading of the play long before post-colonialism was fashionable. Two years later *Romantic Image* (1957) quickly became a fixture on undergraduate reading lists — as it was on mine, taking its place alongside Auerbach's *Mimesis*, Raymond Williams' *Culture and Society* and Sweet's *Anglo-Saxon Primer*.

I first encountered Kermode in 1967, the year he published his seminal work, *The Sense of an Ending*. One obituarist this week has neatly described that book as 'a brilliant investigation of the idea that the longing for an ending brings order to both life and literature, giving shape to the endless flux of time'. I don't think anyone was using the word 'closure' in 1967.

Skip forward forty-two years: *Concerning E.M. Forster*[16] appeared just in time for the centenary of *Howards End*. I think Kermode suspected this would be his last book, but it has a downbeat and ambivalent tone, and it is this ambivalence which he takes as his starting point. He begins by recalling how F.R. Leavis had condemned Forster's novels for 'a curious lack of grasp' and had decided that Forster was 'only too unmistakably minor' before (in *The Common Pursuit*, 1952) surprisingly concluding that 'Forster's is a name that, in these days we should peculiarly honour'.

Kermode's name is also one that anyone interested in the health of English and English Studies 'should peculiarly honour', especially anyone committed to the engagement of the academic English community with the wider public outside their walls. Kermode believed with passion that debates about literature should be carried out in a wide public forum, and that thoughtful literary journalism aimed at the common reader was a moral obligation since academics are largely paid for from the public purse. He was a founding

---

16 Frank Kermode, *Concerning E.M. Forster* (London: Weidenfeld and Nicolson, 2009).

figure of The *London Review of Books*, for which he wrote right up to his death; his work as a reviewer and essayist became increasingly important to him — and to everyone who admired his wide-ranging interests and his advocacy of writers in and out of fashion.

The first part of *Concerning E.M. Forster* reprints Kermode's three Clark Lectures of 2007, themselves revisiting Forster's own Clark Lectures of 1927, famously published later that year as *Aspects of the Novel*. In the first lecture, 'Aspects of Aspects', Kermode defines his central criticism of Forster's career as a writer:

> It remains possible to complain that in a book [*Aspects of the Novel*] on such a subject he ought, perhaps, to have looked about him rather more, and found something more to say about certain works by his contemporaries, especially those who made formal experiments and believed they had found new and better ways of telling the truth in fiction. [17]

This is the nub of Kermode's quarrel with Forster: that he did not pay enough attention to writers such as Conrad and Henry James; he makes no reference to having ever read Kafka and he would not have cared for the work of the French rhetoricians or the Russian formalists. 'Forster's attitude to these innovations' suggests Kermode, 'would probably have resembled his view of the motor cars in *Howards End* — destructive, smelly and intrusive, and associated with the kind of people he felt little need to know.'[18]

Part 2 of *Concerning E.M. Forster* is described as a 'causerie', a more relaxed and discursive approach — though one is never allowed to forget that Kermode is trying to pin down the essential ambivalence in Forster's own work. He has some interesting things to say about the early publishing history of his books, and of the key role that the reviewer Edward Garnett played in promoting the 26-year-old author of *Where Angels Fear to Tread*. He also demonstrates why Leonard Bast is the litmus test for deciding whether or not *Howards End* is a successful novel, and suggests that Forster's hopes for a post-war 'restoration of England's lanes and fields, of a just, old-style England without the old cruelties and hatreds' were dashed by Labour's victory in the 1945 General Election.

Here Kermode allows himself a walk-on part. Recalling the dismay of the middle classes at the election result, he mentions that he was crossing the Pacific by ship at the time: he remembers 'the incredulity with which regular officers heard the news of the Labour landslide' before adding, 'Only I was content.'[19]

At the end of the book Kermode laments again that Forster's reading and sympathies had not been broader. He allows that Forster 'usually knew

17 *Concerning E.M. Forster*, p.18.
18 *ibid.*, p.21.
19 *ibid.*, p.118.

a great book when he saw one' but concludes 'it is useless to complain that he didn't do all the reading we might have wanted from him. His reports on current fiction were dutiful but superficial. They were not creative acts, the only kind that mattered.' [20]

This hardly sounds like advocacy; but Kermode seems unwilling to write off Forster altogether. In the last paragraph of this candid if sometimes caustic causerie he acknowledges — but is puzzled by — the affection Forster's readers 'continue to feel' for him. When he writes that 'as a guide to literature' Forster was 'for a good many years a skilful though not exciting broadcaster, his programmes much admired in India', the mordant tone and appositional syntax sound more like Alan Bennett than Frank Kermode. But when he finally says of his subject that

> He could speak out. He lived to be old and still active, an achievement
> that almost always impresses the public[21]

I can't help wondering whether this ambivalent accolade is actually offered less to Forster than to Kermode himself.

Berlin's empty shelves
25 November 2010

Next month I am going back to Berlin, a city I once knew well and visited often, both before and after the fall of the Berlin Wall. I am very much looking forward to making the return journey, the first time I shall have been back for nearly ten years. On my last visit, I gave a lecture, arranged by the *Deutsch-Britische Gesellschaft* at the Humboldt University, on ideas of Englishness in contemporary British fiction. I concentrated on three novels: *Nice Work*, by David Lodge, *England England*, by Julian Barnes and *White Teeth* by Zadie Smith. I had not expected a large turnout, but the lecture theatre was full, and the audience — German and British alike — seemed to know a lot already about Lodge and Barnes and even Zadie Smith, whose first novel had only just been published.

I should not have been surprised: Berlin, like the rest of Germany, takes books and writers seriously. The annual Frankfurt Book Fair is the biggest publishing market in the world. In 1987 I visited a small bookshop in East Berlin, under the *Friedrichstraße* railway bridge, and was amazed at the care with which the book was wrapped by the assistant. On the counter lay sheets of old wallpaper, cut into squares and rectangles of different sizes. She selected one the right size for the book, and then folded and tucked it into a package neat and intricate enough for origami. No sellotape, no string, just skill and

20 *ibid.*, p.164.
21 *ibid.*, p.168.

dedication. This was all the more surprising because in most East German shops at that time, the service was surly: if you went into a café, even one that was half empty, you'd be routinely told there was no room. Somehow booksellers, by contrast, had retained their belief in the value of what they sold.

Perhaps Berliners have good reason to cherish books now, having staged in the past one of the most aggressive anti-book demonstrations of the twentieth century, the *Bücherverbrennung* in Bebelplatz. This square is just across the Unter den Linden from the Humboldt, where the poet Heinrich Heine was once a student:

Dort, wo Man Bücher verbrennt, verbrennt man am ende auch Menschen.

Wherever they burn books, eventually they will burn people too.

Heine's words were prophetic. On one night in May 1933, Joseph Goebbels orchestrated a bonfire of 25,000 books (it took the combined presence of Brownshirts, SS, Nazi Students and Hitler Youth to keep heaping books onto the pyre). Among the books burned were those of Heine himself. E.M. Forster, in a wartime BBC broadcast, recalled the scene, which had taken place in front of a huge audience:

Most people enjoy a blaze, and we are told that the applause was tremendous. Some of the books were by Jews, others communist, others 'liberal', others 'unscientific', and all of them 'un-German'. It was for the government to decide what was un-German. There was an elaborate ritual. Nine heralds came forward in turn, and consigned an author with incantations to the flames. For example, the fourth herald said: 'Concerning the corrosion of the soul by the exaggeration of the dangers of war! Upholding the nobility of the human spirit, I consign to the flames the writings of Sigmund Freud.' The seventh herald said: 'Concerning the literary betrayal of the World War soldier! Upholding the education of our people in the spirit of reality, I consign to the flames the writings of Erich Maria Remarque.'[22]

On (or more accurately under) the site of the bonfire there is now a remarkable memorial: through a glass panel set into the cobbled pavement of the square, you can look down into a room. The room itself is empty and has no door, its walls being entirely lined with empty bookshelves. Children cycle obliviously over the glass panel; tourists walk past it; Berliners walk around it or avoid the square altogether. But there sit the empty shelves in silent reproach: '*Is it nothing to you, all ye who pass by?*' I have rarely seen a more telling memorial.

---

22 E.M. Forster, *Two Cheers for Democracy*, (Harmondsworth: Penguin, 1951) p.47.

Other literary memorials in Berlin are less austere. My favourite is the statue of Bertolt Brecht, sitting on a bench outside the theatre where his *Berliner Ensemble* used to perform *Mother Courage*, *The Caucasian Chalk Circle* and *The Threepenny Opera*. I owe a lot to Brecht. His plays we used to read avidly at school and they helped me, even then, to understand why literature mattered and why I wanted to teach it. In fact, along with E.M. Forster, it is probably Brecht to whom I am most indebted for the impetus to spend my life in literature. I look forward to saying hello again to him soon.

3.4 On writers, mostly novelists

The first of the posts in this final section of 'World and time' brings together two topics that have been very influential in my teaching: Durham, where I studied for my first degree and where I did my postgraduate research, and Anthony Trollope. I first read the Barchester and Palliser novels while I was a student at Durham and Trollope has become one of my favourite teaching subjects, enabling me to combine my interests in Victorian fiction and ecclesiology. 'Charles Lamb and Cambridge' takes an oblique look at the problem of defining a 'Cambridge writer'. 'Jane Austen and anachronism' arose from conversations with my students and from my sense that these days it is often adaptations of texts that attract more critical attention than the texts themselves. By contrast, 'Charles Dickens stayed here' is an example of a piece I had not expected to write. Nevertheless, it forced me to reflect on an aspect of Dickens' career and reputation which helped to put his novel A Tale of Two Cities *in a sharper focus. 'Coastline' looks at the way two East Anglian writers, W.G. Sebald and M.R. James, have evoked the Norfolk coastline in their fiction and non-fiction writing. Finally, 'The sense of an ending' took as its starting point a newly published work by the novelist Julian Barnes and provided me with a theme for my final post, written the day I retired from the Institute of Continuing Education and Madingley Hall.*

Archbishop Ramsey's treasure
29 October 2009

Anyone who knows Durham will agree that Prebends Bridge is one of the most beautiful bridges in England. Spanning the River Wear, it offers the most famous of all views of Durham Cathedral. It's the view that inspired Sir Walter Scott to exclaim:

> Grey towers of Durham,
> Yet well I love thy mixed and massive piles
> Half church of God, half castle 'gainst the Scot
> And long to roam those venerable aisles
> With records stored of deeds long since forgot.[1]

---

1   Sir Walter Scott, 'Harold the Dauntless', (1816)

Glancing over my neighbour's shoulder on the train last Thursday, I saw in his *Guardian* a picture of Durham cathedral from Prebends Bridge accompanying a story about a collection of treasure found in the river below. When I got to London I bought my own copy and discovered that the treasure was not an Anglo-Danish hoard but gold, silver and other precious items dating from the second half of the twentieth century and belonging to Michael Ramsey, former Archbishop of Canterbury.

Ramsey had retired to Durham, which he loved and where he had once been Bishop. How had his precious possessions found their way into the Wear? One theory suggested they were the contents of a burglary the unworldly bishop, widowed and in his late old age, had failed to report to the police. More intriguingly, others thought he might have deliberately dropped them over the bridge himself.

Apparently Ramsey had once sold some gifts given to him during his episcopate. He'd done this to raise money for the charity Christian Aid, but was mortified when the items later turned up at auction and he was heavily criticised for allegedly profiting from the sale of gifts. Perhaps as a result, the speculation ran, he had just quietly disposed of his remaining unwanted gifts one by one during daily walks in Durham along the riverbanks and across Prebends Bridge. If so, he must have hoped they'd never the see the light of day again.

There have been six archbishops of Canterbury in my lifetime. The first was Geoffrey Fisher, who presided over the Coronation of Elizabeth II. Then came Ramsey, in every way the opposite of his predecessor. He was followed by Donald Coggan and then by the much underrated Robert Runcie, who was famously accused of 'nailing his colours to the fence' but had the courage to stand up to Mrs Thatcher over the Falklands War and the Miners' Strike. After Runcie, Carey; and now Archbishop Rowan Williams, theologian, poet, literary scholar and frequent visitor to Cambridge, where he was once Chaplain at Clare College.

Of these half dozen it is Ramsey who I think would have been most at home in a novel by Anthony Trollope, that great chronicler of the English clergy. Ramsey's moral distress on being falsely accused of selling his unwanted gifts for personal profit reminds me of old Mr Harding in *The Warden*. As warden of Hiram's Hospital, the Rev. Septimus Harding was accused of profiting from his office at the expense of the old almspeople he looked after. Ramsey reminds me too of Mr Crawley, the scholarly perpetual curate of Hogglestock in *The Last Chronicle of Barset*, accused of having stolen a cheque. True, Mr Crawley was an unlovable and unyielding man (adjectives hardly applicable to Michael Ramsey) but — like Harding, like the Archbishop — he was a man of daunting moral and intellectual integrity.

I'm preparing my weekend course 'Barchester re-visited: Trollope's Last Chronicle', and my admiration for Trollope continues to grow: I think his evocation of a cathedral town and provincial mid-Victorian society is one of the great achievements of English fiction. And it's a measure of how much Barchester came to mean to Trollope himself that on the last page (p.891 in the Oxford World's Classics edition) of *The Last Chronicle* he wrote:

> To me Barset has been a real county, and its city a real city, and the spires and towers have been before my eyes, and the voices of the people are known to my ears, and the pavements of the city ways are familiar to my footsteps. To them all I now say farewell. That I have been induced to wander among them too long by my love of old friendships, and by the sweetness of old faces, is a fault for which I may perhaps be more readily forgiven, when I repeat, with some solemnity of assurance, the promise made in my title, that this shall be the last chronicle of Barset.[2]

I'm looking forward very much to revisiting Barchester, the fourth, but perhaps not the last, weekend course that I shall offer on Trollope.

Charles Lamb and Cambridge
1 March 2010

Two invitations this week to lecture later in the year, but sadly both on dates when I already have engagements. The first, to speak on Cambridge architecture for the Open Cambridge Weekend, would have been straightforward: I could have adapted a lecture from my forthcoming day school, *Exploring Cambridge Architecture*; the second, to give a lecture on writers and Cambridge, would have been an interesting challenge: to find a new angle on a well-worn subject.

The number of lectures already delivered on literary Cambridge must be legion: in the past, they often took the form of a chronological canter from Christopher Marlowe (Corpus) and John Milton (Christ's) to Rupert Brooke (King's), E.M. Forster (*ditto*), Ted Hughes (Pembroke) and Sylvia Plath (Newnham), with due deference paid to William Wordsworth (St John's), Samuel Coleridge (Jesus) and Charles Darwin (Christ's again) in between. No doubt many of these lectures are now being updated to include contemporary writers: Zadie Smith (King's), for instance, and Sebastian Faulks (Emmanuel). Faulks would deserve a special mention for having set his 2007 novel *Engleby* in Cambridge itself.

---

2   Anthony Trollope, *The Last Chronicle of Barset* (Oxford: Oxford University Press World's Classics, 2001) p.891

But I'd try a different tack. I think an interesting lecture could be built around writers who were never students here, but wished they could have been. Thomas Hardy, for instance, who was delighted in later life to be made an Honorary Fellow at Magdalene; or Virginia Woolf, whose celebrated lectures, published as *A Room of One's Own*, were tinged with resentment at her having been denied the chance of going to university because she was a woman.

One writer above all would feature in my lecture, the essayist Charles Lamb. I wonder how often, these days, guides taking tourists around the city point to the discreet plaque on the wall of 11 King's Parade? It records Charles Lamb lodged in this house in the summer of 1819.

This was a long overdue visit, though not his first. As early as 1800 Lamb's friend, Thomas Manning, was urging him to make the journey to Cambridge, and Lamb was promising 'that I will come the very first spare week, and go nowhere till I have been at Cambridge. No matter if you are in a state of pupillage, when I come; for I can employ myself in Cambridge very pleasantly in the mornings. Are there not libraries, halls, colleges, books, pictures, statues?'[3]

Lamb always regretted that he could not have gone to university. In his essay 'Oxford in the Vacation' he wrote: 'I can here play the gentleman, enact the student. To such a one as myself, who has been defrauded in my young years of the sweet food of academic institution, nowhere is so pleasant, to while away a few idle weeks at, as one or other of the Universities.'[4]

When he had the chance to spend a few days in Cambridge with his sister Mary, in the summer of 1819, he came back to the same theme:

> Mine have been anything but studious hours,
> Yet can I fancy, wand'ring mid thy towers,
> Myself a nursling, Granta, of thy lap,
> My brow seems tightening with the Doctor's cap,
> And I walk — gowned — feel unusual powers.[5]

Yet, from the time he first met Manning, Lamb began to be known in Cambridge. Dick Hopkins, who was cook simultaneously at Caius and Trinity Hall, sent Lamb a present of Cambridge Brawn, which pleased him mightily:

---

3   Charles Lamb to Thomas Manning, October 16 1800; Alfred Ainger (ed.) *The Letters of Charles Lamb* vol. 1(London: Macmillan and Co., 1891) p.143

4   'Oxford in the Vacation'; *The Essays of Elia* (London: George Harrap and Co. Ltd., 1909) p.15

5   Charles Lamb, 'Sonnet: written at Cambridge August 15, 1819'; in E.E. Kellett (ed.) *A Book of Cambridge Verse* (Cambridge: Cambridge University Press 1911) p.185

He might have sent sops from the pan, skimmings, crumpets, chips, hog's lard, the tender brown judiciously scalped from a fillet of veal (dexterously replaced by a salamander), the tops of asparagus, fugitive livers, runaway gizzards of fowls, the eyes of martyred pigs, tender effusions of laxative woodcocks, the red spawn of lobsters, leverets' ears, and such petty filchings common to cooks; but these had been ordinary presents, the everyday courtesies of dish-washers to their sweethearts. Brawn was a noble thought.[6]

Lamb was one of the great writers on food. I suspect many schoolchildren were first introduced to his *Essays of Elia*, as I was, by reading 'A Dissertation upon Roast Pork', published in 1822. In that year, too, he was writing to Wordsworth's sister about a Mrs Smith, 'the biggest woman in Cambridge', who 'broke down two benches in Trinity gardens' and was 'to be seen in the market every morning, at ten, cheapening fowls, which I observe the Cambridge poulterers are not sufficiently careful to stump.'[7]

In the early twentieth century, Lamb was held in high esteem in Cambridge: between 1909–1914 annual dinners were given to honour his memory. But it was at Cambridge too that his reputation tipped into decline. F.R. Leavis declared him overrated, and dismissed the whole tradition of the essay as *belles-lettres*, beneath consideration as serious literature. Though he has been since somewhat rehabilitated as a key figure of the early Romantic movement, Lamb is not widely read any more. But he was a great essayist, critic and letter-writer. Today he'd have been — perhaps — a brilliant blogger. So, I'm sorry I've had turn down the invitation to lecture on writers and Cambridge. I'd have started with Lamb.

Jane Austen and anachronism
5 November 2009

I started to have misgivings about the latest TV adaptation of *Emma* early in the first episode. As soon as Emma herself began referring to her 'exercise régime' and announcing that she liked to be 'upfront', I knew things were going wrong. I can't see the point of being fastidious about accuracy over costume, settings, dishes served at meals etc. and not thinking that the language matters just as much.

Perhaps this is sheer pedantry? Admittedly, by the last episode I was enjoying the production a lot, though I was never quite convinced that there were nearly twenty years' difference in age between Emma and Mr Knightley.

6   Charles Lamb to Thomas Manning, 24 February 1805; *The Letters of Charles Lamb*, vol. 1, p.211
7   Charles Lamb to Dorothy Wordsworth, Christmas 1822; ibid., vol. 2, p.58

Romola Garai (whose performance as the eighteen-year old wartime nurse Briony in the 2007 film of Ian McEwan's *Atonement* I thought was excellent) seemed older than Emma, who should be not quite twenty one; Johnny Lee Miller, as Mr K, scarcely seemed thirty-seven.

I nearly always watch film and TV adaptations, and these days discussion of adaptation of novels is a legitimate field of critical interest. For the record, I thought that the 2007 adaptation of *Mansfield Park*, with Billie Piper ludicrously miscast as Fanny Price, was the worst Austen adaptation I have ever seen. The best? Undoubtedly the 1995 production of *Persuasion* with Amanda Root as Anne Elliot and a cast that included Simon Russell Beale, Fiona Shaw, Corin Redgrave, Samuel West and Phoebe Nicholls. Phoebe Nicholls had played the part of Cordelia Flyte in the 1981 ITV adaptation of *Brideshead Revisited*, which I count as one of the two best TV adaptations (of any novel) ever made — the other being the 2005 adaptation of *Bleak House*.

Both these adaptations had the luxury of many episodes: 15 episodes for *Bleak House*; 11 episodes for *Brideshead*, running for an astonishing 659 minutes. Perhaps you need this much length to do justice to a novel on the screen. Perhaps this is why film adaptations of novels usually disappoint badly: the 2005 Keira Knightley version of *Pride and Prejudice* was good to look at but unrewarding otherwise, I thought. The great exception was Emma Thompson's own adaptation of *Sense and Sensibility*, which still seems to me to get closer to the essential loneliness of Marianne, Elinor and their mother than any other adaptation of Jane Austen I have seen. Critics and film-makers alike usually fail to stress how much emphasis Austen gives loneliness in a world where getting away from people — even having your own bed, never mind your own room — is very difficult.

But even this 1996 film had an anachronism of interest to super-pedants: Marianne (Kate Winslet) begins to fall head over heels for the bounder Willoughby (Greg Wise) when they read Shakespeare's sonnet 'Let me not to the marriage of true minds' together. In fact, the Sonnets were hardly known to the general reading public of Jane Austen's day, and were certainly not published in the handy little pocket-sized edition over which Marianne and her dastardly admirer pore so avidly.

Marianne famously has a lot to learn in *Sense and Sensibility*; as does Emma; as does Elizabeth Bennett in *Pride and Prejudice* (the 1980 adaptation of which novel by Fay Weldon is still the best, lack of Colin Firth in wet shirt notwithstanding). 'Educating the heroine' is the title of a Jane Austen weekend course at Madingley Hall (15–17 January 2010) which will be exploring Jane Austen's novels in the light of contemporary debates on the education and social role of women. It's not only the heroines, though, who have painful lessons to learn in Jane Austen's novels. Poor Harriet had almost as much to learn as her mentor Emma, but at least she got to marry her original hero, Robert Martin, in the last episode of the latest adaptation, and no one seemed to mind that the stained glass in the east window of the church in which the wedding was filmed happened to be by William Morris & Co. It must have been made at least fifty years after Jane Austen's death.

'Charles Dickens stayed here'
18 May 2010

It's unfair to judge any town by its appearance and atmosphere on a Sunday evening, but Berwick-upon-Tweed was a disappointment. Once upon a time I knew the Welsh borders well, but I've hardly explored the Scottish borders at all and last weekend I was looking forward to visiting Berwick for the first time. I'd been through it on the train to Edinburgh once or twice, but never before by car with the chance to stop and walk around its walls and ramparts, stroll over its bridge or admire its once-elegant High Street.

In its heyday Berwick must have been splendid. Its streets have plenty of imposing eighteenth century buildings, none more splendid than the Town Hall that stands at the end of the High Street looking at first sight more like a church than a temple to trade (a covered market was cleverly built into the rear section of it). It has been enlarged more than once, and each time the Mayor of the moment has made sure his name was prominently displayed on the portico for posterity.

Civic pride, however, was hard to spot as we set off in search of supper. There wasn't much open: a Chinese take-away, and an uninviting staircase leading to some further Eastern Promise. In Hide Hill we found eventually a wine bar which had no one in it, potential customers presumably discouraged — as we soon were — by the loud music thumping away within.

Over the road, however, was an old coaching inn. The place looked less than flourishing; still, on the wall beside the front door a plaque announced that Charles Dickens had stayed there twice, in 1858 and again in November 1861, on which occasion he had also given a public reading in the adjoining Assembly Rooms. On the principle that if the place had been good enough for Dickens to stop at — not once, but twice — then it should be good enough for us, we went in.

Of the meal itself I'll say nothing, but I was intrigued by Dickens. I suspect that more hotels have signs saying 'Dickens stayed here' than you'll find for any other distinguished visitor apart perhaps from Queen Elizabeth I. And of course he often wrote about them: the Angel at Bury St Edmunds, for instance, or the Great White Hart in Ipswich where Mr Pickwick had his disastrous encounter with the lady in yellow curling papers. The biographer *manqué* in me wanted to know what Dickens was doing in Berwick (presumably on his way north or back again) and I resolved to look up my copy of Peter Ackroyd's biography when I got back home to see if I could find the answer.[8] The local newspaper office looked old enough to have a complete run of the *Berwick Advertiser* going back to the 1860s. If it had been open I might have found out what the local reporter had had to say about Dickens's performance in the Assembly Rooms.

'Old Assembly Rooms' said a sign on an inconspicuous door near the entrance to the Old Stables Restaurant where we were dining in solitary state. I expected the door would be locked, but it wasn't and, with a daring I do not often muster, I opened it and went through. In front of me was a huge staircase, very wide and very stately. It would have taken mid-Victorian ladies a long time, dressed in their finest crinolines, to reach the landing, turn for a brief glimpse in the huge mirror, and then enter the Assembly Rooms to take their seats ready for Dickens to appear. But no doubt everyone who was anyone in Berwick turned out for the occasion, and the Assembly Rooms must have been a sparkling sight: three huge chandeliers lighting an enormous hall which could seat three hundred people with ease. Now, as I stood in it, the hall looked merely empty. A tatty bar had been improvised at one end, perhaps on the very spot where Dickens would have stood to give his virtuoso performance. His readings brought him as much adulation as his novels themselves.

I wonder what he read. Probably the death of Nancy from *Oliver Twist* (always a favourite) or the death of little Nell from *The Old Curiosity Shop*. Perhaps he read from his recent best-seller, *A Tale of Two Cities*, which he would have been writing when he'd first stayed at Berwick, for it was serialised in 1859. Did he have them laughing in the aisles with his rendering of the indomitable Miss Pross ('I am an Englishwoman. You shall not pass') grappling with Mme Defarge and then shooting the astonished *tricoteuse* through the heart? Was there a dry eye in the house when he squeezed every last drop of pathos from Sidney Carton's final words on his way to the guillotine: 'It is a far, far better thing I do than I have ever done: it is a far, far better rest that I go to, than I have ever known'? It would be good to know.

November 1861, when Dickens performed in these same Assembly Rooms where I stood now, was the same month that Prince Albert arrived at Madingley to remonstrate with his wayward son, the Prince of Wales, who was living at the Hall while allegedly studying at Cambridge. We doubtless attach too much significance to dates and anniversaries but they are sometimes useful hooks. So, thinking of Dickens in Berwick reminds me that 2012 will be the two hundredth anniversary of Dickens' birth, and great festivities are planned. It's not too soon for us to start planning the 2012 Literature courses at Madingley; and, if for no other reason, I shall think more kindly of Berwick from now on for prompting me to get on with planning our own Dickens celebrations.

---

8   He was on a reading tour of the north of England.

Coastline

25 February 2011

I'm downsizing my library, drastically. Half my books must go. I sit in my shed, surrounded by boxes I have already filled, and let my eyes scan across the shelves, left to right, then back again right to left. There is a word for this: *boustrophedon*. It describes the action of printing, writing or reading from one side of a page to the other, and then back again, as with oxen ploughing a field. And just as a plough will give a jolt when it hits a stone or a root of buried tree, so my eye stops abruptly when it lights on a book I have forgotten, but know immediately I could never give away.

Over and over again, I find reasons for not getting rid of this or that particular book or, worse, of this or that particular author. W.G. Sebald, for instance, whose novel *Austerlitz* I taught when it first appeared a decade ago, and of whom a student said to me only yesterday, 'I'd never have read Sebald, but for you. He changed my life.' Here are all his books on my shelf now, and I pick one at random: *The Rings of Saturn* (1998), a strange hypnotic account of a walk along the East Anglian coast. I have not opened it for several years and to my surprise I find I have annotated it heavily — highlighting, cross-referencing, pencilling notes in the margin. Did I once teach this book alongside *Austerlitz*?

> A quarter of an hour's walk south of Benacre broad, where the beach narrows and a stretch of sheer coastline begins, a few dozen dead trees lie in a confused heap where they fell years ago from the Covehythe cliffs. Bleached by salt water, wind and sun, the broken, barkless wood looks like the bones of some extinct species, greater even than the mammoths and dinosaurs, that came to grief long since on this solitary strand. The footpath leads around the tangle through a bank of gorse, up the loamy cliff-head, and there it continues amidst bracken, the tallest of which stood as high as my shoulder, not far from the ledge, which is constantly threatening to crumble away.[9]

Sebald's book is a meditation on time, and time's changes. The coastline he treads is itself always changing. Cliffs crumble, houses fall; footpaths become too dangerous to follow. Soon it won't be only Dunwich which lies out to sea: Happisburgh is well on the way to joining it, and it will be a sad day when the lighthouse, the church and the Hill House pub (where Arthur Conan Doyle got the idea for the secret code in his short story, *The Dancing Men*) all disappear.

But it's the North Norfolk coast I know better, from Cromer to King's Lynn and round into the Wash. I learned to swim at Hunstanton, which used to boast it was the only resort (does anyone still use that word?) on the east

---

9   W.G. Sebald, *The Rings of Saturn* (London: Vintage 1998) pp.64–65

coast that faced west. When Professor Parkins, in M.R. James's ghost story
'Oh, Whistle, and I'll Come to You, my Lad' sets off from the mythical St
James's College in Cambridge for the east coast to improve his game during
the vacation, I have always imagined that his equally mythical destination,
Burnstow, ought to be Old Hunstanton, and that his golf course of choice
must be the links next to the Le Strange Arms or the Caley Hall Hotel:

> Bleak and solemn was the view on which he took a last look before
> starting homeward. A faint yellow light in the west showed the links,
> on which a few figures moving towards the club-house were still
> visible, the squat martello tower, the lights of Aldsey village, the pale
> ribbon of sands intersected at intervals by black wooden groynes, the
> dim and murmuring sea. The wind was bitter from the north, but
> was at his back when he set out for the Globe. He quickly rattled and
> clashed through the shingle and gained the sand, upon which, but for
> the groynes which had to be got over every few yards, the going was
> both good and quiet.[10]

I admit that there is no martello tower off Old Hunstanton, and I know
that Burnstow is meant to be Felixstowe (sure enough, there is a squat
Martello tower in the middle of Felixstowe Ferry Golf Course), but 'Oh,
Whistle, and I'll Come to You, my Lad' in my imagination will always be set
on the Norfolk coast.

The stretch of this coast, though, that I know best, and often re-visit in
my imagination, is hardly coast at all. It is where the river Nene flows into
the Wash beyond Sutton Bridge, just near the lighthouse where Peter Scott
lived in the 1930s, dividing his time between wildfowling, painting and
conservation. You can follow the line of the coast and of successive waves of
land reclamation by walking the sea wall from here to West Lynn. At high
tide the sea comes almost up to the lighthouse; at low tide it is so far out
you cannot see it. And when the tide is turning, the sound of the contesting
currents is like nothing I ever heard anywhere else.

The sense of an ending
17 August 2011

The Sense of an Ending was originally the title of an influential book of literary
criticism and critical theory by Frank Kermode. Now the title has been
recycled, this time for a new novel by Julian Barnes, published this month.
It's a book I strongly recommend, and I'm not surprised it is already on this
year's Booker Prize long list.

---

10 M.R. James, 'Oh, Whistle, and I'll Come to You, my Lad', *Count Magnus and
   Other Ghost Stories* (London: Penguin Classics, 2005) p.86

The narrator of the novel is Tony Webster, a man in his early sixties who has had a mostly uneventful life until, unexpectedly, he is forced to revisit a period forty years earlier when his close friend at school, Adrian Finn, committed suicide. On one level, it's Adrian's ending of which Tony still has to make sense; however, he is also confronting his own mortality and trying to make sense of what his life has amounted to now that he is retired. He has the uneasy feeling that the life to which he had looked forward with such expectation in the 1960s has already started to slip into the past tense. All of which he finds unsettling:

> It strikes me that this may be one of the differences between youth and age: when we are young, we invent different futures for ourselves; when we are old, we invent different pasts for others.[11]

The creating of a history for oneself, the rewriting of history for others and the recovery – if possible – of the real truth (surely a revealing tautology?) is a key theme of Barnes's novel. So it has also been of a surprising number of other novels and plays from the twenty-first century to date: Philip Roth's *The Human Stain* (2000), W.G. Sebald's *Austerlitz* (2001), Ian McEwan's *Atonement* (2001), Alan Bennett's *The History Boys* (2004) and Aminatta Forna's *The Memory of Love* (2010) among others.

There's always a danger in treating the past that one lapses into nostalgia, and this is a danger of which Tony is well aware:

> I've been turning over in my mind the question of nostalgia, and whether I suffer from it. I certainly don't get soggy at the memory of some childhood knick-knack; nor do I want to deceive myself sentimentally about something that wasn't even true at the time – love of the old school, and so on. But if nostalgia means the powerful recollection of strong emotions – and a regret that such feelings are no longer present in our lives – then I plead guilty.[12]

In this my last week at Madingley, I too have been trying hard to resist nostalgia but it's not easy when you have known a place like this for over thirty-five years. I first came to Madingley on a course in 1974 and have taught here for the Institute of Continuing Education since 1998. It's the best job I've ever had. So I have been focusing on the last lecture I shall give in Cambridge this afternoon. It's on Seamus Heaney's latest collection, *Human Chain*.

There is a strong sense of an ending about this book, too. Indeed, I have called my lecture 'Last Words? Heaney's *Human Chain*'. In these poems the poet looks back over his life from the perspective of someone

---

11 Julian Barnes, *The Sense of an Ending* (London: Jonathan Cape, 2011) p.80
12 *ibid.*, p.81

recently brought face to face with mortality: Heaney suffered a stroke in 2006, and some of the most poignant and powerful poems in the collection are about this experience.

As ever, though, with Heaney, the sense of place is also very strong, whether he writes about the farms and country roads of Northern Ireland he has known all his life or the small communities, villages and towns whose names still resonate from news items about 'the Troubles' any time these past forty years. The places he recalls have sometimes witnessed public grief and private tragedy, but his sense of commitment to them is stronger than ever. (A line from Jane Austen's *Persuasion* comes to mind: 'One does not love a place the less for having suffered in it'.) So there is something wonderfully affirmative – not nostalgic at all - in the conclusion Heaney reaches in 'A Herbal, after Guillevic's *Herbier de Bretagne*':

> I had my existence. I was there.
> Me in place and the place in me.[13]

By any reckoning, that's a good note on which to end.

---

13 Seamus Heaney, *Human Chain* (London: Faber and Faber 2010) p.43

Index